GENDER SHOCK

ALSO BY PHYLLIS BURKE

FAMILY VALUES

ATOMIC CANDY

PHYLLIS BURKE

ANCHOR BOOKS

DOUBLEDAY

NEW YORK   LONDON   TORONTO

SYDNEY   AUCKLAND

WITHDRAWN

'GENDER SHOCK,

EXPLODING THE MYTHS
OF MALE AND FEMALE

AN ANCHOR BOOK
PUBLISHED BY DOUBLEDAY
a division of Bantam Doubleday Dell Publishing Group, Inc.
1540 Broadway, New York, New York 10036

ANCHOR BOOKS, DOUBLEDAY, and the portrayal of an anchor
are trademarks of Doubleday, a division of Bantam Doubleday
Dell Publishing Group, Inc.

BOOK DESIGN BY DANA LEIGH TREGLIA

Library of Congress Cataloging-in-Publication Data

Burke, Phyllis, 1951–
    Gender shock : exploding the myths of male and female / Phyllis
Burke. — 1st Anchor Books hardcover ed.
        p.   cm.
    Includes bibliographical references and index.
    1. Sex role.   2. Sex differences.   3. Gender identity.   4. Human
behavior.   5. Sexism.   I. Title.
HQ1075.B85   1996
305.3—dc20   96-11270
                                                          CIP

ISBN 0-385-47717-1
Copyright © 1996 by Phyllis Burke

Printed in the United States of America

10 9 8 7 6 5 4 3 2 1

First Anchor Books Edition: July 1996

FOR THE CHILDREN WHO HEAR A
DIFFERENT DRUMMER,
AND THOSE WHO LOVE THEM.

ACKNOWLEDGMENTS

This book would not have been possible without Lynn Hendee's creative partnership, and the exuberant presence of my son, Jesse.

I would like to thank my publisher, Martha Levin, for believing in this project at its earliest stages, and allowing me great freedom in developing this book. That will long be remembered. I would also like to thank my agent, Bonnie Nadell, and particularly my editor, Charles Flowers, for his exhaustive work toward making this book the best it could be.

There were also many individuals who, although not mentioned specifically in the book, gave of their time and wisdom: Kevin Gogin; Dr. Barry Wolfe; Kate Bornstein; Sergeant Stefan Thorne; James Green; Sister Mary Elizabeth; Cheryl Deaner and Lori Guidos of the Alternative Family Project in San Francisco; and Simone and Anne of Villa Villa Dorman, who generously came through at an especially difficult crossroad.

CONTENTS

PREFACE

In Western Africa, there is a tribe called the Yoruba. They have a ritual for curing the invisible
"demons" of the mind and soul. These demons
are often embodied by the opposite sex, and the
ritual consists of wearing the clothing of the one
who has power over you, and performing a healing
dance in that clothing. In 1969, after viewing a
film of the ritual, Rollo May described the frenzied
dancing of an impotent young man obsessed with
women. The young man felt "possessed" by
woman's evil power, wrote May, in that he was
overdependent on his mother. He put on his
mother's clothing and invited the feminine demon
into his being. He was assisted by the entire tribe,
who danced along with him. This film also captured a similar ceremony for a teenage girl who
resisted male authority. The demon, for this girl,
took the form of a British census taker, whose hat
and coat she wore during the dance. She invited
the masculine demon into her being, to capture
him, and absorb him into her identity, because the

demon was the part of herself that terrorized her and caused her to resist male authority.

After the ritual, the trappings of the opposite sex were stripped from the young man and the teenage girl, their demons presumably now tucked away and integrated into a secret shadow self. They would now be able to assume their proper gender roles, as interpreted by Rollo May: for the man, masculine sexual potency; for the girl, feminine sexual submission.

Western society has also had its ritual gender role reversals, from the ancient Roman Saturnalia to Halloween, from the theatrical cross-dressing of Harvard's Hasty Pudding Club to Sadie Hawkins' Day. Underlying these rituals is an experience of special power: the powers ascribed to the opposite sex.

The first defining moment in a human being's life occurs in the birth room, and in medical terminology it is called "the announcement." Not concerned with health, or weight, or fingers and toes, the announcement consists solely of the sex of the infant's body. From the moment of birth, the baby is handled in a way considered appropriate to the body's sex. Appropriate colors are chosen, appropriate toys are selected, appropriate religious and social rituals are performed. Who among us has not hesitated when asking if a child is male or female, worried that the parent will become insulted if we guess wrong. We have all seen the elaborate lengths to which most parents go to adorn their children in sex-specific garb so that there will be no mistake.

Before my son was born, his sex was known to me, and in his nursery, the major primary color was blue. Any pink was incidental, suppressed. Yet, if the baby had been a girl, you would not have seen a flood of pink in her nursery. I considered myself feminist, and although there would have been some pink in my girl's room, other colors would have dominated. While I would have been more than willing to offer my girl a gender independent world, where the choice of activities and colors was up to her inclination and not her sex, I hesitated to offer my son anything pink, and I panicked when someone gave him an outfit that could be mistaken for a dress.

There were special complications in my case. My partner and I were lesbian mothers, using donor insemination. I would be trying to adopt Jesse as his second legal mother, and I knew that gender appropriateness, both his and mine, would be an important factor in the success of that adoption. At least that is how I rationalized to myself my early gender training of my son, and I had good cause to believe that this training would be crucial to securing our legal relationship, a journey I recorded in a memoir, *Family Values.*

As my son grew, I began to believe in the gender roles, forgetting that I had made a conscious choice to train him as a boy. I marveled at how he seemed so very involved in rough and tumble play, and that he was the best at throwing a ball, and that he wasn't a bit whiny. He was a "boy's boy," a remark often made by his friends' fathers and mothers, and I was proud of this.

Something happened, however, when the story of our family became public. During my first book tour for *Family Values,* no matter where I went, the most impassioned and inevitable question was always: Who is going to teach him to be a man? I found myself telling the interviewers, in an apologetic tone, that there were men in his life. Yet the questioner would persist: Who would teach him to play baseball, or football? I assured them that someone would, without telling them that a number of women had already taken care of that, but after a while, their questions began to dig inside of me. I began to wonder if there *would* be things that no woman would be able to do for Jesse. I asked myself if I had been wrong not to have provided him with a man. Although Jesse had two mothers, I related to the single heterosexual woman who is told she must find a man for her child, particularly if she has a boy. I became almost apologetic about the fact that I was a woman with no man and a son. I promised on radio and television programs that I would provide Jesse with male role models and surrogate father figures. I found myself watching with great interest a public service television advertisement alerting me to ways of providing a male role model for my son. There was a phone number to call, and they showed a young, sullen teenage boy, withdrawn and on the verge of self-destruction, until over his shoulder came the shadow of a man. I wrote down the number, but I did not call it. I read books about the "deep masculine," and the special problems of boy children, and I read Robert Bly's *Iron John.*

Bly writes, "Standing next to the father . . . the son's body has the chance to retune . . . the son's body-strings begin to resonate to the harsh, sometimes demanding, testily humorous, irreverent, impatient, opinionated, forward-driving, silence-loving older masculine body . . . Sons who have not received this re-tuning will have father-hunger all their lives . . . Such hungry sons hang around older men like the homeless do around a soup kitchen. Like the homeless, they feel shame over their condition, and it is nameless, bitter, unexpungeable shame. Women cannot, no matter how much they sympathize with their starving sons, replace that particular missing substance." Although I was per-sonally devastated as I read Bly's words, my feelings took a back-seat to my fear for Jesse's future. What had I done to my child? I began to look at any male who came within a short radius of Jesse as a potential father figure. I told no one, but I became obsessed with providing him a male. I did not want him to be ashamed, bitter, starving. I did not want him to hate me for bringing him into the world.

On the second book tour, a year later, the question was still there: Who will teach him to be a man? I made my usual prom-ises of providing Jesse with a male role model, but as the inter-views continued, and I went from city to city, there was some-thing very wrong, and I could not deny it. I was saying that I could not raise my own child, and that it would be best for me to phone a number on a television advertisement and acquire a man, any man, for my son. This man might have nothing in common with Jesse. This man would not share his life with him on a daily basis. But if I loved my son, I'd better get a man in my house. The inner turmoil was tremendous, in stark contrast to Jesse's jubilance.

Finally, I got a reality check with an experience of tough love from a very wise elder at a Unitarian church gathering. I was asked to give a talk about being a lesbian mother, and then to take part in a question and answer session. I did my usual speech, being respectful of the presumed social norms of the group to whom I was speaking, trying to make them feel comfortable with me. An elderly gentleman stood and said that he felt there was a problem with not providing a man in the house for a boy. He had been to the home of a single woman friend, and the children were running wild. He explained that this would not happen with a man in the house, and furthermore, that the experience of the deep masculine, as dictated by the work of Robert Bly, would not be possible for my son. Without the adult male presence, my son would never be able to become a full man or a mature sexual being. I nodded and assured the man that I would provide Jesse with men as the need arose, and that I appreciated his comments.

It was then that an elder of the congregation, a usually reserved woman well into her sixties, slammed her hand down upon the table in front of her and demanded of me from across the room, "What is wrong with you?" I braced myself. "When I was married," she said, "and I was married for fifteen years, I played housewife, and I did the roles I was expected to do. But when my husband died, I learned the hard way that there had never been a single thing that he did that I could not have done. I raised my sons, and there's nothing wrong with them, because I used all the parts of me to do it. What kind of a mother can you be, if you think because you are a woman that you are incapable of raising your own child?" The elderly gentleman challenged her: "What about Robert Bly? What about the deep masculine, and Iron John?" The woman looked him straight in the eye and said, "The heck with Iron John."

The man sputtered, and I flushed with embarrassment. I was supposed to be giving the lecture, and instead, she gave me one of the greatest lessons of my life. She helped to propel me into a journey through the world of gender with a powerful experience of gender shock. Whereas the child makes an agreement, somewhere along the line, that he or she will suppress and deny a feeling or activity considered inappropriate to their gender, the adult, often in a state of crisis or confusion, has the experience of feeling the shadow self move inside. That shadow self is the trapped half of our identity, where we have hidden those parts of ourselves that are considered gender inappropriate.

I became determined to look at everything about gender, to not shy away from anything, no matter how uncomfortable it made me feel, no matter how much it challenged my identity. I was determined to find inside myself the things that I had suppressed, and the first thing I had to do was be honest about why I had gender-trained Jesse so carefully as a boy. I *did* believe that there was something intrinsically different, beyond the obvious physical differences, about boys and girls. I *did* believe, especially in the case of boys, that it was wrong to transgress those boundaries. Now, I can honestly say, without a doubt, that this is not true. There are, indeed, behavioral differences between individuals, some striking, some subtle, but the major determinate of these differences is not the sex of the body. If I had found that the body *did* determine gender behavior, I would have fully accepted that knowledge, because I want to give my son everything he needs to realize his full potential and become a vibrant part of the world. I would deny him nothing. But what I have learned, instead, is that he needs as many fully developed people in his life as possible, people who will show him ways of being that bring him, and the people in his life, joy and compassion. These people might be men, and they might be women, but the fact that they are male or female is the least important fact of all.

I have also learned that everyone falls along a gender continuum, but where they are on that continuum, which expresses the fullest range of human experience, has nothing to do with their sex, or their sexuality. The questions I now ask about the people who come into my son's life are: Does he have heart? Does she have strength? Does he know how to handle power? Does she believe in the essential goodness of humanity? Those are some of the things I look for now, but the journey was long and complex, and on the road I got confused, and had to question absolutely everything, as if for the first time.

In our early gender training, we are taught that there is something we are able to do, but are forbidden, because of our sex. Every child has this experience, sometimes consciously, sometimes not. It is a moment when the mind stops, experiencing a break in time, as a crucial facet of our identity is socially decreed: our behavior, or gender role, is determined by our sex, or body. Although the assigned gender role is declared absolute, definite, permanent and immutable, most of us secretly do not believe in every aspect of the role. A boy is told that boys do not skip, or jump rope, but he knows that his body is capable of skipping. A girl is told not to physically fight because she is a girl, but she knows that her anger is as real as her fist. Nevertheless, gender role is a daunting thing for a child to challenge, and children most often compensate by becoming involved with the socially ordained special powers of their sex. For example, the boy might be fascinated by the power of the body to conquer, and the girl might be fascinated by the power of the body to attract. The gender role then becomes so deeply embedded into identity that it feels as if it were a part of the body. The gender role seems innate only because we have forgotten that we agreed to it. This agreement was made so early in our lives, and was so powerfully reinforced by our culture, our parents and our peers, that we usually have no memory of the moment when our sex (or body) and gender (or behavior) first fused.

Anything that threatens our gender identity, any excursion beyond the line of demarcation between the sexes, is vigorously resisted, because it seems to threaten the foundation of identity, and puts into play the question: What am I? We might even feel that to challenge the gender roles is to invite chaos, the chaos of identity in flux, because we are trained to see the world as divided into two groups, men and women, who have split reality down the middle. When we are deeply committed to this state of identity, we are sex-typed, and cannot help but project upon the world a version of reality that upholds that sex-typing.

The young child may or may not be conscious of the struggle to suppress behaviors that do not belong to his or her assigned gender role. Most often, however, the child is fully aware of the role, and we often hear that child disdainfully declare, with absolute authority, "That's for girls," or "That's for boys." When traits or behaviors, as simple as wrestling, or combing a doll's hair, give enjoyment to a child but are not considered gender appropriate, the child might experience guilt, panic, anger or shame, doing whatever he or she can to remedy the unwelcome feelings. The boy might pick the doll up by the legs and bash its head on the edge of a table. The girl might curl her legs beneath her, squeeze her knees together and become obsessed with wearing dresses. The adults watching these children will often smile and shake their heads, sometimes saying, "Just like a girl," or "Just like a boy," reinforcing the appropriateness of what the child has just done. If the child does not recognize his or her gender-inappropriate behavior, however, that guilt, panic, anger or shame is often experienced by the parents, who then turn to psychologists and psychiatrists that they might cure their children.

Most children are successful at suppressing the unwanted behaviors, if not the feelings. Yet as they grow and try to establish relationships with the opposite sex, reality becomes a split screen arrangement, with each child secretly suppressing the unwanted feelings, while trying to find someone else who will express them for him, for her. They are off on a lifelong journey to find the other half of themselves. They try to build adolescent and adult relationships with each other, but they rarely work, because no one else can ever give us the other half of our identity. They turn to the books of gender gurus like Marianne Williamson's *A*

Woman's Worth, or John Gray's *Men Are from Mars, Women Are from Venus,* where they are told that their anxiety over their masculinity or femininity, and their concerns and fears about their relationships with the opposite sex, can be cured by believing that gender roles are innate and natural.

These books advise becoming even more involved with the socially decreed, mythical special powers of their sex. Williamson writes that womanhood is "a mass pain of unspoken depth" which would be resolved if only it were accepted that the "masculine is active, the feminine passive, the masculine dynamic, the feminine magnetic, the masculine *does* while the feminine *is.*" If you do not accept Williamson's definitions, then you are suffering from "Amazon neurosis." John Gray writes that sometimes a seminar couple will relate to the examples of men and women "in the opposite way," the woman relating to his descriptions of men, the man relating to his descriptions of women. "I call this role reversal," Gray writes. On the one hand, he assures the couple that everything is alright, and suggests that they either ignore what they do not relate to and move on to something else, "or look deeper inside yourself," where they will find that, rather than having traits of the "opposite sex," they have suppressed their true masculinity or femininity.

In this way, the gender gurus offer a rationalization for why relationships do not work. They make the reader, who is often in pain, feel a temporary, transient relief. By repackaging old myths in order to build up our self-esteem, they enable us to believe that our relationships are not in trouble. We always feel better for a little while when we try something new, but the quick fixes offered by the gender gurus are little more than the equivalent of fad diets for relationships. In the long run, these gurus intensify the psychic damage caused by forcing all men and all women into the two categories of masculine and feminine, and by implying that if a man feels a "feminine" trait, or a woman feels a "masculine" trait, there is something wrong with them, and that they are in denial about their true selves.

This type of reasoning had long been problematic for a Minnesota radio host who was interviewing me toward the end of my second book tour. She asked me, "Who will teach your son to be a man?" At that point, I had begun to talk about the gender continuum, along which men and women of all sexualities express themselves. I explained that it was my job to nurture my son so that he could express himself in as true a range as was natural for him. I had noticed that the host had what could be considered stereotypical "butch" mannerisms and style, although she was wearing a comfortable shift dress. Her haircut was short and practical, her shoes flat and durable, her body movements full and confident. On her ring finger was a wedding band, and she mentioned her husband. In the lingo of academic gender studies, she could be referred to as a heterosexual gender blender, blending together certain elements of both gender roles into the fullest expression of who she is. I took the opportunity to explain that a person could be a biological woman, with a masculine gender expression, and be heterosexual. She seemed almost vindicated as she explained to her listeners that it drove her crazy trying to convince gays and straights alike that she was heterosexual, "masculine" and female at the same time, and that she was not, thank you very much, in denial about her sexuality. This is probably one of the most difficult and important concepts explored in *Gender Shock:* the connection between gender behavior and sexuality. This Minnesota radio host was not suffering from Williamson's "Amazon neurosis," and when she looked "deep inside herself," as Gray advises, she did not find a suppressed feminine identity, but a wide range of human traits, many considered masculine, some considered feminine, but all of them properly belonging to her.

Gender Shock investigates three major aspects of gender: Behavior, Appearance and Science. Within each of these categories are the seeds of gender identity. Within each of these categories is an explosion of myths. One myth holds that gender (or behavior) is a result of sex (the body itself); another that gender and sexuality are linked within the body and are the same thing. Perhaps the most surprising myth of all is that there are only two kinds of bodies: the male and the female.

By investigating the forces operating the gender system, by ignoring nothing, by listening and reading, by sending messages out on the Internet and by traveling from coast to coast to attend gender conferences and interview those on the cutting edge of gender studies, I saw clearly that gender, sex and sexuality are three distinct domains, and the variance within each domain is extraordinary.

Every journey has a turning point. I began by trying to figure out what to do with my son, how to best prepare him for the world. In searching for the answers I could give to my own child, I stumbled upon a shocking pocket of psychiatric practice called Gender Identity Disorder. I found myself reading stacks of case histories of very young children whose behavior was deemed gender inappropriate, and as I read their stories, my vision of gender would never be the same.

Gender Identity Disorder is a microcosm of the whole gender issue. Children as young as three years old undergo "therapy" both at home and at school, oftentimes with government funding, for not adhering to accepted notions of "girl" or "boy" behavior. Their stories frame much of *Gender Shock.* These are the children who remain oblivious to, or defiant of, their "gender-inappropriate" behaviors. These are the children whose parents turn them over, in shame, to the psychiatrists and psychologists, that they might be cured. Some of the children have died. Some have come to adulthood with terrible anger. Many have shut down whatever part of themselves was deemed inappropriate, as they try to walk in lockstep with the teachings of the gender gurus. A few defiantly continue to express themselves honestly.

While most of these children have disappeared from the case history books and are unavailable for follow-up, their doctors are still operating in clinics and private practice all over the world. It is my goal to see the removal of the diagnosis of Gender Identity Disorder in children from the world's psychiatric manuals, and although I do not expect it to happen tomorrow, I do not think it an impossible task.

The refusal to live the masquerade of half an identity is surfacing in a cultural revolution, while the incidences and experiences of gender shock are accelerating. Gender roles are being challenged every day, from sex-segregated institutions like the Citadel, to the emotional and psychological capacity of a man to "mother" his child, girl or boy, with just as much tenderness and caring as a woman.

I did not, however, want to write a book that would only examine dilemmas and point out problems. *Gender Shock* offers a new path, beyond the myths, and a window on the coming revolution in human identity, sparked by gender independence. At the beginning of this preface, I spoke of the Yoruba tribe, of the demons embodied by the clothing of the opposite sex and of how these demons were controlled through ritual. But what would have happened if the teenage girl, after experiencing the special power of the British census taker, then refused to take off his hat and coat? What would have happened if the young man had refused to relinquish his mother's clothes? Would their demons have been satiated, or angered? What penalty or accommodation would the tribe have provided? We cannot know what they would have done, but perhaps we can ask ourselves: Who is the demon, what is it? What will we do when we see it in ourselves, in our children?

The demon has come to be defined as an evil being or spirit that possesses and afflicts a person, but if we go back in time, we find that the demon was not always a creature of destruction and torment. In Roman mythology, the demon was an attendant spirit, or power, with unusual drive and vitality. It was the raw gift from the divine, and it often went by the name of "genius." That genius lies dormant within us all, as we shut it out and try to live as "real men" and "real women." That genius is waiting to be acknowledged.

BEHAVIOR

When the child emerges into the world, every physical movement and spoken word, every toy touched and game imagined, are colored by the power of gender role expectations. The taboos are powerful, and they can be viciously enforced. The boy knows he must not wear pink, that he must not wheel the doll carriage. The girl knows she plays football at her own risk and with the disapproval of many, and that she must wear a dress for special occasions. Soft baby dolls, Barbies, G.I. Joe's and ferocious steroidal action figures populate childhood's gender pantheon, and transgressions in toy selection are swiftly dealt with by peers, parents or teachers.

Who we are is often judged by what we do, and what starts as play develops into the work of a lifetime. The child is asked what he or she would like to "be" when grown up, and the child learns that the answer to that question has a powerful charge for the adults who ask it. Nothing influences the child's answer so strongly as gender role expectations. Understanding the implied and explicit norms, and the penalties for challenging those norms, most children give gender-correct answers, and they are rewarded with social approval. By the time they can give these verbal answers, everything about them, from what they wear to how they walk, has been through rigorous and constant gender training.

What can happen, however, in the offices and clinics of psychologists and psychiatrists all over the world, to the child who refuses to behave "like a girl" or "like a boy"? In the words of Dr. Susan Coates, a clinical psychologist who runs the largest childhood gender identity clinic in the United States, "You'd be shocked."

Dr. Coates is not exaggerating. The case histories that follow are true and accurate representations of documented treatment and experimentation on children as young as three years old, most of it government-funded. All quoted dialogue is taken directly from the case histories, and has not been changed or enhanced in any way. The record has always been from the point of view of the doctors, of the parents and of the teachers, but whenever possible, I have attempted to portray the events through the eyes of the child.

It is my belief that by looking at what society pathologizes, we can see the clearest common denominator of what society demands of those of us who wish to be considered normal. It is also my belief that although most children do not undergo formal gender training to the extremes experienced by these children, almost every child receives this training informally, often at the hands of the most liberal of parents and teachers.

BECKY

SEVEN YEARS OLD

In 1978, one month short of her eighth birthday, a little girl began experimental behavioral treatment under the auspices of the United States Public Health Service and the National Institute of Mental Health, which had provided funds for this purpose to Dr. George Rekers. A UCLA- and Harvard-trained clinical psychologist, Dr. Rekers diagnosed Becky as having "female sexual identity disturbance" which manifested as "deviant gender behavior." He was intent upon demonstrating with this child that he could produce "a reversal of pronounced cross-gender identity to a normal female sexual identity." That a seven-year-old girl can be described as *having* a sexual identity, normal or otherwise, and that the United States government funded this experiment, and many others like it, is alarming.

Becky liked to stomp around with her pants tucked into her cowboy boots, and she refused to wear dresses. She liked basketball, and climbing, and if she wore a dress, she didn't like the idea that the boys might see her underwear. She liked "rough-and-tumble play" which, in psychological terminology, is the hallmark of the male child. She liked to play with her toy walkie-talkies, rifle, dart game and marbles. She stood with her hands on her hips, fingers facing forward. She swung her arms, and took big, surefooted strides when she walked. Becky's mother told her, "I'm taking you to a doctor because you act too much like a boy. I don't want you to be like a boy when you grow up."

Dr. Rekers was assisted in Becky's treatment by an individual who listed herself as "Miss Shasta Mead," of the Division of Child and Adolescent Psychiatry, and a Ph.D. candidate in Clinical Psychology at the University of Florida. Dr. Rekers and Miss Mead wrote in their report that girls like Becky are at risk for transsexualism, adult homosexuality, neuroticism, personality disorders, drug and alcohol abuse, an unstable work record, depression, suicidal ideation, suicide attempts and schizophrenia. Their most dire prediction was that when girls like Becky reach puberty, "psychiatric hospitalization is frequently required."

Becky was described as "consistently rejecting feminine clothing (e.g. dresses) and jewelry," and as displaying "excessively aggressive behavior." She was given the usual intellectual functioning tests, and scored in the "high-average range." She was also given several tests to determine her gender identity. One of the tests is called the Machover Figure-Drawing Test, where the child is given a piece of paper and asked to draw a person. If a girl draws a boy, she has a gender problem, and if a boy draws a girl, he has a gender problem, since the sex of the person the child first draws is supposed to reflect their gender identity. In my own teaching of creative writing to adolescent girls and women, I have found that they will often have first-person male personas from which they write. This has nothing to do with their personal gender identity, but rather reflects the more active role of males in society in general, and in dramatic narrative in particular. For a girl to pick a boy as a persona has no certain connection to her rejection of being a girl.

Becky, however, much to the doctor's surprise, did draw a female figure first, but Dr. Rekers hastened to qualify it. The figure, he said, "had a frown on its face" and was "without arms." Becky next drew the male figure, with a smile, and with arms. Even though Becky drew a female figure first, Rekers interpreted the figure as damaged and deficient, and it became another check mark on the list of Becky's symptoms of deviance.

Becky was also administered the IT Scale for Children, a fascinating exercise in which a child is shown a stick figure, "IT," which is assumed by the creators of the test to be "neuter." As almost any female knows, and most girls intuit, the default for "unknown sex" or "neuter" or "objective" is "male."

Holding the picture of the stick figure in her hand, Becky selected various cards which depicted toys, accessories or clothing. For IT, she then selected pictures of boys and girls to represent IT's friends. According to the test, girls should pick girls, and boys should pick boys. The test is scored in the following way: If Becky makes "masculine" choices, she gets points. If Becky makes "feminine" choices, she does not get any points. The subtext to this scoring method is amusing: a little girl is being treated for not valuing a female identity, and the test that determines this devaluation does not award "feminine" choices any points.

When "normal" boys take the test, they score about 68 out of a possible 84 points, and when "normal" girls take the test, they score about 33. Becky scored 80 points, and earned yet another check mark on her list of sexually deviant symptoms.

The evaluation that sealed Becky's diagnosis was the Barlow Gender-Specific Motor Behavior Form, which "revealed that she was almost exclusively masculine in her manner of sitting, standing, and walking." What does "exclusively masculine" mean, and what objective, scientific criteria were used to arrive at this distinction?

Dr. David Barlow, who now directs the Phobia and Anxiety Clinic at the State University of New York at Albany, devised the experiment, along with colleagues at the University of North Carolina at Greensboro. Two undergraduate males were selected as the gender raters at Greensboro. They walked through the North Carolina campus, "rating passers-by on a 7-point scale from −3 (extremely masculine) to +3 (extremely feminine)." The two young men who were assigned the job of gender judges selected at random twelve Caucasian subjects for four categories: masculine males, feminine males, masculine females and feminine females. Tall, thin and well dressed were the two gender raters' criteria for feminine males. It is also interesting to note that no African American subjects were chosen. The study does not state if this was deliberate, but it is likely that there was some concern that the African American subjects might differ substantially from stereotypical Caucasian masculine and feminine body gestures, and so interfere with the expected results of the experiment.

The twelve selected subjects were videotaped first without their knowledge, and then with their knowledge. When they knew they were being videotaped, and why, *all* of the subjects showed a decrease in "feminine" body movements, which reflected a devaluing of these movements, even among feminine females.

The raters used their checklists for the following categories:

Standing. If you stand with your feet apart, you are masculine. If you stand with your feet together, you are feminine. If you swing your arms from the shoulder, you are masculine; from the elbow, you are feminine. If your wrist is limp, you're feminine; if your wrist is firm, you're masculine. If your hands are in your pockets, or in your belt loop, or under your belt, you are masculine. If you have "two distinct arm or hand motions in a fifteen second period," you are feminine.

Walking. If you take "long, free strides," you are masculine. If you take "short, controlled strides," you are feminine. Swing the hips, it's a girl. Walk as stiffly as possible with no hip motion, it's a boy. Your feet placement is also highly relevant. "A subject was said to be 'stepping on a line' (feminine) if some part of the feet fell on an imaginary one-inch-wide line which indicated the subject's path, a sort of mincing motion. If not, 'straddling the line' was checked (masculine)." If your arms hang loose and relaxed, that's masculine. If your upper arms are tucked against your body, that's feminine.

Sitting. If while sitting you show "precise hand motions," that's masculine, while "graceful hand motions (fingers bent, often at different angles)" reflect the feminine. An added feature of sitting was legs uncrossed and apart (boys); legs uncrossed or crossed at ankles, legs together (girls); legs crossed, foot on knee (boy); legs crossed, knee on knee (girl).

But Dr. Barlow's observations on the buttocks deserve special attention for sheer absurdity:

"Buttocks away from back of chair versus buttocks close to back of chair . . . If the distance between the buttocks and the back of the chair was four inches or more, 'away from the back of the chair' (keyed as masculine) was scored. Otherwise, 'close to the back of the chair' (keyed as feminine) was scored. Since the view was head on, this item was sometimes difficult to rate. Raters were told that if a person is leaning back, the buttocks are generally away from the back of the chair. If sitting up straight, the subject's buttocks are generally close to the back of the chair. Watching a person as he or she first sat down also gave some valuable clues. Some subjects sat down and leaned back while at the same time sliding their buttocks away from the back of the chair. Others sat down and then wiggled back into the chair, moving their buttocks close to the back of the chair. If both behaviors were shown, the one occurring most was scored."

These minute observations and measurements serve as the "objective" scientific standards that define our behavior as gender appropriate. A little girl who favors cowboy boots and basketballs is probably not destined to come out too well on the Barlow Gender-Specific Motor Behavior Form, which, of course, found Becky to be "exclusively masculine."

Dr. Rekers painted a picture of Becky as a very disturbed child. She was described as masturbating in public, and rubbing her body up against other girls. How often, the context of this behavior and an exact description of this behavior are never rendered. Dr. Rekers further stated that Becky "often projected her voice very low so that she sounded like a man." (In subsequent descriptions of Becky's case, rather than being described as "often" sounding like a man, she is described as "frequently" sounding like a man.) It is hard to imagine a little girl being able to pull off such a feat of mimicry.

Becky was described as not interacting well with other girls, particularly her younger "feminine" sister, and as preferring male roles in play. She was finally pictured as expressing the desire to be a boy. What this meant to Becky was never explored. Did she want to have the body of a boy, or did she simply want the masculine privileges accorded to boys?

Most revealing of Becky's true condition are Dr. Rekers' own words: "However, [Becky] apparently did not exhibit enough of these behaviors in the school environment to warrant the concern of school personnel since they did not report significant behavioral problems to her mother. Becky's mother attributed this discrepancy to Becky's fear of the teacher . . . Becky's behavior at school apparently did not represent a significant problem."

Whether or not Becky was afraid of her teacher, it seems blatantly impossible that a young girl who is rigidly masculine, with a "strong male identification which she consciously defends," could, upon arriving at school each day, just simply drop these behaviors. If Becky were really so compulsively masculine, she would not be selective of the environments in which she would "defend" her identity. At school, she was not experiencing any serious social consequences for her "boy" behavior, but neither was she putting in enough hours with her dolls at home to make her seem sufficiently feminine to her mother and to the doctors.

The first phase of Becky's treatment involved assessment, in order to obtain a baseline, or norm, of her behavior. This baseline assessment took place in a clinical "playroom" which featured a one-way mirror and two child-sized tables, such as are found in typical grammar schools. One table featured "dress up" items for the child to wear in fantasy play, and the other table featured "affect" toys, with which the child was supposed to act out masculine and feminine roles.

On the dress-up table, "girl toys" and "boy toys" were segregated at opposite ends. The dress-up table designed for Becky consisted of "feminine clothing and grooming items, including two wigs, a small pair of high-heeled shoes, a child's-size robe, a cosmetic set (lipstick, compact, and blush-on), and a set of jewelry (bracelets, necklaces, rings, and earrings)." The masculine items were "a plastic football helmet, a sea captain's hat, an army helmet, an army fatigue shirt, an army belt with hatchet holder and canteen holder, and a play electric razor."

The affect table also segregated the "masculine toys" and "feminine toys" at opposite ends. The masculine toys on Becky's affect table were "two dart guns with darts, a small target, a rubber knife, play handcuffs, and a set of plastic cowboys and Indians." The feminine affect toys for her to choose among were "a baby doll in a 3-foot crib, a baby bottle, baby powder, and a Barbie doll with two sets of clothes."

Behind the one-way mirror sat two observers selected by Dr. Rekers. The observers operated a multiple-response panel by pushing buttons to signal feminine or masculine behaviors performed by Becky, while a closed-circuit television monitoring and videotaping system recorded the sessions. The observers pressed

Key #1 to indicate the length of time that Becky was in contact with a masculine toy on the affect table, and Key #2 was pressed to indicate the length of time that she was in contact with a feminine toy on the affect table. Keys #3 and #4 were used to indicate masculine and feminine play performed by Becky at the dress-up table.

What Becky actually did with a toy could also influence her masculine and feminine rating. For example, if Becky put on the sea captain's hat, and then picked up Barbie to take her sailing, Becky would not have received a feminine point, as she would have been acting out a masculine role, even though she was in contact with the Barbie doll.

Baselines were obtained for Becky, with and without "probe" conditions, which did not particularly affect her behavior. Probe conditions meant that a noninteracting adult was in the room with Becky to see if her choice of toys changed with their presence. The noninteracting adults alternated among a male stranger, a female stranger and Becky's mother. The fact that the probe conditions were reported to have no consequence on Becky's choice of toys supports the idea that the schoolteacher could not have had that much power over Becky's behavior, since the presence of adults in the clinic playroom, whether male or female, produced no changes in her actions.

Determined from behind the one-way mirror, Becky's baseline scores reflected, of course, overwhelming interest in the masculine dress-up and affect toys, yet they did not indicate exclusive masculine play. In fact, although the feminine affect toys were consistently rated very low with Becky, the dress-up toys were variable, suggesting once again that Dr. Rekers' descriptions of Becky's compulsive and obsessive masculinity were exaggerated.

Becky knew that her mother was bringing her to the clinic because she "acted too much like a boy," and that her mother and the doctor did not want her to grow up to "be like a boy." Becky believed that there was something wrong with her because her mother said so. She trusted her mother, and the doctor who was going to help her. She was almost eight years old, and a girl that age would certainly have had a clear grasp of what was going on.

Little girls who are "tomboys" are often intrepid souls who have tremendous faith in their bodies. They can have heroic visions of themselves, and they often possess above average to excellent hand-eye coordination. Their desire to play with boys might not be because they want to *be* boys, nor should it be thought to indicate that they hate their bodies, or that they are practicing for their future male role identities. They might prefer playing with the boys because males are always more highly trained in athletics than girls. For the talented tomboy, to play with the boys can be fun because it is more competitive and challenging.

Since only boys are truly encouraged to participate in athletics, a girl like Becky who can, or likes to, dribble a basketball might assume that she actually *is* a boy, except for the penis. In fact, according to Dr. Laura Allen at UCLA, there is no biological basis for a lack of climbing, throwing or other athletic skills in any girl. What is lacking is serious athletic training and a cultural milieu encouraging their participation.

It is important also to note the concern over Becky's future sexuality, based upon her being a tomboy. There have been many claims, as recently as 1995, that lesbians do not play with dolls when they are girls, and that most lesbians were tomboys. The fact that most tomboys grow up to be heterosexual, and that adult heterosexual and lesbian women report playing much the same way during childhood, does not grab the headlines, and does not convince doctors like Rekers, who surmise to this day that there is a connection between persistent "tomboyism" and lesbianism. Because of this belief, they mistakenly reason that if you change the tomboy's play behavior, you will enhance her chances for a heterosexual future.

Cross-cultural studies on tomboys, however, have concluded that "tomboyism" is not an accurate predictor of sexual orientation. Women in Brazil, Peru and the Philippines, "irrespective of their sexual orientation as an adult, reported low rates of tomboyism as a child." In an Australian study, "77% of the bisexual women and 77% of the lesbian women recalled having been considered tomboy as a girl," but so did 63 percent of the heterosexual women. Nonetheless, Dr. Rekers and many of his colleagues base, in part, the diagnosis of gender disturbance, or sexual deviance in tomboys, upon a girl's body language and superior motor skills.

As soon as Becky's baseline "masculine" and "feminine" play behaviors were obtained, her treatment in the playroom began, with some Orwellian twists. Miss Mead was the primary contact for Becky, since she represented an appropriately feminine female role model. Under the supervision of Dr. Rekers behind the one-way mirror, Miss Mead showed Becky a wrist counter. On the side of the wrist counter (similar to those used to keep golf scores) there was a little button, and when Becky pressed it, she saw a number come up: the number one for the first press, the number two for the second press and so on. As Miss Mead attached the counter to Becky's wrist, she told her, "You may play with any of the toys that you like, but you can only press the wrist counter when playing with girls' toys."

Miss Mead then pointed out to Becky the various treatment toys, which were mixed together on the table. As Miss Mead picked up each toy, she told Becky if it was a "girls' toy," or a "boys' toy." The boys' toys featured "a highway road scraper, a plastic race car, a plastic tugboat, three miniature plastic soldiers, five small airplanes, and a dump truck," and the girls' toy choices were "a baby doll with clothes and baby bottle, a doll crib and doll, a bathinette with doll, two purses, a highchair and doll, plastic tea dishes, and a doll buggy with doll."

Becky was now shown an additional device, a "bug-in-the-ear," which was an earphone hooked up to a microphone behind the one-way mirror. Even though Becky would not be able to see her, Miss Mead explained that she would talk to Becky through the device, which she now inserted into Becky's ear.

We can only imagine how peculiar this entire setup must have been for Becky, as she was left alone in the mirrored observation room, wearing the wrist counter and the bug-in-the-ear. As soon as Becky touched a toy, Becky heard Miss Mead's voice through the device: "Becky, if you played with only the girls' toys since I last talked to you, you can press your wrist counter." If Becky wanted to get any points, and have the opportunity to press the button on the wrist counter, she knew she would have to play with the "girls' toys." A few moments later, she again heard, "Becky, if you played with only the girls' toys since I last talked to you, you can press your wrist counter."

Rekers observed, "At the end of the clinic visits, Becky often asked the therapist, 'How did I do?' Regardless of her actual performance, the therapist invariably answered, 'Fine,' in as neutral a voice as possible. However, it was clear that Becky realized what behaviors were expected of her since she would reply, 'No, I didn't. I played with the boys' toys,' whenever her play was not exclusively feminine. It should be noted that over the course of treatment, Becky became emotionally attached to [Miss Mead] and seemed to be generally eager to please her." The fact that Becky was able to form a sincere attachment to another human being was ultimately used against her, and this ability would be used against the child even more dramatically toward the end of her treatment.

For the initial treatment sessions, Becky was prompted once every minute, five times per session, and instructed to press her wrist counter only if she had played exclusively with the girls' toys. The Orwellian nature of this experiment on an eight-year-old child is truly remarkable: invisible strangers monitoring your every move, voices coming into your ear, being told what is being done is for your own good.

These "prompts" were gradually decreased, and when they were at three per five-minute session, Becky was given a new instruction. "You can press the wrist counter whenever you think about it after playing with the girls' toys." This was the beginning of the "self-regulation intervention."

Rekers reported that after only three of these "self-regulation" sessions, Becky exhibited "a consistently high level of feminine sex-typed play." But Becky began to exhibit a behavior which the doctor found to be as disconcerting as it was unexpected. True, Becky was playing mostly with the feminine sex-typed toys, but "the observers reported a persistence of instances of aggressive play." The doctor and therapist seemed confused. They had believed that if Becky played with "girls'" toys, she would become "feminine," which to them meant nurturing and passive. Instead, Becky "would occasionally throw a doll up into the air or bang its head against the table." In response, Rekers added two new keys, #5 and #6, onto the observers' response panels to record aggressive play, both with masculine and feminine toys.

After thirty-two sessions in the clinic, the next phase of Becky's treatment occurred within her home, specifically in her bedroom, where the researchers separated her toys into two piles. They put the "girl" toys on one end of her bed, and the "boy" toys on the other end of her bed. The feminine toys that Becky owned consisted of "two baby dolls, a Barbie doll, and jacks," and her masculine toys were "walkie-talkies, a rifle, a gun with a holster, model cars, a foam-rubber car, a basketball, a basketball game, a dart game, and marbles." The three observers, including Miss Mead, who had all been concealed behind the one-way mirror, were now in Becky's bedroom, making check marks on lists as she played. Also present was a fourth person, who held a stopwatch to determine the end of a five-minute play period. After six of these sessions, the home gender-play baseline was established.

We can only imagine how peculiar and dramatic this must have seemed to Becky. Three people were checking off her every move, a fourth person was timing her with a stopwatch, and her mother, who had let them in, was probably hovering in the background. The pressure for Becky to conform to the feminine mystique was truly overwhelming, and she must have sensed that she had to comply, or risk this constant intrusion.

After the six baseline sessions in Becky's home, the seventh session showed a "high level of feminine sex-typed play, which was maintained as prompts were gradually faded out." By sessions thirty-two and thirty-three, however, Becky indicated "satiation with the feminine toys," explaining, "I'm tired of playing with these toys." The team decided that she did not have enough girls' toys, and so the therapist took her to the toy store, explaining, "Since you've been so good playing with girls' toys, we're going to buy you some more girls' toys as a reward." While at the toy store, Becky was again prompted. For example, as they toured the aisles, Miss Mead would stop at a feminine item, such as a cosmetic kit or a set of plastic dishes, and she would say, "When I was a girl, I used to play with this." She would then point to the item, which Becky would then select. This was referred to as an "intervention."

Becky's voice projection was also intensively monitored, as were her motor behaviors, although no specific punishments or rewards were given. The doctor noted that as her sex-typed play became more feminine, there was a moderate change in her voice and manner of sitting, walking and standing. Since everything she said during a session was tape-recorded over the monitoring system, we learn that Becky seemed confused, or torn, over the changes she was noticing in herself: "She was often heard to make such verbalizations as 'I look ugly in dresses. I get sick in dresses 'cause I like to play with boys' stuff.' "

Rekers described Becky's early "ambivalence toward her new feminine behaviors" in the following way: "She reacted to her use of feminine cosmetics by saying, 'I'm getting this stuff off of me, and I ain't kidding. I better not smell like a girl,' but when a different set of toys was presented, she asked, 'Where's the makeup? You should have gotten the makeup. Doesn't a lady wear makeup?' "

After seven months, Rekers then offered proof of Becky's remarkable cure: "Becky spontaneously began wearing jewelry and perfume at home." With ninety-six sessions in her bedroom, in addition to the one hundred and two sessions in the clinic, "spontaneous" might not quite be the correct word to account for her use of jewelry and perfume. Rekers further stated that Becky "presented the research assistant with a list of 'boyfriends' in her class. Her mother reported that Becky had never indicated any interest in a boyfriend previously."

Becky's original diagnosis explicitly stated that she played almost exclusively with boys, which was interpreted as a clinical sign of her sexual identity disorder. Once she was taught to display faux-sexual interest in boys, her male friends were transformed into a sign of her mental health. Rekers goes on to cite her mother and grandmother's confirmation that Becky had "changed remarkably," with a "decrease in excessive aggression and an increase in general compliance. The pretreatment deviant sexual behavior was no longer occurring." Once she became compliant and appropriately sexualized, Becky was pronounced cured; yet perhaps, in Becky's case, her change in behavior was an act of love. One could infer that she suppressed her natural play behaviors to please and comfort the two women for whom she cared: her mother, and Rekers' colleague, Miss Mead.

Immediately after treatment, Becky was tested, as she had been before treatment began. In the Machover Figure-Drawing Test, Becky again drew the female figure first. Unfortunately, her female figure, like its pretreatment predecessor, had no arms. The figure did, however, have a "big smile on her face." No arms, but happy? Common sense tells us that this is a less than desirable result in terms of Becky's self-esteem, but according to Dr. Rekers, the drawing was proof of further progress.

The repeat of the IT Scale was especially startling. On pretreatment testing, Becky scored 80 out of 84 possible points, revealing a strong masculine identity. Post-treatment, "when asked which pair of shoes IT would like to play dress-up with, Becky chose the high-heeled shoes and said, ' 'Cause I'm a girl, ain't I?' " Becky now scored 4 out of 84 points, making her almost exclusively "feminine." Again, this was taken as true progress, despite the fact that "normal" girls score 33, displaying some degree of gender independent behavior, at least as far as the IT Scale goes.

Becky's physical movements were again rated, and according

to the Barlow scale, Becky was now predominantly feminine in her movements. There are no specifics given as to what this meant. Was she limping a wrist that never before limped? How did this affect her basketball game? Was she mincing down an invisible line one inch wide in play high heels? How did this influence her ability to climb on the jungle gym?

Fourteen weeks later, Becky had follow-up testing. She was once again put into the playroom with the one-way mirror, but this time she had a new set of toys: "The masculine sex-typed toys included a football, a softball with a baseball hat and mitt, a plastic S.W.A.T. car, a model hot rod, and a toy rifle." The feminine sex-typed toys included the usual doll with a carrying chair, and a Playskool doll house with doll figures. Your heart has to go out to Becky when you see the remaining toys she is offered as appropriate and healthy for a little girl. Please remember that the boys' toys included a softball and a baseball hat and mitt, toys excruciatingly appealing to this tomboy, or even to a gender independent girl who likes sports. We know from the toys Becky had at home that she had a number of model cars, but she probably knew that she could not now touch the model hot rod. Instead of the car or the balls, the final choices on Becky's toy table were "a set of pots and pans, and a toy iron."

Dr. Rekers now reported that Becky "played 100% of the time with feminine sex-typed toys." Being made gender-rigid represented a cure. The IT Scale was administered to Becky for a third time during this follow-up, fourteen weeks after the psychic and physical invasion of her home. Becky now scored 84 points, the highest recordable masculine identity score on the IT Scale. How is this possible? She walked like a girl, she talked like a girl, she played like a girl. Rekers explained that Becky's earlier scores reflected a pretreatment hypermasculinity (undesirable), and a post-treatment hyperfemininity (desirable). The final IT Scale discrepancy, he contends, was because "the literature on normal children indicates that a high frequency of female subjects perceive the 'IT' figure as male."

Since he rejected this explanation for Becky's high pretreatment score, one wonders if Dr. Rekers simply interpreted these last results to find what he wanted to find. Since Becky is now "normal" in his eyes, her follow-up test score, although virtually identical to her pretreatment score, becomes a sign of her mental health, rather than deviance. It would seem that, rather than being "cured," Becky's self-esteem was destroyed by wrist counters, stopwatches and a bug-in-the-ear. Her true desires and feelings had been worn down, split off from her everyday world, only to become hidden within a secret and shamed place inside her. Becky valiantly strove for acceptance and to do what was necessary in the face of overwhelming odds. She wanted to earn back love, and if that meant choosing the pots and pans over the softball mitt, so be it.

Becky's mother proudly wrote to the doctor at Christmastime to report that Becky had asked for dresses and a Barbie doll, but most telling is the doctor's final report of Becky's miracle cure. "Becky was enamored with the male examiner and wanted to give him her phone number so that he could call her 'every night and every day.'" Becky was eight years and six months old at the end of her treatment, and Dr. Rekers considered her cured because her relationship with an adult man was consuming, obsessive, even sexualized.

In 1995, Rekers published the *Handbook of Child and Adolescent Sexual Problems,* which is available in many medical school libraries. The handbook is designed to assist the general practitioner and pediatrician when he or she is presented with a nonconforming child. The same treatments that Becky underwent are recommended, and Becky's case history, in abbreviated form, is cited. This child's case, rather than an aberration, is now being presented to young pediatricians as a diagnostic and treatment model.

JERRY

NINE YEARS OLD

While girls like Becky often display high levels of hand-eye coordination, and therefore a talent for sports, boys who are considered gender deviant often have poor hand-eye coordination, and are viewed as disliking "rough-and-tumble play." Because of this lack of coordination, they are described as being more like girls, and their every movement can become suspect.

Nine-year-old Jerry could not have been sure, might not have even known, but his teacher was watching him carefully at recess as he moved toward the girls who were playing four square. If he had looked over his shoulder, he would have seen her making a check mark on her clipboard. The teacher in the lunchroom did the same thing. Typical for suburban Florida in 1969, the lunchroom was bright yellow with a series of long maple tables. Jerry sat with his friends: the girls. He was the only boy who sat with the girls, and his teacher stood nearby, with her clipboard, watching him eat. Whenever his laughter sounded, to the teacher, like the girls', she drew her clipboard up and made a check. During physical education class, the PE teacher also had a clipboard. When she saw that Jerry was jumping rope with the girls, or participating in any of their activities, she made a check on a piece of paper, and looked at the clock in order to note the time and duration of his play with them.

These observations went on for a week, and no one ever spoke to Jerry about his play patterns or his friendships. Jerry was about to become the case study of a man he would not meet, Dr. Robert D. Myrick, who, in 1970, published the results of his experiment with Jerry in "The Counselor-Consultant and the Effeminate Boy." The study intended to demonstrate "how deviant children, such as this effeminate boy, can be aided through consultation with teachers and through learning experiences within the regular school program."

Working out of the Department of Counselor Education at

the University of Florida in Gainesville, Dr. Myrick wrote: "In general, females are more nurturant, passive, dependent, and inhibiting of verbal and physical aggression; males are more rebellious, mechanical, independent, and physically active . . . The effeminate boy is one who has failed . . ." Dr. Myrick also cited research that showed "effeminacy" to be incapacitating in a boy, and linked to the development of excessive anxiety, peer rejection, isolation, even schizophrenia. (The schizophrenia warning for "masculine" girls and "feminine" boys was very popular for most of this century, but seems to have dropped out of sight in light of recent schizophrenia studies which no longer cite feminine or masculine (mis)behaviors as indicators of the condition.)

Jerry's classroom teacher initiated contact with Dr. Myrick, who decided to work behind the scenes, assuming that Jerry would have no idea that anything was happening. Jerry had been playing quite a bit, although not exclusively, with the girls. His teacher believed Jerry's self-esteem was suffering, despite his solid academic performance, because when he tried to play with the boys, some of them would reject him because he could not throw the ball properly. The teacher also felt that Jerry was adopting some of the girls' mannerisms, and she was alarmed for his future, since some of the boys had begun to make fun of him "for being a sissy." It is interesting to note that the children who are doing the teasing and name-calling are not assessed or treated for bullying behavior patterns, because these patterns are considered "normal." Dr. Myrick also believed that Jerry was at risk for homosexuality because "a high percentage of homosexual men . . . were less likely as children to play baseball." Myrick here erroneously conflates a child's hand-eye coordination with his future sexuality.

When Jerry underwent testing, he scored high (120) on the California Test of Mental Maturity, and his achievement tests showed him to be "above grade level." Although there was nothing wrong with Jerry academically, he became the subject of an experiment which would take place, unbeknownst to him, for a period of seven weeks.

For the first and the last of these weeks, Jerry's behavior was evaluated by his teachers in three specific venues: the playground, the lunchroom and physical education class. A chart was made to indicate how often Jerry played with girls and how often he played with boys, before and after the five-week treatment period. There were also two pre- and post-experimental measures: the first was a class sociogram, the second a Semantic Differential questionnaire.

The sociogram, which is basically a popularity and self-esteem questionnaire, was administered to all of the children in Jerry's classroom. "Pupils were asked to list in order the names of three classmates whom they would most like to (a) play with, (b) have on a team, and (c) work with on a class committee . . . They would also list three people with whom they would least like to do any of these activities." Out of thirty-three pupils in the class, Jerry was ranked only twenty-seventh out of thirty-three in desirability (first being the most desirable). Two children, however, did select Jerry as a child they would most like to play with, while *no one* selected him as a child they would least like to play with.

The second measure, the Semantic Differential questionnaire, was administered only to Jerry. Jerry was asked to answer several questions, using "bipolar adjectives" for his answers: pleasant-unpleasant, loud-soft, cold-hot, ugly-beautiful, delicate-rugged, fast-slow, good-bad, weak-strong, dull-sharp, deep-shallow, heavy-light, dark-bright. The questions required him to rate, on a 28-point scale (28 being the highest score), the girls, the boys, his teacher, the school and the principal. He gave his teacher the perfect score of 28, and chose the girls as the ones he liked the best. The last questions on the test were fill-in-the-blank: "As I see me" and "As I'd like to be." The second question might have made him feel uncomfortable, since it could mean that he didn't like himself just as he was, or that an adult in power thought he did not.

For the next five weeks, Jerry met his physical education teacher for a special tutoring session. He did not enjoy rough contact sports with the boys, and he knew that the PE teacher did not approve of his playing with the girls. She explained the rules of touch football to him, and showed him how to throw and catch the ball, something which he found difficult to do. The football wobbled in the air when he threw it, and when it hurtled toward him, he would shy away. The ball he actually preferred to play with was the four-square ball, but he was discouraged from touching it, since it was a girl's ball.

Frustrated by Jerry's lack of athletic talent, his teacher decided to train him to be the center for the football team. He just had to stand with his legs apart, bend over and throw the ball up through his legs to the quarterback behind him. He did it over and over again, and then she taught him how to block and rush. Contact sports were not something he liked, yet his teacher wanted him to do these things. Most likely, he cooperated because, as with Becky, Jerry had never misbehaved at school.

In physical education class, Jerry's teacher decided not to ask him to throw or catch the ball, because she knew he still could not do that, but she did make him play football with the boys. She coached him intensively, explaining to him that it was his job to block, and to rush the boy who was facing him. Jerry did not like shoving his body against the other boy's, and he did not want to knock him over, but he heard the teacher's voice: "That's the way, Jerry," "Good job that time, Jerry." She had never said his name like that, but Dr. Myrick had instructed the PE teacher to speak like this, and to be sure to say Jerry's name when affirming his "boy" behavior. The other boys would certainly have noticed this attention, and "That's the way to hustle in there, Jerry" must have sounded very strange indeed, not just to the other boys, but to Jerry.

When Jerry went to his classroom, he found that his seat had been changed. He was now sitting beside the most popular boy, whom we'll call Mike. Mike was the one who played sports best, the one everyone liked, the one everyone wanted on their team. Mike was now Jerry's partner on classroom projects, such as bringing things to the office, or preparing for a math test. The problem was, Mike began to dislike Jerry. They did not enjoy the same activities, and they did not excel at the same things. After a

week or so, when Jerry walked into the classroom in the morning
and went to take his seat, Mike rolled his eyes, smirked and said
to the other boys, "Oh, boy." Mike had never done this before,
but after having Jerry foisted on him in such an artificial way, he
began to rebel.

Dr. Myrick explained, "This pairing provided Jerry more opportunity to identify with a model boy." Clearly, Jerry was not a
model boy, and after one week, he probably felt his difference
even more acutely. Everything was done to steer him away from
the girls and toward the boys, and he began to play exclusively
with the boys at recess.

On one particular day during his five-week treatment period,
Jerry walked into the cafeteria, carrying his lunch bag. He entered
the lunchroom and saw the teacher with the clipboard, watching
him. Jerry stayed close to Mike, who rolled his eyes and turned
away, but for the first time, Jerry went to the boys' loud and
messy lunch table. Even though Jerry was playing with the boys
now, and never with the girls, some of the boys were still calling
him names, such as "sissy." One of the boys challenged Jerry:
"Go sit with the girls," but Jerry did not move. By now, the girls
must have seemed distant to Jerry, and perhaps threatening, in
that he knew his attraction to them and their play signaled to
others that there was something wrong with him.

He sat at the boys' lunch table for a couple of weeks, but the
suspicion persisted that he did not belong. The other boys might
have detected that Jerry's disdain of girls and girl behavior was
only on the surface. To test him, Mike challenged Jerry to go with
him to the girls' table, to "tease" the girls. Mike stood, and Jerry
got up to follow him. He probably did not feel very good about
himself, since he had enjoyed and appreciated the girls. But he
followed Mike anyway, because he knew that this was what a boy
was supposed to do, and he had to prove that he was a boy. The
details of the "teasing" are not given, but teasing among nine-
year-olds is usually belittling. A behavioral problem typical of
boys that affects the self-esteem of girls is here considered a developmental milestone for Jerry on his road to boyhood.

Dr. Myrick reported: "He continued to sit and talk with the boys during lunch period . . . he went to the girls' table on only two occasions and that was with another boy to tease the girls." Jerry was no longer exhibiting deviant behavior. The girls were separate and distant from him, objects suitable for teasing and proving his masculinity. He had become appropriately gendered by shutting down, at least from public view, that part of himself which enjoyed the company and friendship of girls.

The two experimental measures were again administered. On the class sociogram, Jerry now ranked eighth in the class, and fourth among the boys. He had many more positive responses, yet, for the first time, he received two negative responses, both from boys. What is most disturbing, however, is the post-treatment result of Jerry's Semantic Differential. Dr. Myrick wrote, "The later SD also indicated a significant change in how [Jerry] felt other boys and girls perceived him—less valued, less potent, and less active." On the scale of 1–28, pre-experiment Jerry perceived his popularity among boys at 16, and among girls at 16. Post-experiment, he scored himself among boys at 7, and among girls at 7. This was a precipitous drop of 9 points. Even more crucial and disturbing was the revelation, through the question "As I see me," that Jerry had suffered "a perceived loss of self-esteem." On the same scale of 1–28, pre-experiment he perceived himself as a 20, post-experiment as a 14.

Finally, there was a chart of Jerry's pre- and post-experiment playground behavior, showing how often he played with girls, how often he played with boys. (Not shown was the small percentage of time that Jerry played by himself.) Pre-experiment, Jerry played with the girls 57 percent of the time, and with the boys about 37 percent of the time. Post-experiment, Jerry played with boys 97 percent of the time. The line that signified his post-experiment play with girls was a solid bar along the bottom of the chart, indicating absolute zero.

When I contacted Dr. Myrick, who still works in the counseling department of the University of Florida at Gainesville, he explained that the serious drop in Jerry's self-esteem could be understood in light of the new "ideal self" that Jerry now wished to attain. He added, "When we matched Jerry up with [Mike], the star student got kind of tired of him. The top kid was a good athlete, good-looking, one of those golden boys. We created almost bogus situations that would put Jerry with the star. Ironically, when we finally did do another sociogram at the end, Jerry's popularity increased tremendously, but one of the kids who rejected him was the star! Some of the researchers were concerned that the star would lose status by being forced to associate with Jerry, but we did not find that to be true."

Dr. Myrick explained what he believes to have been the positive aspect of Jerry's loss of self-esteem. "It's part of a defensive posture. They pull in, have a mask. He is put into a position where he is confronted with who he is. He is not content to be an isolate, to not play with boys, not be in sports. But he has to face up to the fact that he's not a star athlete. Therefore, all this would contribute to lower self-esteem." We now learn that Jerry's cure involved accepting that he was socially, perhaps constitutionally, inferior to the "star." As a mother, I would find it difficult to understand how making it clear to my son that he is "less than" the other children, particularly the boys, could possibly be good for him, even if it did correct his supposed "gender deviance."

"The last follow-up was in high school," Dr. Myrick told me. He hesitated, then said, "He was reasonably involved with activities. It won't surprise you that these are artistic activities. The annual [yearbook]. Drama. He never lost his predilection toward art. He was never a star athlete. He never had the coordination. We're not talking a 180-degree turn here."

I asked Myrick if there were any specific mannerisms that the teachers reported that first caused them to perceive Jerry as "effeminate." "He was not flaunting his mannerisms," answered Dr. Myrick. "It was more like a lack of physical aggression. He wouldn't slug it out, or physically push people. He would be gentler, rely more on his brain. He did not have effeminate speech. But people would view him as a gentle person."

When asked if he believed that by changing a child's gender

play, or mannerisms, their future sexuality could be influenced, Dr. Myrick replied: "From where I'm sitting, that's an old theory with a hard time proving. You can only do so much with a Jerry. There was something innate in him, there was the gentle, effeminate part of him that goes with femininity. He was more artistic. It was part of who he is . . . The bottom line would be, if we were to use the biological chromosome theory in term of homosexuals, he may have that gene."

Dr. Myrick seemed anxious to distance himself somewhat from this study, especially in regard to spotting the prehomosexual child. Dr. Myrick declared a lack of homophobic thought on his own part, and explained that the study was a sign of the times, and that some things have changed. For instance, he would now probably use different language to *describe* Jerry. Yet, when asked if he would treat Jerry in the same manner in 1995 that he did in 1970, he said, "Exactly." Throughout the research for this book, I have found that although the doctors have modified their rhetoric, attempting to distance themselves from blatantly sexist and homophobic statements and theories, their assessment and treatment of children remain identical to their past practices.

When I asked Dr. Myrick if he still does this type of work with children, he said, "It's not a popular thing to study now." Perhaps this is due to the elimination of homosexuality as a mental illness from the *Diagnostic and Statistical Manual of Mental Disorders* (DSM), which was voted upon in 1973, and implemented in 1980. Dr. Myrick's latest research, although not focused on "effeminate boys," still concerns gender and self-esteem. His recent article "From Barbie Dolls to Board Rooms" tackles the problem of girls' plummeting self-esteem in the middle school years, and targets academically able girls. How ironic that a doctor who spent time subliminally teaching a boy to reject "girlish" activities because they were threatening to his boyhood and dangerous to his future mental health and academic performance is now researching self-esteem problems in girls.

In Jerry's case, much of his perceived deviance was due to an emerging style of physical movement labeled "effeminate," which

Dr. Myrick acknowledges was actually a lack of hand-eye coordination. Jerry exhibited no "flaunting" effeminate behavior or speech, and never expressed a wish to be a girl. The only "mannerisms" Jerry had, and held on to even after treatment, were a lack of physical aggression expressed by not wanting to "slug it out" or physically push people.

As early as 1959, specific children's body movements were cataloged to determine gender norms, and substantial work on this subject has been compiled by George Rekers. In 1977, he devised a list of gestures by observing boys whom he considered "gender-disturbed." Building on the 1977 study, and financed by a United States Public Health Service Research Grant awarded to him through the National Institute of Mental Health in 1978, Rekers and an associate at the Fuller Theological Seminary in Pasadena, California, conducted an experiment with 180 boys and girls in three age groups to determine sex and age differences in physical gestures. They created a childhood body gesture litmus test for mental health or disturbance based upon Rekers' "Operational Definitions of Gestures":

Hand Clasp: Touching the hands together in front of the body.

Hyperextension: Moving the hands in the direction of the posterior surface of the forearm while the elbow is either flexed or extended.

Limp Wrist: Flexing the wrist toward the palmar surface of the forearm and/or upper arm while the elbow is either flexed or extended.

Flutters: A rapid succession of up-and-down movements of the forearms and/or upper arm while the wrist remains relaxed.

Palming: Touching the palm(s) to the back, front or sides of the head above the ear level.

Hands on Hips, Fingers Down or Back: Resting the palm(s) or back of the hand(s) on the waist or hip with fingers pointing down or back.

Flexed Elbow: Walking or standing with the arm(s) held such that the angle between the forearm and the upper arm is between 0 and 135 degrees.

Arm Fold: Placing hands on the opposite arm on the area above the elbow.

Rekers determined that five of the gestures had significantly higher occurrence among girls: Limp Wrist, Arm Flutters, Flexed Elbow, Hand Clasp, and Palming. He also observed that boys and girls had no significant difference in Hyperextension or Arm Fold. Another difference was noted and became a new subcategory: Hands on Hips, Fingers *Forward.* Since older boys did it more often than younger boys, and more often than all girls, this gesture was designated masculine.

Published in 1978, this list continues to have a powerful impact upon what is perceived as normal or abnormal behavior in children. These strict categorizations of physical gestures are the hallmark of the bipolar gender system, in which boys are believed to have naturally masculine mannerisms, and girls to have naturally feminine mannerisms. Dr. Rekers recommends that boys between the ages of four and eleven undergo further evaluation for gender disturbance if their mannerisms include frequent Hand Clasp, Limp Wrist, Flutters, Palming, or Flexed Elbow. Body gestures otherwise considered normal in a girl, and indicative of her mental health, can put a boy at risk for a psychiatric diagnosis when he is as young as four years old. The same holds true for a girl like Becky who does not display adequate frequencies of Flexed Elbow, Hand Clasp, Palming and so on.

The year after Dr. Rekers published the childhood body gestures study, he replicated a classic study in which he analyzed book-carrying behavior differences between the sexes. He confirmed that females cradle their books against their bodies either with one or two arms, whereas males grip them to their side with one hand. Dr. Rekers added a new behavior: backpack carrying. He found that males use backpacks more frequently, and that "females were less consistent than males in the book-carrying method they employed and were more likely to vary the method with the size of the load carried." These results could have two interpretations: superior intelligence among females, or fear among males of attack due to perceived homosexual cues. What were the U.S. Public Health Service and the National Institute of Mental Health thinking when they doled out the money for these studies? What possible significance can "book-carrying behaviors" have to the health and welfare of the citizenry, other than to perceive deviance and engage in witch-hunts against those who do not conform? In 1988, Rekers went so far as to suggest that observation of a child's book-carrying behaviors would serve to "quickly assess [the child] for potential gender disturbance."

In terms of body movements, what we have seen in Jerry's case is the assumption that lack of hand-eye coordination in a boy is a sign of effeminacy, which our culture interprets as a sign of homosexuality in boys. Jerry, who is now in his mid-thirties, was a bright, observant child, who was perhaps drawn to "girl" activities because his natural abilities tended more toward that arena.

As other case histories will show, these boys are generally acutely aware that teachers, parents and therapists are trying to help them avert their assumed fates as adult homosexuals, as demonstrated by their lack of interest, or ability, in athletics. Yet it is this very obsession with perceived effeminate behavior in boys on the part of teachers, parents and therapists that inadvertently teaches these boys to question their sexuality, to fear that, because of their lack of hand-eye coordination, they will grow up to prefer male partners and take on the role of pseudo-women. The same issue was used against Becky, who was penalized for her above average hand-eye coordination, which was interpreted as one sign of her desire to be a boy and to take on the role of a pseudo-man in her adulthood.

The most striking similarity between Jerry's and Becky's cases is the sharp drop in their self-esteem as a result of treatment, even though both of them were experiencing greater social acceptance, at least superficially. Jerry had to "face up to the fact that he wouldn't be a star athlete," and there is no mention of Becky engaging in any competitive sports activities after treatment. Her basketball and softball mitt disappeared, and instead, Becky's assertiveness and independence were swallowed up. When she became "enamored" of the male examiner, giving him her phone number that he might call her "every night and every day," she was exhibiting appropriate "feminine" psychological dependence.

I asked Dr. Myrick if Jerry's parents were notified that their son was being behaviorally treated for "effeminate deviancy" while in school. They were not. They knew he was seeing a school counselor, but the "effeminacy" issue was never presented to the parents. "They didn't know the details," said Dr. Myrick. "They never signed off on the treatment. The teacher never told the parents, you have a homosexual or gay son." That lack of hand-eye coordination equals prehomosexuality in a nine-year-old boy is an alarming and distorted psychological diagnosis, a message that Jerry would certainly have gotten, both directly and indirectly, at a very vulnerable time in his life.

There has been no follow-up on Jerry, but he definitely received messages that he was a homosexual from the very people who perceived themselves as trying to insure him a heterosexual future. No teacher, counselor, judge or psychologist should be given the right to treat a child for perceived gender deviance, particularly without informing the parents, and a child's physical movements should never be regarded as indicators of his or her future sexuality.

Perhaps sensing my shock that Jerry's parents were not fully informed of the behavioral experiment being performed on their son, Dr. Myrick emphasized just how horrible life had been for Jerry, and how isolated and miserable he was, declaring that Jerry played 100 percent of the time with the girls before treatment. As with Becky, a child's condition becomes exaggerated to justify treatment. Dr. Myrick's own pretreatment baseline chart shows that Jerry played, pretreatment, 57 percent of the time with the girls. Myrick explained that, without treatment, Jerry faced a downhill future, because the girls, when they approached middle school age, would reject him, and he would find himself alone.

"Girls don't want sensitive and caring. They want the jerks," said Dr. Myrick. "It's the only fatal flaw of women," he added. "They're drawn toward these kinds of men."

No wonder we so often fall into the trap of believing men are from Mars and women are from Venus. Tragically, that a girl's attraction to "jerks" can be "fatal" is not simply metaphoric. The boys are taught to disdain that which is girlish, and to fight off, within themselves, anything that could be so defined, because it is inferior. This fear sends many a boy into frenzied behavior as he attempts to distance himself from girls in any way available, which includes attacking girls, and other boys. The girls, on the other hand, are taught to form dependent, sexualized relationships with the boys, turning themselves over to them in order to prove their girlhood, learning how to manipulate with "feminine wiles," pretending to be weak, even physically uncoordinated, to enhance a perception of "femininity." By looking carefully at the stories of Becky and Jerry, we can see, in broad strokes, the training we have all received, and the price we continue to pay.

THE FEMININE BOY PROJECT AT UCLA

Anything that challenges the definition of girl and boy fuels our cultural anxiety around gender. So deep is that anxiety that our government has sponsored many studies and experiments on children who do not fit the norm. Government records indicate that, since the early 1970s, at least 1.5 million dollars was awarded from the National Institute of Mental Health (NIMH) alone for this purpose. For the most part, on the occasions when "normal" children were studied with these funds, it was to determine treatment goals for the "abnormal" children. The institutions that received these funds include UCLA, the State University of New York at Stony Brook, the Roosevelt Institute in New York City,

Fuller Theological Seminary and the Logos Research Institute. The last two organizations name George Rekers as the principal investigator.

In most cases, the original NIMH grant proposals have been destroyed, leaving behind only single-sentence descriptions. For example, the only surviving description for a 1976 grant of $96,153 to Fuller Theological Seminary, with George Rekers listed as the Principal Investigator (PI), is "behavioral treatment of childhood gender problems." Rekers himself claims that the NIMH has funded him "over half a million dollars . . . to conduct research on the early identification and treatment of childhood gender problems . . . ," which leads me to believe that 1.5 million dollars awarded to institutions is probably the tip of the iceberg. Tens of thousands in additional funds have been awarded to individual researchers through agencies such as the Foundations Fund for Research in Psychiatry, the Research Scientist Development Award fund, the Public Health Service's clinical research grants and the National Institute of Health's Biomedical Research Support grants. The single largest and most heavily documented government-funded experiment in the United States with nonconforming children took place in the 1970s at UCLA, under the direction of O. Ivar Lovaas, Richard Green and George Rekers, and the target population was the feminine boy.

KRAIG

FOUR YEARS OLD

One night, when Kraig was putting his infant sister's clothing on her stuffed animals, his father became furious and spanked him while his mother stood by, watching. This incident might have been what this mother needed to convince her husband that Kraig should be taken to the clinic at UCLA, where they would be able to help him overcome his feminine behavior.

In 1973, Rekers and Lovaas devised a behavioral treatment

plan for the feminine boy project. The study required access to feminine boys, and they needed to show dramatic improvement in the boys' conditions as a result of their behavioral treatment. In this same time period, Dr. Richard Green was at UCLA's Neuropsychiatric Institute, where he was the principal analyst for the feminine boy project.

Dr. Green was the one responsible for procuring the boys, and so he sent letters announcing the feminine boy project to psychiatrists, psychologists and family general practitioners in the Los Angeles area. In the letter, he described the features of such a boy as: "frequent dressing in girls' or women's clothing, a preference for traditional girls' activities, and statements of wanting to be a girl." He stressed that the boys had to be prepubertal, in order to "better study the association between early gender-role behaviors and later patterns of erotic preference." Green appeared on a television talk show to discuss the effeminate boy and the UCLA project that might help him. Also on television was a man who explained to the viewers that, because he played with dolls as a boy, he grew up to be homosexual. The message could not have been clearer: feminine boys were suspected of being prehomosexual.

Kraig's mother was watching television that day. We do not know what she thought of her son's behavior before she saw that television show, but it is clear that she became alarmed, and began a campaign to convince her husband that Kraig should be taken to UCLA. (There is sometimes a contention that men are more gender-phobic than women, but the truth is that women are just as involved in inculcating gender roles, particularly in young boys, and that women did, and still do, figure prominently among the researchers and clinicians involved in this field.)

When he was four years and eleven months old, Kraig's treatment began with a genital examination to determine if he had any physical abnormalities that the doctors felt might otherwise account for his feminine behaviors. To this end, researchers working for the feminine boy project also tested his chromosomes, and performed a sex chromatin study. His mother knew that they were testing to see if Kraig was really a boy, or if there were some hidden girl component in his body. They found that Kraig was an anatomically normal male.

Kraig was then sent by Richard Green to George Rekers and O. Ivar Lovaas, and a ten-month behavioral treatment began. Rekers later wrote, "Before treatment, [Kraig] had been described by a psychiatric authority on gender identity problems as one of the most severe cases he had assessed . . . [Kraig] continually displayed pronounced feminine mannerisms, gestures, and gait, as well as exaggerated feminine inflection and feminine content of speech. He had a remarkable ability to mimic all the subtle feminine behaviors of an adult woman . . . He appeared to be very skilled at manipulating [his mother] to satisfy his feminine interests (e.g., he would offer to 'help mommy' by carrying her purse when she had other packages to carry)." It is difficult to know what condition Kraig was actually in when he was first brought to UCLA, but much is revealed in the transcripts recorded by Dr. Green in his retrospective study of these boys, which he published in 1987 as *The "Sissy Boy Syndrome."*

Green's transcripts include interviews with the parents at the time they brought Kraig to UCLA, and with the mother and Kraig when he was seventeen, and again at eighteen years old. (It should be noted that Kraig's name was changed by Dr. Green to "Kyle" for *The "Sissy Boy Syndrome,"* and most recently, in 1995, by Dr. Rekers to "Craig" for his *Handbook of Child and Adolescent Sexual Problems.)*

What of Green's determination that Kraig wanted to be a girl? It was the Vietnam era, and at seventeen, Kraig recalled, ". . . before I started kindergarten I was afraid that all boys had to go to the army and be killed. I thought I had to go to the army and be killed, so then I wanted to be a girl 'cause I didn't want to go get killed." This was clearly not a prehomosexual or pretranssexual desire being expressed, and in particular, nowhere in the transcripts or reports does it anywhere state that Kraig was disturbed, or even unhappy, about his anatomy. Kraig also remembered playing with a "mixed" group of children, and that his best friend was a boy. This was not a boy who played only with girls, another symptom of "deviant sex-role."

At the intake interview with Kraig's parents, Dr. Green asked them if Kraig had a history of cross-dressing, and if he ever expressed the belief that he was a girl. The parents had some memories of Kraig with a shirt on his head, pretending he had long hair, and a few other instances of mop and towel play. Kraig also wore his father's T-shirt to bed one night, and the next morning, looking at himself in the reflection of a glass oven door, Kraig said he was wearing a dress. These incidents were enough for Kraig to be labeled as "cross-dressing since he was two years old." Green and Rekers never documented if this child refused to wear boy's clothing.

"Sex-role deviant" boys are also depicted as refusing to engage in any male fantasy roles and as believing that they will grow up to be women. Kraig's mother did report, at the time she brought her son to the clinic, that he wanted "to grow up to be a mommy." Yet, when she explained to him that "daddies go out and work . . . to make money—that's father's role," Kraig was also reported as saying, "Well, I want to grow up and be like daddy." No one ever asked Kraig what it meant to him "to be a mommy." From what has been written about his case, there is nothing to indicate that he wanted to have a woman's body when he was grown up.

When the parents were asked if Kraig had ever said he wanted to be a girl, they said that he did. When they were asked if the boy had ever asserted that he *was* a girl, they said, "No." A dozen years later, when the mother was asked if her son, at the time she brought him to UCLA for an initial evaluation, was confused as to whether he was a girl or a boy, she answered, "I think so. Oh, I'm sure . . . He saw nothing wrong with picking up a doll instead of a car." She also stated that Kraig did not know if he was supposed to play with the teacups or the cars. Perhaps, in the years that followed her son's treatment, this mother had a strong investment in rationalizing having turned her son over to the doctors, and to do this, she created a memory that he was confused about his anatomical sex.

Kraig was the first child to be treated by Rekers and Lovaas for "deviant sex-role behaviors," and the treatment took place both in Kraig's home and at the clinic. Many other young boys would follow in Kraig's treatment path. Rekers and Lovaas go to great lengths to explain why it was important to behaviorally treat a child like Kraig. The first reason was that the child will be scorned by his playmates, and that it is easier to change the child, rather than the society in which he lives. Secondly, the doctors believed Kraig to be at risk for adult transsexualism, transvestism and "some forms of homosexuality." (Homosexuals whose gender identities conform to their sex are not considered to be quite as pathological as those homosexuals whose gender identities do not conform to their sex. Therefore, a gay carpenter is not as sick as a gay hairdresser, and a lesbian nurse is not as sick as a lesbian plumber.)

The most chilling claim by Rekers and Lovaas, which would certainly have alarmed any parent, was that Kraig was at risk not only for depression, but for "arrest, trial, and imprisonment" in association with his possible future as a transsexual. Their most remarkable assertion, however, is the following: "self-mutilation in the form of autocastration or autopenectomy was attempted in 18% and accomplished in 9% of one series of adult cases." Nowhere in the literature of Kraig's case is there a single statement, by the child or the parents, that even implies that this five-year-old wanted to cut off his penis, or that his feelings about being a boy, or a girl, had anything whatsoever to do with his body. Rather, Kraig's thoughts about being a girl or being a boy seem to be based on socially sanctioned gender roles, including his strong self-preservation instinct which told him he did not want to die in war.

Rekers and Lovaas designed the primary clinical feature of this treatment, which Rekers later replicated in treating Becky, and continues to recommend: the play-observation room with the one-way mirror, and the masculine and feminine toy tables. To obtain baseline play behaviors, Kraig's dress-up table featured various clothing and grooming toys. "On one side were girls' cosmetic articles and girls' apparel, consisting of a woman's wig, a long-sleeve dress (child's size), a play cosmetic set (lipstick and manicure items), and a set of jewelry consisting of bracelets, necklaces, rings, and earrings . . . On the other side of the Dress-Up Table were boys' apparel: namely, a plastic football helmet, an army 'fatigue' shirt . . . an army belt with hatchet holder and canteen holder, and a battery operated play electric razor . . ." The affect tables in Kraig's playroom featured: "girl toys associated with maternal nurturance; namely, a baby doll in a 3-foot crib with sliding side, a baby bottle, baby powder, and a Barbie doll with two sets of dresses, shoes, hat, and miniature clothesline . . . On the other side were placed articles associated with masculine aggression, consisting of two dart guns with darts, a small target, a rubber knife, plastic handcuffs, and a set of plastic cowboys and Indians . . ."

Kraig was left by his mother at the door to the play-observation room, where a doctor, presumably Rekers, led him into the room. Kraig's memory of the doctor is that he had very big ears that stuck out. When Kraig entered, he saw the large mirror and the two tables of toys. The doctor instructed Kraig, "When I leave this room, you may play with any of the toys on this table." He pointed only to the affect table, the one with the baby doll and the handcuffs. "Even though you will not see me," said the doctor, "I can see you play; so, I will know if you are playing with this table or a wrong table. So remember, choose toys to play with from this table only." Kraig watched the doctor with the long ears leave the room and close the door behind him. It might have been difficult for this four-year-old to understand exactly how the doctor would be able to see him, and he might have wondered why he did not simply stay in the room if he was going to watch him anyway.

Kraig did not display interest in the "masculine" toys, although his attraction to the army belt was noted. In fact, he took the army belt and tied it around his head. Kraig did not receive a masculine play point on the observer's scorecard for playing with the army belt, however, because what he did with it was considered "inappropriate play (e.g., cross-gender role use of same-gender toy object, such as army belt for a bonnet)." A variety of "probe" conditions were used, to see if Kraig changed how he played depending upon who was in the room. The only time Kraig engaged in exclusive masculine play was in his father's presence, which is not difficult to understand considering the father's response to his dressing up the stuffed animals.

This was not a particularly difficult phase of treatment for Kraig, and the observations established a baseline of his gender behavior, which was predominantly feminine. Kraig's assessment then moved to his home. A checklist of deviant effeminate behaviors was made, and for four ten-minute periods every day, Kraig's mother would watch him, and make check marks to indicate if he had engaged in the behaviors on the checklist, which were: "(a) plays with girls, (b) plays with female dolls, (c) feminine gestures, which included limp wrist, swishy hand, arm or torso movements, sway of hips, etc., and (d) female role play, which included impersonating or pretending to be a female (like actress, mother, female teacher) when playing games (like house, school, etc.)." Every three weeks, research assistants went to Kraig's home to watch his mother watch him, to be sure she was catching the behaviors and recording them correctly. After the baselines were established, the therapy began at the clinic, three times a week, for three ten-minute sessions in an hour.

In his early sessions, Kraig and his mother were alone inside the observation room with the one-way mirror. Kraig's mother wore a set of earphones, and she had a book on her lap. The toy tables were again present. The doctor entered the room and said, "You may play with any of the toys you like on the table, until I come back. You may talk with your mommy, too, if you want to. I'll be back in ten minutes." He then left the room.

Initially, Kraig engaged in some type of feminine-identified play behavior. Maybe he picked up the plastic tea dishes, and poured imaginary tea from the teapot. He would have taken a pretend sip, and then offered his mother some. She would have bent toward him, smiling. Kraig would have seen her suddenly jerk upright, and look away from him toward the one-way window. His mother was being prompted, through the earphones, by the doctor. She was told to completely ignore him, because he was engaged in feminine play. Kraig would have no understanding of what was happening to his mother. On one such occasion, his distress at her behavior was such that he began to scream, but his mother just looked away. His anxiety increased, and he did whatever he could to get her to respond to him, but she just looked away. She must have seemed like a stranger to have changed her behavior toward him so suddenly and for no apparent reason. He went to her, pulled on her, did anything he could to get her to speak, even if she were just going to reprimand him, but he could get no response. He was described as being in a panic, alternating between sobs and "aggressing at her," but again, when his distraught mother finally looked at him and began to respond, she stopped mid-sentence and abruptly turned away, as if he were not there. Kraig became so hysterical, and his mother so uncomfortable, that one of the clinicians had to enter and take Kraig, screaming, from the room.

Dr. Rekers explained, "During the session, the mother was helped to extinguish feminine behavior (verbal and play) by instructions over the earphones such as 'stop talking to him now,' 'pick up the book and read,' 'ignore him now,' 'look away from him.' Immediately after the mother's correct response, the doctors verbally reinforced that response; e.g., 'good,' 'great, that's what we want,' 'that's right,' 'excellent' . . . Before sending Kraig back to the playroom, we reassured the mother empathetically that she was doing the right thing . . ."

Back in the playroom again, whenever Kraig touched a masculine toy, his mother was instructed over the earphones, " 'quick, look at him now,' or 'talk to him now.' " If the doctors had understood that one of the main reasons Kraig did not want to be a boy was that he did not want to go to war and be killed, perhaps they might not have provided such toys. As it was, for rehabilitation of his gender deviance, Kraig was offered miniature plastic soldiers, a submachine gun, a rubber knife, an army helmet, an army fatigue shirt and the army belt. In effect, to get his mother's love back, Kraig had to be aggressive, willing to play at war, to "die" or "kill" in a boy's toy land.

Kraig's deviance was also addressed within his home, creating what Rekers described as a "24-hour" program, with "investigators . . . 'on call' at all times," and frequent visits to his home by research personnel. The home phase of the behavioral treatment consisted of a token system: when he was good, his mother gave him blue tokens, and when he was bad, she gave him red tokens. Before the token system was put into place, Rekers and Lovaas decided to start with "non-gender" behaviors which would be "clinically safer." These included brushing his teeth for a blue token, tracking dirt on the carpet for a red token. After he stopped those behaviors which earned red tokens, they moved on to the feminine gestures, and initiated a system of consequences, or "back-up reinforcers," for the blue and red tokens. Blue tokens could be cashed in for favorite candy bars, watching television or other treats. Getting a red token for a feminine outburst such as "Oh my goodness," or playing with dolls, might result in Kraig's losing some of the blue tokens he had accumulated, getting a time-out, or not being allowed to watch television. For the first four months, a research assistant was sent to Kraig's home three times a week to be sure that his parents, particularly his mother, were fully implementing the token system. The most effective red token back-up reinforcer was selected in "consultation" with the doctors: "physical punishment by spanking from the father." Each red token earned Kraig one "swat," and Rekers and Lovaas concluded that spanking was the only red token back-up reinforcer that successfully affected Kraig's behavior. The final feminine play behavior extinguished by Rekers and Lovaas, using the red tokens, was "plays with girls."

According to Rekers and Lovaas, Kraig experienced an almost miraculous turnaround, although there was some suspicion that "he was 'going underground' with his deviance, suppressing his femininity in the company of adults." By the beginning of session 56, Kraig would enter the playroom and say aloud, "I wonder which toys I will play with. Oh, these are girls' toys here, I don't want to play with them." Rekers and Lovaas actually refer to this as Kraig's "spontaneous verbal labelling." Here is a child whose every movement and voice inflection were being charted. He was probably dreaming of blue and red chips after a few months of this. As with Becky, Kraig is finally described, by session 60, as engaging in "exclusively" gender-appropriate play. Rekers, perhaps in a bid to continue funding for this type of treatment, claims in his 1995 *Handbook* that he would never want a child to have rigid gender play behaviors. Yet his two hallmark cases, Becky and Kraig, are respectively described in their post-treatment play as rigidly feminine and rigidly masculine.

In follow-up, twenty-six months after treatment had begun, Kraig's mother expressed concern that her son had become a "rough neck," and was acquiring the destructive behaviors of the boy next door. Rekers and Lovaas wrote, "We reassured the mother that such 'mildly delinquent' behavior was much easier to correct in future years than feminine behaviors would be." The doctors described how Kraig no longer cared if his hair was neat and, most significantly, no longer engaged in the deviant behavior of "color-coordinating his clothes." They do reserve some judgment, however, because it is their clinical impression "that he may still be less skilled in some desired masculine play behaviors (e.g., throwing, catching, and batting a softball) than his same-aged peers." Again, the specter of poor hand-eye coordination is raised.

A disturbing aspect of Kraig's "turnaround" concerns how his relationship with his father is depicted. The father and son are described, post-treatment, as happily going off to Indian Guide club meetings and weekend campouts. Yet when Kraig was seventeen, and his mother was again interviewed by Dr. Green, she said that as a result of his experience at UCLA, Kraig and his father ". . . drew further apart." If anything, his son's diagnosis as gender deviant only served to intensify this father's rejection of his child. The mother went on to defend her husband, saying that Kraig "can really shut somebody out if he wants to." After the invasive treatment this boy received, the ability to shut someone out could be perceived as an instinct for self-preservation.

Ten years later, Rekers continued to describe fifteen-year-old Kraig as the poster boy for behavioral treatment of boyhood effeminacy. Richard Green's follow-up interviews with Kraig paint a very different picture. Kraig became a young man terrified of his sexuality, worried that if he wore his hair wrong it might make him appear feminine, and obsessively alert to any kind of overture by a male. If Kraig thought a man might be gay, and was trying to make contact with him, Kraig was driven to feelings of physical violence, which he would soon turn against himself. At eighteen, when he called his own sexuality into question, he responded by taking fifty aspirins in a suicide attempt. The word "shame" runs throughout the dialogue he had at that point in time with Dr. Green: shame for "everything about UCLA," shame for playing with dolls, shame and confusion about his sexuality. He specifically remembers about the UCLA behavioral treatment experience at the clinic and at his home: "I felt really ashamed, and I didn't want anybody to know, and when the research guys would come to check on me, I didn't want anybody to see me with them."

Once again, there is evidence that much of Kraig's childhood behavior, specifically his avoidance of "rough and tumble play," the hallmark of boyhood legitimacy, was connected to a lack of hand-eye coordination. This subject was not addressed during Kraig's treatment, but Dr. Green asked him at eighteen, "If you were a woman now, magically, what advantage would you have?" Kraig replied, "I can't really think of any. Except for maybe since I am uncoordinated everything would fit my sex better if I was a woman."

Kraig's suicide attempt and subsequent confusion and anxiety about his sexuality do not affect Dr. Green's conclusion that none of the children in the feminine boy project were "harmed by treatment." Ironically, despite the publication of the follow-up studies with Kraig, George Rekers, in his 1995 handbook for pediatricians, continues to use Kraig's case history as a treatment model, although he has modified some of the initial case report. Gone is the statement "Kraig had been described by a psychiatric authority on gender identity problems as one of the most severe cases he had assessed." Gone is the description of Kraig as using his "mother's" clothing, which is now described as "girl's" clothing. Referring to Kraig's use of his "mother's" clothing would have been a way of backing up an extreme attachment to his mother, one of the popular theories at the time on the cause of gender deviance in boys. Now, however, that is no longer quite as fashionable, and it is "girl's" clothing that Kraig is described as wearing. Once again, although Kraig never is reported to have repudiated his anatomy, Rekers writes in 1995 that "Such boys exhibit many cross-gender behaviors in conjunction with a cross-gender identity evidenced by persistent repudiation of their male anatomic status." The reason for Rekers' emphasis on the child's repudiation of his penis is that the specter of transsexualism is far more powerful at this point in time than the specter of homosexuality.

There was a long succession of boys in the UCLA study, and among them was an eight-year-old named Carl. He refused to go along with playing in a room with a one-way window, but his treatment was essentially the same, with one important addition: the red and blue tokens appeared in his classroom, under the control of his teacher. According to his case history, Carl's deviances included enjoying Flip Wilson, "a [black] male comedian who cross-dresses and assumes a female role." He also had a tendency to use such phrases as "Oh, my goodness" and "Goodness gracious." One of the "play acting" categories of behavior that Rekers and Lovaas included in deviances to watch out for was Carl's "feminine role" of "pretending to be his mother washing dishes." Observers went to Carl's home on the average of two evening visits each week, and they helped his mother to record Carl's masculine and feminine speech content, activities and body gestures. Carl's treatment lasted for fifteen months.

One of Carl's treatment components included athletic training, to cure his "deficits in throwing a football." At follow-up twelve months after the treatment program had ended, the parents' "only remaining concern was that Carl would occasionally make self-critical remarks about his athletic abilities." Hand-eye coordination problems were marching again under the psychiatric flag of gender identity disorder of childhood in boys.

Carl was another of Dr. Rekers' and Dr. Lovaas' miracle cures. We do not have the extensive cross-references about Carl that we have about Kraig. We do know that they found him at risk for transvestism, transsexualism and probably autopenectomy. They also wrote, "After our behavioral treatment, the two independent psychologists could find no evidence of feminine behavior or identification in Carl's test responses or interview behavior." Perhaps Carl's feminine behavior had gone underground, as the doctors suggested with Kraig, yet of all the things in this report, the most disturbing are Carl's own "volunteered" words, that he "used to be a queer, but not anymore."

One of the strangest phases of treatment for these boys involved their group therapy. Picture a large group of feminine boys on a playground with male coaches reinforcing any sign, however minuscule, however "inept," of masculine behavior, shouting constantly with deliberate emphasis on masculine nouns: "That's a good *boy*." "Come on, *guys*." "You're getting taller; you're going to be a big *man* when you grow up." When feminine gestures are exhibited by a boy, the therapist/coach says, "Hey, don't run like that." We are told that "the boys know what the admonition refers to." Any type of female role taking, which typically surfaced during rest periods from sports or enforced "rough housing," was met with immediate negative reinforcement: "You don't *look* much like a stewardess. You look more like a *pilot*. I think you'd make a better pilot." According to Dr. Green, who supervised this arena of therapy, there was a particularly distinct advantage to this type of treatment. At first, the boys would allow each other to take on female roles, but soon, they turned on each other, and in Dr. Green's view, this was an important aspect of their rehabilitation. "For example, one boy with an effeminate lisp took severe exception to another boy's speech, citing a lisping quality. When the therapist wondered whether the criticizing boy had ever *also* had difficulty in his manner of speaking, this was adamantly denied."

These boys also turned on themselves, exhibiting what Green describes as "Identifying with the aggressor. A potentially feminine toy, such as a stuffed animal, may be, with great display, rejected as a 'sissy' object, a feminine boy thus identifying with the masculine boys who usually tease him." Oppressed individuals often turn on each other in frustration and shame, and they often try to take power by identifying with their oppressors. It is disheartening that the National Institute of Mental Health underwrote this treatment.

In the course of my research on UCLA's feminine boy project, the name of O. Ivar Lovaas was prominent. Dr. Lovaas still works at UCLA, where he is the head of the Clinic for Behavioral Treatment of Children. His specialty at present is autism, and he now dissociates himself from what now is known as Gender Identity Disorder of childhood. Dr. Lovaas agreed to be interviewed on the condition that he tape-record our conversation. During the conversation, Dr. Lovaas was defensive and frequently explosive. Like others in the field, such as Dr. Myrick in Florida, who treated Jerry, Dr. Lovaas wishes to distance himself from this work in regard to questions of sexuality.

Dr. Lovaas began by claiming that the feminine boy project took place in the early 1960s, and that his role in the project was minor. I refreshed his memory by pointing out that the National Institute of Mental Health grant checks to UCLA for all of the research on the children in 1973, 1974 and 1975 were written with the understanding that he was the principal investigator. He often interrupted, raising his voice as if being attacked, in a bid to prevent this simple fact from being acknowledged: over and above the funds that Richard Green brought with him from SUNY-Stony Brook, $218,945 went to UCLA from the NIMH with Dr. Lovaas as Principal Investigator (PI) in this project. For the early 1970s, this was an extraordinary amount of money for such a research grant, and because he was the PI, Dr. Lovaas was also the kingpin, the one whose reputation secured the grant, and the one who determined how the money would be allocated.

He now describes his role as tangential, explaining that he was simply on a committee that evaluated the research of a young assistant professor, George Rekers, who was working on gender deviation. Dr. Lovaas says that gender deviation was of absolutely no interest to him, which might be news to the National Institute of Mental Health.

When asked who specifically examined the children's genitals before they were admitted into the program, he became enraged, denying that anyone had ever looked at the children's bodies in any way. When told that it was reported by the NIMH, and in Dr. Rekers' own studies, that the children's genitals were examined by *someone,* along with other physical tests to rule out anatomical deviances in feminine boys, he denied knowledge of that.

He then explained that at the time this research was performed, UCLA was heavily involved in psychosexual reassignment. He believes that transsexualism results from living a life of rejection and accusation by peers, which drives these men to undergo hormonal treatments and genital changes, that they might live as women. Dr. Lovaas contends that these men were so seriously emotionally disturbed by the time they were thirty years old that they contemplated suicide, and wanted to have their bodies changed. Dr. Lovaas said that some of those who underwent the reassignment were pleased, and others were not. In the 1970s, he believed that if he could prevent the children from experiencing peer rejection, such as being called a sissy, they would not grow up to be disturbed to the point of wanting to change their bodies. This statement would indicate that gender deviation actually was of interest to him.

When asked why Kraig's treatment included spankings by his father, he stated that the father or mother decided to do that, not him. When asked why he, as the UCLA psychologist in charge of a government-funded study, did not insist that hitting the boy was not a sound psychological tool for growth and self-esteem, he stated that he just gave parents advice on what to do.

During the interview with Dr. Lovaas, my suspicions were confirmed that the boys in the study were not necessarily in as dire a condition as the reports might lead one to think. "Many of the boys did not exhibit any cross-dressing or any behaviors like that in the presence of the father. Only in the presence of the mother," said Dr. Lovaas. "When the issue came up, the father said, 'I never saw that.' That was a common observation of ours." Yet the children were portrayed in the case studies as compulsively performing these behaviors, with little or no choice. One could speculate that this would enhance the position of the researchers by highlighting profound gender deviance. The more deviant the child is to begin with, the more impressive their post-treatment, gender-appropriate behavior would be to funding sources.

Lovaas described the boys as playing with cosmetics, wigs and other female grooming items, which were made available to them on dress-up tables. "They were like superwomen," he said. The concept of these boys performing like "superwomen" is very revealing. Kraig is described as "swishing" around the clinic, "fully dressed as a woman with a long dress, wig, nail polish, high screechy voice, slatternly, seductive eyes . . ." (Another UCLA gender behaviorist, Lawrence Newman, used the phrase "slovenly seductive eyes" when describing Kraig's case.) This behavior suggested to the doctors that Kraig was suffering from "irreversible neurological and biochemical determinants." If a five-year-old girl were performing as Kraig did, she would not be diagnosed as gender deviant, although she might be viewed as practicing to be

48

a "superwoman." Perhaps these boys were treated because they frightened the adults around them when they reflected an exaggerated and stylized female gender role performance in such a devastatingly accurate manner. Ironically, many doctors still believe that this type of behavior is caused in some girls and women by "irreversible neurological and biochemical determinants," when it is actually the product of a series of choices and coercions, conscious and otherwise.

In terms of the boys who engaged in this behavior, Dr. Lovaas stated that they would not be able to develop friendships until they were seventeen, eighteen or nineteen years old, at which time "they could meet people like themselves." Dr. Lovaas said it was very, very easy to change behaviors, but that it was simply "just not interesting" after the first three or four children were seen. Despite this observation, he allowed treatment to proceed with sixty-six boys between the ages of four and twelve, at taxpayers' expense.

After six to twelve months of treating the boys, Lovaas said, "they'd dress like boys, talk like boys, gesture like boys. To me, this was easy to do, and as far as I was concerned, that fulfilled the intent of the study." When asked about treatment goals regarding the boys' adult sexualities, he responded hotly, "The issue of sexual orientation is of no interest to me." It seems disingenuous of Dr. Lovaas to claim a "disinterest" in sexual orientation, when his own reports on Kraig and Carl reveal a very clear agenda. For example, in June of 1974, Dr. Lovaas coauthored the article on Carl, in which Carl stated that he " 'used to be a queer, but not anymore.' " The doctors follow up his statement with: "The treatment has clearly changed Carl's overt gender-related behaviors, suggesting that his sex-role development may have become normalized." In the spring of 1977, Lovaas was coauthor of a study of a child with gender behavior disturbance which speculated: "He may also be high risk for a homosexual adjustment."

I again broached with Dr. Lovaas the fact that Kraig had been touted as a poster boy for gender treatment, only to become suicidal. By self-report, Kraig said that he knew he was being brought to UCLA to prevent him from growing up to be a homosexual because, among other things, he played with dolls and wanted his hair to be neat. Dr. Lovaas said, "I am not responsible for that. I don't know what happened to these kids in follow-up. My responsibility was to help George Rekers set up a scientific study." I asked Dr. Lovaas if he had read Richard Green's book, from which this follow-up information on Kraig comes, and he answered, "I think I did. It didn't provide any information to me which I thought was all that helpful."

When pressed on the subject of sexual development, and specifically in terms of preventing any deviance from heterosexuality, which Rekers has clearly stated was his goal in treating these boys, Dr. Lovaas became inflamed. "I lived in Norway during the war when Adolf came. And it's the last thing you want to do . . . A real psychologist would encourage variability . . . Some persons contribute a lot to society, as scientists or artists. And those people deviate from the average. For the survival of the culture, you want all kinds of persons. But you don't want to assign them that role at five years of age." This was a surprising outburst. Lovaas was conceding that he connected boyhood play behavior with adult sexuality, something he earlier denied, and he also seemed to think that I was accusing him of some form of genocide.

BLAMING THE PARENTS

The most revealing insight gained from my talk with Dr. Lovaas, however, was his experience with the parents. Dr. Lovaas explained that there was a strong psychoanalytic etiology at the time which featured "horrendous accusations of the mother," including pathological penis envy. According to Lovaas, the psychoanalyzing of the mother "was the alternative to the [behavioral] treatment of the children. The mothers came to us with enormous guilt. They thought they had caused this problem.

They might have gotten the idea from psychoanalysts. You make a statement like that to a mom, and she would pay any amount of money to take care of that!"

When the mother was blamed for her son's femininity, she typically became "totally panicked whenever her child would put on a skirt. Initially, when it first occurs, it's common. At the beginning, [parents] think it's funny. But some persons act anxious around it. The impression I had was that the kids would sometimes control the mother. Kids are extremely good at manipulating the parents. From the beginning, the kids want this control."

Lovaas described a typical mother and son scenario, which was reminiscent of Kraig and his mother. "The mom and the kid are sitting in the waiting room. I come and ask, 'Can I talk with you now in the office?' Very quickly, the kid would pick up the purse and carry it, and mother would be panicked! To help mother disengage from these behaviors was quite a task. Mother has been told by the analyst that she has penis envy, that she couldn't handle a boy because he has a penis, and that she controls her aggression toward this by pretending her son is a girl." Lovaas scoffs at this analysis, feeling it has caused only harm.

Dr. Lovaas is quite clear on this scenario: the mothers of these children are willing to pay any amount of money to correct the situation. They are also willing to subject themselves to treatment, as are many of their husbands. Kraig's mother had to sign a contract guaranteeing that she would faithfully record Kraig's feminine behaviors, that she would use the blue and red token system as the psychologists instructed and that she would allow observers in her home at least twice a week. Other parents were required to attend group therapy sessions, in which they discussed the reasons for their sons' deviant behavior, as well as their role in it.

During the UCLA sessions, which were controlled by Dr. Richard Green, the mothers also discussed their feelings about homosexuality, which they clearly connected to their sons' play behaviors. They struggled with questions of biochemical versus environmental causes. They were chastised for laughing at their sons' feminine behavior, such as pretending to be a "stewardess," because their laughter, they were told, was encouraging him. Another mother remarked that the only child who wanted to play with her son was a tomboy who "will outgrow it." One mother rebelled: "I'm not going to follow him around saying, 'Don't do this and don't do that.' 'Keep your hands down.' 'Don't put your hands on your hip.' I'm just not going to reduce myself to doing that." This mother was made to feel guilty for her self-indulgent negligence. Another mother reported on her son's progress in rejecting girl playmates. "There is one little girl who calls him up to play with him, and he says, 'I don't want to play with her. She's a dumb broad.' I don't know if he is doing it to please me or if this is typical of boys that age." The therapist answered, "It could be both." Mother responded, "It really pleases me. He hasn't done anything in months and months and months that has even worried me a bit." That this mother was convinced by a government-funded psychologist that her son's referring to a little girl as a "dumb broad" can be taken as a sign of his psychological progress is a powerful commentary on the institutional roots of gender-based extremism.

In contrast to the blame and shame sessions with the mothers, the fathers' group therapy sessions focused on getting the dads to spend more time with their sons, particularly by joining "Indian Guides." Unlike the Boy Scouts, which are often run by den mothers, Indian Guides was limited to fathers. This organization was preferable, Dr. Green explained to the parents, because "Feminine kids don't need their mothers around." The success of Indian Guides in reaffirming the father-son bond must be taken with a grain of salt. We learn from Dr. Green's own follow-up with Kraig that his membership in the Guides only covered up his true relationship with his father, which, according to his mother, actually deteriorated as a result of his UCLA diagnosis and treatment.

During the group therapy sessions, one father expressed confusion that his son's desire to play with girls was considered symptomatic of psychological disturbance. Dr. Green explained,

"These kids don't choose girls as playmates because there is something tremendously attractive about girls; they choose them because they are not a threat to them, they don't tease them." A recent interpretation suggests that these boys are inherently bossy, and can take charge when they play with girls.

Two areas stand out vividly in these ministrations to the parents. First, there is the devaluation of all that is traditionally feminine when it appears strongly in a boy. Girls are not chosen by the boys because they like them; they are chosen because they can be dominated, or are not a threat. Activities are chosen not because they are enjoyed, but because the boys fail at masculine activities, because if the boys could succeed at masculine activities, why would they bother with feminine activities? Second, a true emotional bond or friendship between a boy and a girl is ridiculed and devalued. Green explained that "before adolescence your companions are sort of reflective of your self-image." He reasoned that a preadolescent boy who wants to play with a girl has a self-image as a girl. Therefore, the boy is disturbed, and his relationship with the girls is a reflection of his illness, or gender deviance.

There are many theories on parent culpability for their child's gender nonconformance, from delayed naming of a newborn to prenatal gender preferences of parents, neither of which holds up to scrutiny. One of the most influential theories came from Robert Stoller, Richard Green's mentor at UCLA. Stoller believed that the mother and son experienced a "blissful symbiosis" because the boy represents for the mother "her treasured [feminized] phallus" which results in the boy feeling himself "to be somehow female despite knowing that he is male." Stoller also accused the mother of what he called "bisexuality." As he used the term, bisexuality referred to the mother having a combination of masculine and feminine traits in her childhood, which often included "periods of cross-dressing" and "competing with boys in athletics or at school." These mothers have been accused of being covert tomboys who adopted, at puberty, "feminine facades." The mother's mother can be blamed for her grandson's behavior, even if she is not present. Grandmother is described as " 'empty' and unable to be a model for identification," leaving the mother's father to fill the void, which leads the mother to a state of "intense penis envy and rage," not to mention "penis awe." To treat these mothers, Lawrence Newman suggested that a masculine therapist be enlisted, one who is "perhaps feared by the mother." Newman reports that, when the boys are successfully treated with behavioral techniques like those of Rekers and Lovaas, ". . . the boys become more verbally and physically aggressive toward their mothers in almost all reported cases."

In 1991, Janet Mitchell conducted a comparison between the mothers of feminine boys, the mothers of boys with other clinical disorders, and the mothers of normal boys. She found that there were no remarkable differences in childhood cross-gender identity among these three groups. Yet the theories described above were powerful ones at the time of the feminine boy project, and they have lingered on in the popular imagination. Many mothers believe that their own secret pathologies, which they themselves might not recognize, have contributed to their child's behavior and his bleak prognosis.

In 1991, despite Mitchell's research which they themselves cite, Richard Green and Dr. Kenneth Zucker, head of the largest childhood gender identity clinic in Canada, speculated that "other aspects of psychosexuality need to be studied, such as the mother's current attitude toward men and her concurrent views regarding masculinity and femininity." Mothers are also seen as misguided in their attempts to institute nonsexist environments for their sons as well as their daughters. Follow-up observations of feminine boys have described their mothers as not properly bonded to their sons, who as a result display separation anxiety disorder, which is somehow connected to "boyhood femininity." Only one thing is clear: feminine boys have a range of mothers. Some mothers are psychologically stronger than others, but they share no common deviances that can account for their sons' behaviors.

Fathers, although not focused on with as much intensity until later years, were also held responsible, but the blame did not stop with them being unavailable for their sons due to work commitments. They were accused of not performing their "wedge" function, according to Robert Stoller, a UCLA psychologist who, in the mid-1960s, began to study gender issues in childhood. In this scenario, the father is supposed to insert himself by driving a wedge, as it were, between his wife and his son. It is assumed that the boy will then develop normally, and not become overwhelmed by a fear of castration after viewing his mother naked, seeing she has no penis and identifying his body with hers. The father of the feminine boy is further accused of not presenting himself "as a rival for mother's affection," which is considered normal development.

Along with the mother, fathers are guilty of tolerating nonconforming gender behavior, and thereby encouraging it. Most revealing, they are described as having less recall of masculine behavior during childhood. Although they engaged in boyish activities, they also enjoyed solitary pursuits, such as reading, or artistic activities. The subtext is that these fathers are inadequate in their masculinity, and have passed that defect along to their sons. Finally, fathers were accused both of not spending enough time with their feminine boys, and of doting on them.

Echoes of these parental diagnoses remain strong in popular culture, particularly for the single mother who has a son. She has been warned of the dangers she poses to her child's development if she is too close to him, which range from deviance and weakness to violence and drug addiction. The tragic results of this advice are described by Olga Silverstein in her book *The Courage to Raise Good Men*. She explains that, with fewer men in their lives, boys need more attention from their mothers, not less. Mothers often abandon their sons emotionally because they don't trust themselves to raise them as legitimate men. Their biggest fear is that if they are affectionate, or emotionally close, they will turn them into "mama's boys."

Silverstein points out that by pulling away from their sons, these boys are often left with no one. In effect, they must raise themselves. She has also found that these emotionally abandoned boys are trained to be self-absorbed and highly competitive. Pushed away when they are very young toward a hypermasculine male image for training, they question their self-worth because they view their family life, with a mother at the hub, as shameful and inadequate. Ironically, it is a message given to them by the mother herself, who has been inundated by the psychological theories that have penetrated society and popular culture from the study of feminine boys.

A mother might think she is creating a strong and self-sufficient son by not becoming attached to him emotionally, but it is this same emotional attachment that teaches him empathy, and gives him the ability to recognize his own emotions. Without self-knowledge, and the empathy that brings, a boy will truly be lost; with it, he can overcome adversity and reach his full potential, for both himself and the world in which he lives. Yet the mothers pull away, in an attempt to protect their sons and help them construct a "masculine" identity.

And what of the theory that a mother cannot raise a child by herself, particularly a boy? If a mother shuts down everything inside of her that seems "masculine" because it threatens her feminine self-image, there may well be some truth to it. If any child, male or female, is exposed only to one adult, and that adult exhibits rigid sex-typed behavior, then that child is not going to develop into the strongest, most integrated individual he or she can be.

The image of the suffocating, passive-dependent mother and the controlling, distant, aggressive-dominant father as the epitomes of feminine and masculine serve to split a child's inner world, and set up false oppositions in order to conform with what seems to be real. This inner split is brought into adulthood, and the negative effects on well-being are severe, affecting everything from romantic relationships to physical health. Beneath our awareness of this split there is the knowledge that we are, to a powerful degree, constructing our identities. We know that it is not necessarily "natural" to be exclusively masculine or exclusively feminine. Our culture, however, and its advertising insist that such roles are "natural" for everyone. It follows that if we have to work at being masculine or feminine, then there must be something wrong with us. When we become parents, we often work even harder at conforming to our prescribed gender roles, because everything tells us that the most crucial factor in rearing a child is the child's gender training.

Parents' fears of gender nonconformity in their children are powerful. Many studies have shown that even parents who do not subscribe to strict roles or attributes often engage in subconscious gender training. In one experiment, two female and two male six-month-old babies appeared in both sex-appropriate and cross-sex clothing, and they were given gender-appropriate names for their apparent sex. Women, who were themselves mothers, then interacted with the babies, whom they had never before seen. The sex they *perceived* the baby to be changed their behavior toward it. When they perceived that they were playing with a boy, even if they were not, they verbally encouraged the baby in its gross motor activities, responding significantly more often to the "boy" baby's movements. The researchers concluded that it would be no surprise that boys tend toward higher rates of activity and physical prowess, not because of a natural tendency toward it, but because of stimulation during infancy.

Another study identified an infant as "Adam," and dressed "him" in blue overalls. The same infant was later identified as "Beth," and dressed in a pink dress. Three toys were made available for the adults to give the baby: a duck, a doll and a train. The adults were parents who had both girls and boys of their own. The mothers gave the doll significantly more often to the baby when identified as "Beth," yet espoused the view that boys and girls should not be trained in sex-stereotypic roles. Most fathers reported themselves aware of playing more physical games with their sons, but the mothers showed no awareness of their differential treatment of "Adam" and "Beth."

In 1980, there was a study entitled "Baby X Revisited." The infants used in the study were from three months to eleven months old, and they were dressed in gender nonspecific clothing of T-shirts and diapers. The same baby was introduced at different times as male, female, or with no gender information. Sixty undergraduate subjects at Hunter College were told that they were in a study concerning "young infants' responses to strangers." The subjects ranged in age from seventeen to forty-five years, and the racial composition was White, Black, Hispanic and Asian. Three toys were made available for the subjects to present to the babies: a small rubber football, a Raggedy Ann doll and a teething ring.

None of the men presented a "girl" baby with the football, and 89 percent of them presented "her" with the doll. Eighty percent of the women presented a "boy" baby with the football, and 73 percent of them presented a "girl" with the doll. Besides the obvious gender stereotyping in terms of toys with children who are presumed to prefer them because of their "apparent" sex, I think the study reveals something very important that the researchers were not necessarily measuring.

The men presented the baby "boy" with the football only 50 percent of the time. They gave the "boy" the doll 20 percent of the time, and the teething ring 30 percent of the time. The women presented the baby "girl" with the football 28 percent of the time, but *never* presented "boys" or "girls" with the teething ring. When the women were not told what sex the baby was, they then presented the baby with the teething ring 43 percent of the time. In this study, men did not stereotype boys as strongly as women did, while women did not stereotype girls as strongly as men did. This suggests that men and women seem to believe in the stereotyped preferences of the opposite sex, but when it comes to their own sex, they seem aware of flexibility. A man knows that he can be nurturing, although society has forced him to hide that part of himself. A woman knows that she can be competitive and athletic, but she has to mask that part of herself as much as possible. However, when a man looks across the great sex divide at his daughter, or a mother at her son, there is an "otherness" about the baby, a question, a concern by parents that simply by virtue of being male or female, they cannot know something intrinsic about their own child, and so they rely on stereotypes as a guide.

This study also reflects that women may be even more involved in stereotyping children than men, since they never presented the teething ring, which was the "neutral" toy, to a baby unless they were given no information as to its gender. While women bear the brunt of discrimination based upon sex, they seem to be as actively engaged as men, and sometimes more rigid, in the gender training of their children. This might be because women are held more responsible for this training, and they want the children to be appealing to their fathers.

Yet what happens if the parents do not bow to these norms? If their child's behavior is not gender conforming, and is more than simply gender independent, showing a marked "cross-gender" tendency, that child is at risk for being labeled deviant and disordered. His or her future adult sexuality is called into question. Sometimes the child's body itself is called into question, as if deviant doll or truck play lurked in the chromosomes. The parents, however, are often blamed for not training their child in a more rigid fashion. Traditional gender training hangs like the Sword of Damocles over the heads of well-meaning, loving parents, who feel they must teach their boys and girls gender-appropriate roles in order to protect them, even if they sense that gender independence, whatever it may bring, would be a healthier, truer route.

What then of the children who, for whatever reason, slip through the cracks in gender training? In 1995, Dr. Green quipped, "Barbies at five. Sleeps with men at twenty-five." Is that really true, or did Dr. Green and his cohorts simply reinforce for these boys the popular notion that, because they liked "feminine" roles and activities, and disliked "masculine" roles and activities, they were, or would become, homosexual? This is an extraordinary, absurd leap to take with a young child's growing identity. In effect, they trained these boys to believe that they were gay, and psychologically crucified their parents as being responsible for their child's deviance. The parents were accused of being lenient, phallic, distant; too masculine, too feminine; negligent, competitive, empty. They were portrayed as suffering from bad marriages, penis envy, rage, jealousy and impotence. The bottom line was, they had sons who, at their most flamboyant and for a wide variety of reasons, mirrored back to the world a vividly accurate cartoon of socially constructed gender roles. The artificiality of these roles is terrifying for the adult to witness, because we are taught that these roles are biologically natural and linked to sexuality. Our personal identity is threatened when we realize that what we took as a given, because of our sex, was really a choice, a choice we forgot we made, a choice that might have been made for us.

THE CREATION OF
A MENTAL ILLNESS

As funding for the study and treatment of gender nonconforming children increased, a need arose to create a specific psychiatric diagnosis for the condition in the *Diagnostic and Statistical Manual* (DSM) of the American Psychiatric Association (APA). The DSM is the handbook used by mental health professionals to officially diagnose a psychological disorder, and without a DSM diagnosis, insurance companies will not pay for treatment.

Complicating the issue of treating the gender nonconforming child was the 1973 decision by the APA to eliminate homosexuality as a mental disorder. If homosexuality was no longer a mental disorder, then treating children for gender deviance with an eye to preventing homosexuality did not make sense. Those who wished to continue treating nonconforming children had seven years in which to develop a new category of illness, because in 1980, the third edition of the DSM would be published (DSM-III), officially removing homosexuality as a disorder. The new strategy was to focus on these children as "pre-transsexual" rather than prehomosexual. Because they played with the "wrong" toys, for example, or had the "wrong" body movements, they were now labeled as having such profound distress about being a girl or boy that they literally hated their bodies and would grow up to request sex reassignment surgery.

While the publication of the DSM-III was hailed by gay activists as a significant breakthrough, which it was, without much fanfare a new mental illness appeared in the book: Gender Identity Disorder of Childhood. It was defined in boys in the 1980 DSM-III, and again in the revised 1987 DSM-III-R, as follows:

> A. Persistent and intense distress about being a boy and an intense desire to be a girl or, more rarely, insistence that he is a girl;
> B. either (1) or (2):
> 1. preoccupation with female stereotypical activities, as shown by a preference for either cross-dressing or simulating female attire, or by an intense desire to participate in the games and pastimes of girls and rejection of stereotypical male toys, games, and activities;
> 2. persistent repudiation of male anatomic structures, as indicated by at least one of the following repeated assertions:
>> a. that he will grow up to become a woman (not merely in role);
>> b. that his penis or testes are disgusting or will disappear;
>> c. that it would be better not to have a penis or testes;
> C. the boy has not yet reached puberty.

Dr. Susan Coates, a clinician in the field, described the stereotypical female behavior that is most often seen in GID boys:

1. cross-dressing
2. doll play (Barbie dolls)
3. interest in cosmetics and jewelry
4. preference for the female role in play acting
5. preference for female peers

6. female mannerisms

7. avoidance of rough and tumble play.

Elaborating on the DSM-III-R description of these boys, Coates wrote: "GID boys have greater interest in female heroines in children's books and on TV. In early childhood, favorite stories include Cinderella, Snow White, and Rapunzel. In middle childhood, characters such as Wonder Woman, Bionic Woman, and She-Ra become favorites." Dr. Kenneth Zucker observed that the DSM-III-R also added a new criteria for girls, "which emphasized the gender-disturbed girl's aversion to normative feminine clothing and involvement in cross-dressing."

The DSM-III and the DSM-III-R both drew a strange distinction between GID in boys and girls: for a girl to be diagnosed, there had to be a *"stated* desire to be a boy," but for a boy to be diagnosed, there had to be an *"intense* desire to be a girl." Unlike a girl, the boy did not have to verbalize his desire to literally have another body. His repudiation of his anatomy could be interpreted from a sentence such as "It would be better not to have a penis," whereas the girl would have to say "that she has, or will grow, a penis." This distinction was probably the result of feminist lobbying on behalf of girls, and the insistence that it was impossible to separate a girl's wish "to be a boy" from the cultural advantages of being a boy. The tomboy, therefore, became technically more difficult to diagnose with GID, but no one was speaking for the boys. That a boy might see cultural advantages to being a girl, such as the condoning of nurturing behavior and no requirement for physically aggressive play, was not taken seriously until the publication of the DSM-IV in 1994, when controversy over the diagnosis of GID in children intensified.

In the current criteria for GID in childhood, a strong and persistent cross-gender identification must be present in a child, as manifested by four or more of the following:

(1) repeatedly stated desire to be, or insistence that he or she is, the other sex;

(2) in boys, preference for cross-dressing or simulating female attire; in girls, insistence on wearing only stereotypical masculine clothing;

(3) strong and persistent preferences for cross-sex roles in make-believe play or persistent fantasies of being the other sex;

(4) intense desire to participate in the stereotypical games and pastimes of the other sex;

(5) strong preference for playmates of the other sex.

Today, a girl or boy can be diagnosed with GID without ever having stated the desire to be, or that he or she is or will be, the opposite sex. What had been the *primary feature* of the diagnosis when it first appeared in 1980 is now not even necessary. The psychiatrist or psychologist is free to make the assumption for the child. The rationale is that the very young child "may have poor verbal abilities," and is therefore not necessarily able to articulate this desire, which is nonetheless there. Yet why does the six- or seven-year-old child also not have to state the desire explicitly? According to the doctors, the child knows enough not to admit to it, and might vigorously deny the desire "in order to avoid negative reactions" or "perhaps for social desirability factors." The doctors contend, however, that the desire is there, having gone underground. They must make this contention, or they have lost what has now become the primary rationale for treatment of GID in children: the prevention of adult transsexuality. Ironically, in terms of GID, the overwhelming majority of these children do not become transsexual. (There remains one odd distinction between girls and boys: A girl must *insist* on wearing only boy's clothing, whereas a boy needs only a "preference" for "simulating female attire.")

The doctors have never been able to decide in what section of the DSM this disorder should appear. Since the diagnosis was invented, it has been moved to a different section of the DSM for each new edition. In the 1980 DSM-III, GIDC was in a new section entitled "Psychosexual Disorders." In the 1987 DSM-

III-R, GIDC appeared in yet another new section: "Disorders Usually First Evident in Infancy, Childhood, or Adolescence." Finally, in the 1994 DSM-IV, the Subcommittee on Gender Identity Disorders decided to delete the phrase "of Childhood." Children are now included under an adult diagnosis of Gender Identity Disorder, in yet another section: "Sexual and Gender Identity Disorders." The removal of GID from the children's section was done in order to create "one overarching diagnosis that can be used . . . across the life cycle."

Complicating matters for the children, GID is the diagnosis necessary for adult transsexuals that they might receive hormone treatment and sex reassignment surgery (SRS). This final DSM placement of childhood GID has, in effect, welded together a child's nonconforming gender role behavior and transsexuality, as if one were a typical, "across the life cycle," logical outcome of the other, yet there are no studies to confirm this claim. The fusing of these diagnoses has also unfairly pitted those who wish to prevent the involuntary gender treatment of children and youth against adult transsexuals who must have this diagnosis before they can receive treatment.

It is now possible that government funding is being provided to treat children for perceived gender role and future sexual deviance under the guise of the developmental study of the prevention of adult transsexualism. This would make the tracing of these funds extremely difficult, since there is no longer a diagnosis of Gender Identity Disorder of Childhood, but only Gender Identity Disorder, which could apply to children, adolescents or adults.

This could easily happen as a result of the 1994 DSM-IV's elaboration on the symptoms of GID: "In children, the disturbance is manifested by any of the following: in boys, assertion that his penis or testes are disgusting or will disappear or assertion that it would be better not to have a penis, or aversion toward rough-and-tumble play and rejection of male stereotypical toys, games, and activities." What could these people have been thinking when they devised this new criteria? They have equated a boy who is intensely distressed with his body to a boy who does not like to play roughly with "boy" toys or in "boy" games.

The criteria for GID in girls is equally troubling: ". . . in girls, rejection of urinating in a sitting position, assertion that she has or will grow a penis, or assertion that she does not want to grow breasts or menstruate, or marked aversion toward normative feminine clothing." The American Psychiatric Association has given equal pathological weight to a little girl who believes she will grow a penis and a little girl who refuses to wear a dress.

In the more detailed sections of the diagnosis, little boys improvising long hair and skirts with towels, aprons and scarves is listed as a symptom, along with love of the dreaded Barbie doll and preferring to play with girls. The little girls are often described as oppositional, in that they have "intense negative reactions to parental expectations or attempts to have them wear dresses or other feminine attire." These girls like Batman or Superman, and "prefer boys as playmates, with whom they share interests in contact sports, rough-and-tumble play, and traditional boyhood games." Is it not logical and rather normal for a child to seek out playmates who want to play the same games? While the DSM-IV now states that, for boys as well as girls, the child's strong and persistent cross-gender identification must not merely be "a desire for any perceived cultural advantages of being the other sex," determination of a child's desire is open to extraordinary interpretation, because there is no way to objectively come to a conclusion regarding motivation.

What this new diagnosis does is cast a much wider net, especially for the tomboy, who was more protected in the earlier versions of the DSM, in that she was supposed to explicitly state the desire to have the body of a boy before she could be diagnosed or treated for her "masculine" behavior. Tomboys are now as vulnerable as "feminine" boys. Girls, in general, have become more assertive, and as they begin to engage in what has classically been referred to as "rough-and-tumble play," as they display "intense negative reactions" to attempts to force them to wear dresses or other feminine attire, the number of girls vulnerable to GID diagnosis skyrockets. Their resistance to wearing dresses or displaying feminine mannerisms could easily earn them the label "oppositional defiant," which leads to a GID diagnosis of "a sense of inappropriateness in the gender role" of their sex. That there are appropriate gender roles for the sexes, and that these roles emanate from the body itself, is the unspoken assumption. How can small children be expected to separate their bodies from their assigned gender roles, when most adults cannot? How can a small child feel "appropriate" in a gender role the body ordains but the mind and spirit reject?

HOSPITALIZING THE CHILD

That the net has been cast wider, and the number of children vulnerable to this diagnosis has increased, can be confirmed by the DSM text itself. In the DSM-III, Gender Identity Disorder of Childhood is described as "apparently rare," and estimates at the time of children affected were in the 1 percent range. In the DSM-III-R, GIDC is described as "apparently uncommon." "Uncommon" is, arguably, a more inclusive word than "rare." In the DSM-IV, there is no longer any language describing the number of children who could be diagnosed with the disorder. What does this mean? We can look to the recent work of two world leaders in the field, Susan Bradley and Kenneth Zucker, both of whom were members of the GIDC committee that revised the disorder for the DSM-IV. In 1990, they wrote: "One could argue that GIDC or its subclinical variants may occur in two percent to five percent of children in the general population." Therefore, in the United States alone, the figures for children twelve and under in whom GID may occur have gone from 54,443 in 1980 to 272,215 in 1995. If children and youth under the age of eighteen are considered, the figures have gone from 640,000 in 1980 to 3,200,000 in 1995. No longer does this diagnosis seem so "rare" or even "uncommon," and nothing better demonstrates childhood vulnerability to the diagnosis than the story of an eleven-year-old girl as told to me by attorney Ruth Cohen, a patient's rights advocate.

K I T

ELEVEN YEARS OLD

In Albuquerque, New Mexico, a group of attorneys represents minors and adults who are involuntarily committed to psychiatric hospitals in Bernalillo County. They work on a round-robin basis, one day a week, representing those individuals with court hearings that fall on a particular day. In 1992, a case file landed on Ruth Cohen's desk concerning an eleven-year-old girl who was on an "emergency hold" at a psychiatric hospital that treats minors. An emergency hold lasts seven days, during which a child can be kept hospitalized if there is reason to believe that they are in need of treatment, that they will benefit by treatment, and that it is the least restrictive way of providing treatment.

The eleven-year-old girl, whom we will call Kit, was being held because a family member had filed a Petition for Involuntary Commitment. The diagnosis for the girl was depression and Gender Identity Disorder. The depression was described as having been caused by the death of her uncle, with whom she was very close, but the most alarming reported symptom, and the one that propelled her onto the children's psychiatric ward, was that Kit was acting confused about her gender. The allegations included that she had gone to her new school and on the way had changed from being dressed as a girl to being dressed as a boy. The petition also stated that some people at the school had believed she was a boy, particularly another little girl, who became romantically infatuated with her. There were no allegations that Kit ever touched the other girl in any way, or that the girl ever touched Kit. The fact that the other little girl had a crush on her, and believed her to be a boy, helped Kit to earn the diagnosis of GID.

Ruth Cohen was surprised when she read this petition. The leap from wearing "boy's" clothing to prepubertal lesbianism seemed extraordinary. In any case, it did not seem possible, because Cohen was under the impression that homosexuality had been removed from the DSM. There must be some mistake. How was it that this child could be diagnosed in this fashion, and be put on an emergency hold on a locked ward at a psychiatric hospital?

The weather was cool when Cohen went the next day to visit Kit, who was brought from the children's ward to an administrative office. Kit had dark hair, a deep complexion and brown eyes. She clearly felt very much alone, and was relieved that someone had shown up to defend her. What Cohen observed was a shy, depressed child. She was able to determine that Kit had been put on psychiatric medications during her emergency hold, which could now be contributing to her depression. There was some truth to that part of the diagnosis. Kit was depressed at the loss of her uncle, because she came from a chaotic family situation and he had been a source of strength and stability for her. But Cohen suspected that the depression had been exaggerated in the petition, and used as a pretense to hospitalize the child for gender nonconformity as an indicator of future sexual deviance. Not only had Kit lost her uncle, she had been taken to a psychiatric hospital where she was locked up against her will. Of course she was depressed.

In terms of Kit's dressing "like a boy," what Cohen saw was a little girl who needed to have this option. Cohen determined that "the clothes allowed her to take on what are considered stereotypical masculine behaviors, instead of always acting, one hundred percent of the time, 'like a girl,'" which in Kit's circumstances, left her feeling utterly vulnerable.

I asked Cohen to describe Kit's body movements. Were they masculine, or exaggeratedly boylike? She said that they were neither. Kit just seemed comfortable in her body. I asked Cohen if Kit believed she was a boy, or if she ever stated or implied that she wanted to have a boy's body. Cohen is absolutely certain that this was not the case. Rather, said Cohen, "I think she knew that boys are perceived as being more powerful in society than girls," and at that point in Kit's life, she needed to feel some power. Kit knew that boy's clothes, which thousands of feminine girls wear every day without penalty, would have a certain effect, but she did not know that she could be locked up for it. The clothes alone, of course, were not enough, until linked to the "romantic" attraction she inspired in a classmate, and the belief of some children that Kit was a boy.

Cohen showed Kit the papers that had been filed against her. She was not a highly verbal child, and she seemed frightened. She wanted to be released from the hospital. The psychiatric ward scared her, and she was shy, overwhelmed by the charges against her, especially without the support of her uncle. The nightmare lifted for Kit when Cohen walked through the door, and Cohen herself felt that she would be able to help her.

Cohen left Kit at the hospital, went home and opened up the DSM to read about the diagnosis of GIDC. Angry and frustrated, she called a therapist she knew to discuss it. Cohen told me, "The therapist explained that although homosexuality had been officially removed from the DSM-III, there were still diagnoses that could be used to punish people for things that could be perceived as relating to sexual orientation."

The next day, Cohen stood beside Kit for her appearance in front of a hearing officer. The district attorney represented the hospital, with the hospital therapist as his expert witness. Cohen argued that the symptoms that were being identified in Kit were not the basis of a mental disorder, and that Kit had no confusion as to her sex. She just, at times, felt more comfortable acting and dressing as she did. As far as the depression went, Cohen contended that Kit could be treated in a more humane manner, through some kind of outpatient therapy with a counselor.

The district attorney and his expert witness argued that Kit's symptoms were indicative of a mental disorder, and that Kit needed to be evaluated and treated in a locked children's ward. The State based their opinions on the authority of the DSM.

Although this was not argued, I noted that locking Kit up would also have the effect of keeping her out of school, and out of the presence of the other girl who was infatuated with her. Once again, that which generates cultural anxiety about gender issues, such as other children mistaking a girl for a boy, must be treated, and until treated, exiled and humiliated.

The hearing officer contemplated the arguments as Ruth Cohen and Kit sat before him. He closed the file and said that the requirements of the mental health code were met. He decided that Kit would benefit by treatment in the locked psychiatric ward as the least restrictive way of supervising her care. As she was led from the hearing room, the child made little or no response, perhaps because she was drugged.

Ruth Cohen had been holding out for a reasonable, rational decision, but after reading the description of Gender Identity Disorder of Childhood, she knew that the State would be able to make its case, based on the DSM. She appealed to the district court judge, but that judge also ruled against Kit, deciding that there was enough evidence of depression to institutionalize the child. The judge did warn the hospital that when the depression started to lift, they should strongly consider releasing her, although they were not ordered to do so. While Kit was on the psychiatric ward, the doctors had the option of treating her, as they saw fit, for Gender Identity Disorder of Childhood, since it was part of her diagnosis.

Cohen did not appeal to a higher court, because by the time the appeal would be heard, Kit would be leaving the hospital. On the first commitment of a minor, the State can hold the child for up to sixty days. Cohen never saw Kit again, and she does not know if there were subsequent, and longer, involuntary commitments. Today, Kit would be about fourteen years old.

When proponents of childhood Gender Identity Disorder are confronted with cases like Kit's, the response is always the same: misdiagnosis. But was it? Kit did insist on wearing "stereotypical masculine clothing." Kit did engage in "cross-sex roles in make-believe" by pretending at school that she was a boy. Kit did have an intense desire to "participate in the stereotypical games and pastimes" of boys, and apparently preferred playing with boys. In 1992, she did not meet the first criteria for GIDC because, unlike a boy, a girl had to explicitly state the desire, or belief, that she was a boy. Kit fit enough additional criteria, however, to earn the diagnosis. Since 1994, with the doctors now free to interpret her motivations because she is seen as incapable of communicating them or refusing to do so, she could now be declared, based on her other behaviors, as wanting the body of a boy, or believing that she really was a boy. Kit would now fit every single criterion for the disorder.

There exists, in popular culture as well as the scientific literature, a belief that the gender nonconforming child is pathological, with criminal potential suitable for the psychiatric hospital. A historic record of this pathologization can be found in the 1938 work of Martha Wilson MacDonald, M.D., who practiced at Michael Reese Hospital in Chicago. Her work came to my attention when I followed up on the references cited by Dr. Myrick, who in 1970 treated Jerry, the nine-year-old Florida boy who was not very good at athletics. Myrick's goal was to show an alternative type of treatment to that suggested by MacDonald. He wrote, "Several years ago, MacDonald described effeminate behavior as a serious psychological problem which necessitated segregation of the child and individual therapy over an extended period of time." By "segregation," Dr. MacDonald meant incarceration of children in psychiatric hospital schools, since they were deemed too dangerous for outpatient clinic treatment.

The profiles of the eight boys in Dr. MacDonald's study depict depravity and psychosis of an extraordinary proportion, with a high degree of "unprovoked" physical attacks of startling magnitude by these children upon other male children. These "criminally aggressive, passive effeminate boys" are further described with other behavior difficulties, including "thumb-sucking, nail-biting, gluttonous appetite, making 'filthy mouth noise,' con-

stantly fighting about food, enuresis [bed-wetting], expelling fla-
tus, soiling, temper-tantrums, night terrors, stealing, truanting,
telling fantastic lies and using obscene language." Interestingly,
upon closer examination of the material, we find that of the eight
boys studied, "three are definitely small and undernourished." In
those cases, "fighting about food" could denote that they were
trying to get enough to eat, hardly a criminal behavior in a child.

The primary word the doctor chose to describe these boys
was "fear," coupled with "an overwhelming feeling of physical
inferiority and fear of physical attack from other boys and men
with anxiety of the type commonly seen among little girls who
fear the burglar and kidnapper." (Fearful girls were considered
normal.) All of these boys were examined physically, and found
to have "no marked deviations from the average. One has rheu-
matic heart disease, another a malformed ear, and a third has
scars from burns." Since the source of these burns is not mentioned, and many of these children lived under the fear of physical attack, this doctor may have been describing abused children,
not children who abuse.

These boys were profiled as extremely violent, yet when in the
company of women or girls, without exception they were cooperative, calm, kind and courteous. Dr. MacDonald specifically
noted that "when permitted to assist mother or grandmother with
such household activities as cleaning, dusting, washing, sewing,
embroidering, and cooking, they are happy, cooperative, and 'the
nicest boy a mother could want.' In play with girls, coloring,
drawing, making cutouts, dressing dolls, dramatizing women's
roles, wearing girl's dresses and hair ribbons, they have been the
model playmates." Yet when alone in the company of boys, seem-
ingly without provocation, these children erupted into diabolical
creatures. The doctor noted that their eruptions always resulted
in their being *severely beaten* by the other boys, yet she drew no
connection between their "fear" and the reality of their physical
endangerment for exhibiting "feminine" traits. Nor did she attempt to consider their behavior as a form of preemptive strike to
discourage the beatings to which they were regularly subjected.

Instead, as evidenced by their ideal behavior when in the company of girls, Dr. MacDonald asserted that "One is again reminded of the suspicion and cunning alertness of the adult paranoid." With truly perverse reasoning, since these boys were relaxed, cooperative, even charming in the presence of girls and women, Dr. MacDonald interpreted them as deranged, even precriminal.

Dr. MacDonald believed that studying these children would be "a valuable contribution in research in the dynamics of adult criminal behavior as well as schizophrenia." There was nothing in her report about healing the child, and finally, with absolutely no clinical research, she wrote these words: "The writer suspects that they [the boys] were attempting to overcome strong passive homosexual drives in which they would play a masochistic role with resulting projection of the aggressive, sadistic role to the exterior and identification with the fantasied aggressor."

That Dr. Myrick, in 1970, could invoke MacDonald's work as having even the remotest relevance to Jerry is astounding, as well as dangerous. Jerry's sin was poor hand-eye coordination. He was a child who never exhibited a single instance of violence or precriminal behavior. He was in fact a good student, and was not "dangerous" in even the wildest of evaluations.

When Dr. MacDonald advocated psychiatric hospital schools for these children, it was the first time in the literature that such treatment was prescribed. At the time that she wrote her recommendations, she lamented that no such facilities existed in Illinois for the "study or treatment of these boys."

By 1941, boys and girls between the ages of four and twelve were incarcerated on a ward at Bellevue Hospital in New York for various reasons. Among them were twenty-one children who were thought to be "homosexual." Their personalities were evaluated as a means of tracking "homosexual trends in children," although many of them had never engaged in any sexual acts. For example, Dora was eleven years old. After her mother's death, her alcoholic father took up with "Mr. X," an "effeminate" homosexual who cared for Dora and her brother while their father was at work. Mr. X "displayed a great deal of affection for them, called them his babies." When Dora was nine, her father remarried, Mr. X was forced to leave and she and her brother were sent to a boarding home. Dora ran away, and was placed in Bellevue, where she expressed the desire to live with Mr. X. "I wish he was my father," she said, adding that Mr. X liked to knit, cook and crochet. She thought that made him "half man and half woman," and Dora said of herself: "I am half man and half woman too. I like to take things apart and put them together, but I like cooking too. I wouldn't marry no drunk. I want to be a surgeon and I'll marry a doctor." Dora was described as "a happy affectionate girl and was no problem on the ward." Then why was she there? She was suspected of being prehomosexual.

Gloria, eleven years old, was described as Italian, and having been rejected by her mother because of her "sturdy," hence masculine, body build. Gloria "wanted to be a boy and an aviator." Edward, also eleven, "preferred to play with girls and dolls, and loved to rock tiny babies to sleep . . . Afraid that he might be assaulted by boys, he sought protection in the nursery. Obscene words of anal connotation alarmed him, sexual discussions excited him, threw him into tantrums and provoked him to defensive physical assault. His dreams were filled with ghosts who stuck knives into his back." John was eight. His last boarding mother complained that, among other offenses, he played with dolls. He was described as small, poorly nourished and "wore his shirt over his pants," which seems to imply an attempt at crossdressing. On the ward, John "made a small clay figure and said: 'It's crying for its mother.' "

There is no indication of further documentation on these children, and so they fall into the technical category of "lost to follow-up." The story of an individual I will call Jamie is therefore an important one, because it is remembered by the adult who survived fifteen years of hospitalization, beginning in the late 1950s, for the treatment of childhood gender deviance.

JAMIE

SIX YEARS OLD

Jamie remembers the red brick, the turrets, the overwhelming height of the building. It rose up like a forbidding castle, surrounded by pine woods. The windows had black bars, closely spaced. Not even Jamie, with such a small body, could slip through them. The sky that day was a brilliant blue, and there were birds swooping through the trees, then landing to scream and rock from foot to foot upon the branches.

Mother and Father left Jamie in the hospital admitting area. They went outside, and did not return. They had spoken to a doctor about Jamie's troubles with being a boy, and the doctor had told them to take Jamie to the hospital. It was because of dolls, and tea sets, and feeling too sad to move, that Jamie was there. Feeling lost as the nurse took the papers, Jamie followed her through the hospital corridors. Jamie knew what this was all about, and said, "I'm a girl," even when they said, "No. You're a boy." Jamie did not do boy things, and would not lie about it.

Jamie followed the nurse through the yellow hallway, where the linoleum smelled like ammonia, and the nurse's uniform reflected off the floor in a white blur. She had a pile of keys hanging from her pocket, and she unlocked a door. The door had a little, thick glass pane in it, but the opening was too high up for a six-year-old to see through.

The nurse said, "This way," motioning for Jamie to follow, to step inside, across the threshold into a child's nightmare. The children Jamie heard and saw moved more slowly than other children do, and only later would Jamie understand that they were all drugged. On that day, they stopped to watch the newest arrival stand before the nurses' station.

There was an open window frame in front of the station, without any glass. Some of the nurses sat behind it with clipboards in their hands, and some of them held trays of little paper cups. One nurse handed a paper cup to Jamie. There was a pill in it to swallow, and Jamie recalls that it looked like an M&M.

Brought to a ward room which held eight children, Jamie was shown a bed. The beds were narrow, the sheets tight, and the blankets coarse. The rest of the day was unclear, long and short at the same time, perhaps because there were more paper cups with little pills.

Surely Mother and Father will come back, Jamie thought. Surely they will see that this is not good, and that I am not bad.

But then it was night, and they had not come. The child lay in the locked children's ward, frightened by the broken shafts of light flowing through the barred windows, wearing green hospital pajamas that were clean but stained by the bodies of other frightened children who had come to this place where sleeping and fainting were indistinguishable.

Jamie awakened, mouth dry from medication and nerves. Some days had passed, but it was hard to count. Mother and Father had not yet returned. Two nurses walked through the boys' ward. Through the window bars came sunlight, but it gave no warmth. On this morning, a nurse stopped at the foot of Jamie's bed.

"Do not eat breakfast," she said.

Jamie watched as the nurses moved through the ward, checking their clipboards. They did not tell all of the children not to eat breakfast. Just some of them. Jamie did not understand why there was no food, no breakfast. Jamie's legs and arms were so heavy from the sadness and the pills. A Black boy stopped at the foot of Jamie's bed. He smiled, his face full of life. He seemed to have captured some warmth inside of himself, even though he, too, could not have any breakfast today.

The boy was wearing the same pajamas as Jamie, but he also had on paper slippers. There was a place for your toes, and then they were just flat, like sandals. The children who could not have breakfast formed a line, and they all wore the paper slippers, which were green. Jamie slipped them on. They felt funny and coarse, not the way you imagine slippers should feel. As the obedient and silent line of children moved out of the ward and along the hallway, there was the sound of paper sliding across the linoleum as the shuffling of tiny feet made a swishing noise.

And Jamie wondered, What is listening, who is listening to this? Does anyone know what is happening? Does anyone see me? Does anyone love me?

Jamie was not the first in line, and did not know where the line was going. It inched forward, the slippers rustling like paper wings. It was not so long before Jamie was next, waiting at a closed door, where the nurse studied her clipboard. The door opened, and Jamie watched a child come out of the room. He was looking at the ground, and one arm was held by an attendant, all in white, who guided him. The nurse did not explain anything. She held the door open, and motioned for Jamie to go inside.

Jamie did not feel real, and thought, Mother and Father will come back. They cannot know what is happening.

Placed upon a hospital bed, Jamie's wrists and ankles were then tied by restraint cords against the metal rails. There was a large black box, on wheels, and there were wires coming out of it. No one said anything. No one said what was going to happen.

The technician spread cream on Jamie's forehead, and attached two electrodes to the temples. It was quiet. This was the first time Jamie had been gently touched since arriving at the hospital. The technician put something in Jamie's mouth that separated the teeth and the tongue. The technician nodded, and then there was sudden pain that could not be coming from anything human as the switch was flipped and electricity traveled through the wires into Jamie's brain, throwing the child's body into grand mal seizure.

It was the late 1950s, before the development of body paralyzers. Jamie's arms and legs jerked and flailed against the restraints, and only the teeth grip stopped the tongue from being bitten off. Jamie's tiny bones were on the verge of breaking until the convulsion stopped, as quickly as it started, as if Jamie were the puppet of a monster who suddenly lost interest.

Jamie's eyes opened as the attendant pried the mouthpiece from the clamped jaws. Helped up from the hospital bed, Jamie was guided to the door and back to the ward bed. Walking felt strange because it was through a wall of pain, and the world no longer seemed clear, but tilted and out of focus.

Shock treatment would always be the same for Jamie: imagine your eyes falling apart inside your head, imagine an arc of pain splitting your skull into pieces. They say that children do not feel pain as adults do. They say this because it makes them feel better. Imagine being six years old and walking into the hospital dayroom a bit later in the day, and everyone, all the other children, are looking at you to see if you can walk, to see how you handle the pain.

The night came, and Jamie fainted into sleep.

The next morning, Jamie was awakened by the sound of the nurses walking through the ward. The sunlight was cold and yellow. The nurse stopped at the foot of Jamie's bed.

"Do not eat breakfast today," she said.

These words were powerful, the precursors to electroshock, a terrible way to say good morning.

And the nurse said it the next day. "Do not eat breakfast." And the next day. And the next. The next. The next.

Jamie understood that Mother and Father were not coming back. The season changed, and changed again.

Before the hospital, Jamie could not play sports with the other boys. There was no way to do this. Some children can learn to pass in the role they are expected to play, and some feminine boys can put on a veneer of masculinity, can appear to be "cured." But there are those, like Jamie, whose bodies and hearts cannot perform the acts the world demands, regardless of the price they are forced to then pay. They are given the psychiatric labels of severely depressed, or fearful, borderline personality, or even schizophrenic and delusional.

Every child in the hospital was called borderline or schizophrenic, Jamie told me. "You're schizophrenic if you think you're something they don't think you are. In children, through imagination, when they want to fly away from all this terror and pain, they make up playmates if they're lonely. That's how to escape. You pretend you have worlds of playmates, and toys, and people who love you. And so they say you're schizophrenic and having delusions."

Jamie was now eight years old, still a beautiful child, delicate and feminine. They again inserted the mouth grip in preparation for another series of eight to ten shock treatments, and as they attached the electrodes, one nurse said to another, "He should have been a girl."

I am a girl, thought Jamie. I am a girl. Can't they see? Can't they let it be?

Jamie would have told them that, but the grip made speech impossible as the switch was flipped and the electricity ricocheted from temple to temple. Shock treatments and drugs were the only "therapy" Jamie received.

The treatments never became less painful, and there was nothing more painful than the shock, not even the rapes by the male patients, not even Mother and Father never returning. There was no way to survive besides surrender, and then to create a pretend world, where there were playmates, and beauty.

Jamie created a beautiful angel father, and could be heard speaking to the angel from the ward bed, when the children were supposed to be asleep. "Come down to save me. Take me home." It was not a big winged being that Jamie spoke to, but "a world of arms that hold you safe."

This confirmed to the doctors Jamie's diagnosis of delusional, although Jamie could come back at any time, and always knew the difference between the real and the imagined. Even the nurses had to admit that Jamie's soprano voice was beautiful, singing songs in the night, and there was one special song, learned in the past, from another world, that was Jamie's favorite:

Sha baba, sha baba, sha wawa,
My bambino go to sleep
Sha baba, sha baba, sha wawa,
My bambino is too sweet.
See the stars up in the sky
Ready to say goodnight.
Sha baba, sha baba, sha wawa,
My bambino go to sleep.

Jamie was now nine years old.

"Do not eat breakfast this morning," the nurse said.

Jamie had heard this phrase dozens of times.

The children formed their line, the paper slippers shuffled out onto the ward corridor, toward the door to the shock room. The Black boy, now ten or eleven years old, so full of light, went into the room. He was always smiling. They brought him out of the shock room, past the day room, toward the nurses' station and its big window without the glass behind which the nurses stood with clipboards and tiny paper cups. Jamie saw something suddenly happen. The boy went into a seizure, and his convulsions were so violent that, through no will of his own, he leaped up into the air, through the open window frame, and into the nurses' station, as if he were flying. But his body fell with a thud back to the floor, to the linoleum, and the clipboards and paper cups came raining down from the nurses' hands. Again, he convulsed, and then he stopped, and as Jamie and the other children watched, he died. There were no more shocks for the children that day, and there were no explanations.

By the mid-1960s, Jamie had been hospitalized for almost fifteen years. Twenty years old, Jamie could not even go to the bathroom in the men's ward without an attendant at the door to prevent rapes. There were, however, ground passes to go to work every day as an assistant in the hospital's beauty parlor, rolling women's hair in the basement shop. For this work, Jamie earned snack bar change.

One particular morning, the nurse stopped at the foot of Jamie's bed and said, "Don't eat breakfast this morning." The series of shock treatments now numbered in the sixties. Jamie knew why this particular shock had been ordered. The day before, a new boy on the ward had called Jamie a girl's name, and had said, "You look pretty today." A nurse overheard their conversation and wrote it down. The new boy was gone, and Jamie never saw him again.

By the 1960s, the drug companies had developed body paralyzers, so that only the feet twitched during shock, lessening the danger of broken bones. The body paralyzers, however, made it possible to use more electricity, which makes the treatment more dangerous. On the morning after the now disappeared boy told Jamie, "You look pretty today," the electrodes were attached to Jamie's temples and the mouthpiece put in place. The electricity began to surge, but something was wrong.

"It's not getting enough juice," said the attendant.

Jamie could hear them talking about it, how there was not enough "juice." Jamie remained conscious but incapable of movement as the electricity ricocheted from temple to temple. Shock should last only a couple of seconds, but on this day it seemed to go on forever.

"Not enough juice," the technician said again, continuing the treatment. The pain was relentless, a pain that Jamie will never, could never forget.

Jamie prayed, and wondered who, what was listening? "Please let this be the last one, or I'm going to die come morning. I can't take it anymore. The shock or the men. No more. I'll fly anywhere. Help me. If I die in the street in the winter, it's better than this."

The new day came, and the gray winter light seeped through the barred windows. The nurse did not say, "Don't eat breakfast," but passed by the foot of the bed. Jamie thought, If I'm so sick, how come they can send me to work every day? Putting on day clothes and taking a jacket from a hanger, Jamie gathered up the change so far saved and put it in the jacket pocket.

This was the day when the beauticians and their assistants,

like Jamie, dutifully went to the women's back wards. Jamie stood at the door to their dayroom and watched the women screaming, urinating on themselves, picking at themselves, wandering through truly delusional worlds that only rarely intersected with anyone else's. To enter the back wards was like walking on shattered glass, and to enter the back wards for the purpose of rolling the women's hair, trying to set and comb it into stylish sixties hairdos, was a level of madness that defied comprehension. It was also a terrible warning of what could come to pass if you did not cooperate.

Jamie tried to calm the women down by rolling their hair, to help them feel pretty and give them a lift. But it was absurd, horrifying, ridiculous, and at the end of this day, it was enough. Jamie put on the jacket and took the ground pass in hand. Each step toward the hospital door and onto the grounds felt like a dream. As discreetly as humanly possible, Jamie turned away from the hospital and walked into the woods, trying not to draw anyone's attention, placing one foot in front of the other, walking into a complete unknown but knowing that moving forward was the only hope.

There was snow on the ground, and the hospital was in an isolated location, away from people. Jamie had no boots, just thin shoes. The ground was hard and the air was bitter. Every coin earned as a beautician's assistant had been carefully saved and counted. Finally, out of sight of the hospital buildings, Jamie ran through the pine woods, slipping, running deeper into the woods, the change jingling in the jacket pocket.

There was a bus stop a mile or so away. It took so long to get there, like running in a dream when you cannot go fast enough to escape and you can feel your pursuers at your back. But the bus stop sign eventually became visible, a square of metal attached to the top of a pole. Jamie hid at the edge of the woods, and waited, not knowing the bus schedule. It was freezing, and the sky was now a hard gray. There was only the sound of birds, but then there was the sound of a motor. Jamie waited at the edge of the woods, knowing it could be a hospital vehicle on a search, but it was the public bus, and Jamie walked toward it with perfect timing for the first time in twenty years. The bus doors opened, and warm air spilled through the doorway onto Jamie's face. Looking quickly at the driver, and then away, in case he might notice something was amiss, Jamie stepped up into the bus, and dropped the coins into the box. There were enough coins left over for a bowl of chili in the city.

Homeless but alive, having survived fifteen years in a psychiatric hospital system for the crime of being feminine, Jamie began a new life, singing jazz in after-hours clubs, finally earning enough money to take the Greyhound to San Francisco, where she has lived ever since as a transsexual woman.

Unlike many transsexuals, she has never had training of any kind in how to move or dress as a woman. That all comes naturally to her, she says. "People talk about a gender continuum, where people change how they walk and act according to how they feel that day." Jamie laughs as she talks. "I'm so far at the edge of the continuum, I fell off! Now, I think it's just wonderful that some of you are running back and forth along the continuum. But I have always been, will always be, this feminine. And I'm not a stereotype. I'm not a patriarchal construct. There are some people who had choices, but I did not. I don't understand why people have a hissy fit that we're born this way. What's wrong with it? There are whiptail lizards that have babies without males. And do you know what's under the sea? The sea horse father who has the babies, and the hermaphroditic barnacle that comes out and decides which one it's going to be that day. This is the biodiversity of nature, and I am part of nature."

Jamie lives in a small corner studio filled with the light she needs for her self-taught art. She took "one of those housewife courses" to learn how to mix paint, but that is all the formal training she has had. Beautiful paintings of fields and children, in the blues favored by the French impressionists, adorn the walls, but there is one painting that draws the eye away from the others. Abstract and frightening, the canvas is not easy to look at. It depicts the images of girl children undergoing electroshock.

There is a teddy bear, split in half, and there is a barred window high up in the right-hand corner, the bars painted blood-red. The legs of one child are wings pushing toward the window, and near the bottom of the painting is another girl, her hands on the back of her head, trying to stop the pain.

Jamie has written in her journal, "the faces of floating children . . . mirrored images . . . of an old girlchild at the end of the world . . . for the sky is full of wings without bodies." She cannot forget these images from her own childhood, and she is determined to save the children who, like her, know that they are different and cannot pretend otherwise. "I just want them safe," she says. "They are the only children I will ever have."

She asked me to find as many of these children as I could. "No one is talking about them," she said. "They don't want to. They don't want to think about it. But there are still kids in the hospitals. They don't want to look at that. It's too hard. But you have to find them. It's still going on. You have to find them, and you have to write about it."

This task proved difficult. Unless there is someone on a pediatric psychiatric ward who is aware of the particulars on a child's case, and who is willing to come forward, the reason for the commitment of a child to a psychiatric facility is not public knowledge. I learned of eleven-year-old "Kit" in New Mexico only because she was automatically given a patient's rights lawyer on the grounds of involuntary commitment, and that lawyer was willing to come forward. A child younger than Kit would not necessarily be provided with such legal assistance, and would probably not understand what was going on.

A safeguard against locking up the gender-nonconforming child has been to forbid institutionalization based solely upon the diagnosis of Gender Identity Disorder. As we saw with Kit, however, there are many other diagnoses available, particularly depression, which when combined with GID render the child eligible for the psychiatric ward or hospital. The treatment that child receives is completely in the hands of the doctor, and so subject to his or her theories on the meaning of a child's gender behavior.

If a doctor believes that there is a link between gender nonconformity and adult homosexuality, something that has never been proven, and further believes that adult homosexuality is a mental illness, that child will be aggressively treated with behaviorism, psychiatric drugs and counseling. This is known as "reparative" or "conversion" therapy, and the American Psychiatric Association has yet to forbid the practice. It is promoted by organizations of psychiatrists and psychologists such as NARTH (National Association for Research and Therapy of Homosexuality), who are also hard-line advocates of Gender Identity Disorder. As a result, hundreds of adolescents, either suspected of being gay because of gender nonconformity or self-declared as gay, are involuntarily locked into psychiatric hospitals. Since lesbian and gay adolescents are more likely to experiment with gender roles because their psychology does not adhere to the heterosexual norm, a disproportionate number of them are swept up into the psychiatric system, often before they have had a sexual experience of any kind.

Ironically, many of these children are not gay, but are simply gender nonconforming. They do not come forward after treatment, because they do not want to be accused of being gay. They are often deeply homophobic as a result of their treatment, and spin into a panic at the sight of a gay man or lesbian, sometimes becoming violent. If they are part of a politicized religious community, they can be put on display as "proof" that reparative therapy works, and that homosexuality can be cured.

The individuals who have come forward after treatment are almost always gay, buoyed up and encouraged to speak out by a strong gay community base. The ones who speak up are the ones who survive. At the same time that George Rekers was treating seven-year-old Becky with a "bug-in-the-ear" device and a wrist counter that could only be pressed if she played with "girl" toys, a young teenager was on her way into a psychiatric nightmare that would last for four years.

DAPHNE SCHOLINSKI
FOURTEEN YEARS OLD
1981

At the age of fourteen, Daphne Scholinski was committed by her parents to Michael Reese Hospital in Chicago, which had the reputation of being the best adolescent treatment facility in the area. Labeled with Gender Identity Disorder and Oppositional Defiant Disorder, a specimen of tomboy-gone-bad, Daphne was incarcerated at the same hospital where, over forty years earlier, Dr. Martha Wilson MacDonald had conducted her research on "criminally aggressive behavior in passive, effeminate boys."

When Daphne was institutionalized, she had never had a sexual experience with anyone, girl or boy. When her parents brought her to the hospital, they were told by the doctors that "girls in your daughter's condition usually spend the rest of their lives in mental institutions." Daphne did not want to go along with society's expectations of a girl: she was athletic, she did not want to wear dresses and she refused to be submissive. Her refusal, coupled with her own anger and the anger her refusal caused in others, earned her the "oppositional defiant" label. Daphne was given psychiatric medications and was held incommunicado with anyone outside of the hospital, including her family, for the first three months. This is a standard procedure designed to break all bonds with the outside world, so that the patient is completely dependent upon the hospital and more likely to cooperate with treatment procedures.

Drugged and confused, she found herself sitting in a lounge with people who wallowed in their own urine. She watched others pace back and forth incessantly, babbling, making no sense, declaring themselves to be Jesus, or Jim Morrison come back from the dead. When she found out that some of the ward residents had been there for ten years, she became terrified that she would never be released.

Her first roommate was Pauline, a very small, sweet woman in her fifties, who was being treated with electroshock, a common treatment on the ward, and still a common treatment for hospitalized older women. Daphne was usually awakened early on the days when Pauline was to be shocked, and told to leave and wait in the hallway until Pauline's treatment was finished. From outside the room, Daphne could hear a humming sound, which she thought might be coming from the large metal box with wires that had been wheeled into their room. Standing and waiting in the hallway, Daphne was bothered by Pauline's shock treatments, but Pauline always looked peaceful afterward. She would sleep for the rest of the day, and sometimes into the night, never remembering anything when she awoke.

One morning, at about six-thirty, Daphne pretended to be asleep. She wanted to see what was happening to Pauline, and what could happen to her. Thinking she was heavily sedated from the previous night, the attendants gave up trying to wake Daphne. Out of the corner of her eye, she then watched them wheel in the metal box. She saw that there was a small shelf on top which had cream, a tongue depressor and a mouthpiece. She watched them smooth the cream on Pauline's head, insert the mouthpiece and attach the wires to her temples. The first sound was a warning signal, then there was a beep for the duration of the shock. Daphne now knew that the humming sound was, indeed, from the engine. It took the weight of six attendants to hold Pauline's body in place as she shook and drooled. Daphne was terrified, and she thought that if they knew she was watching, she too would be shocked. It took every bit of her self-control to close her eyes and keep them closed. After the shock team left, she stayed in the room all day, waiting for Pauline to wake.

After three months, Daphne attempted suicide by drinking Sea Breeze, a facial astringent. She had gotten into a fight with her parents on the phone. She did not want to speak with them at all, she was so angry at them for committing her. Her parents had divorced, and her mother was involved with a dangerous man who attempted to kill her and Daphne's sister. He had called Daphne at the hospital and threatened to kill her and her family.

Eventually, he was gone from their lives after he hijacked a plane with his dinner fork and knife and ended up deported.

Daphne, however, was the identified patient, and it was determined that she was suffering from a "gender disorder." She was also considered uncooperative because she did not want to wear a dress, she did not want to talk about sex with her therapist, and she did not want to be a good girl. The psychiatrist in charge of her case decided that she had an "unstable" gender identity. At Christmas, she found herself on the most secured unit, decorating a limp, fake Christmas tree. The staff had removed the metal supports that held up the branches because they were concerned that the patients would tear into the tree, rip out the supports and use them as weapons against others or themselves. Since Daphne and her fellow inmates could not have thread, which was also considered dangerous, Daphne found herself taping popcorn to the tree.

After a year of treatment at Michael Reese, Daphne and a friend on the ward, Amy, were given brochures. They were going to be sent to "long-term institutional learning facilities," and they could choose between the Wilson Center in Faribault, Minnesota, or Menningers in Topeka, Kansas.

"You know how people plan their vacations?" Daphne asked me. " 'Where are we going to go camping this summer?' Amy and I are sitting in the lounge of a psych unit, deciding which mental institution we want to spend the rest of our lives in, if need be. We chose the Wilson Center because it was the only place that didn't have fences. It said it didn't. It was described as being 'on a wooded bluff.' "

Before Daphne would end up at Wilson Center, she was transferred to Forest Hospital in Des Plaines, Illinois, which served as a holding tank for Daphne, since her treatment needed to be continuous for insurance purposes. She had not yet been "accepted" by Wilson, and she is not certain of the reason for her transfer to Forest. Daphne's record does show that she was sent from Michael Reese to Forest Hospital on April 2, 1982, and that her diagnosis was identity disorder and chemical dependency. She showed me her records which described her as experiencing "severe withdrawal," which is ironic, since she could only be in withdrawal from psychiatric medications administered to her by Michael Reese Hospital. Her records read: "Psychotherapy: Patient was initially treated in substance abuse program, and subsequently transferred to psych unit in order to deal with issues of identity." Substance abuse is always a convenient diagnosis for insurance purposes, even if the hospital itself created the chemical dependency, and by the descriptive phrasing of Daphne's "psychotherapy," we can see that "issues of identity" were considered her underlying problem.

At Forest Hospital, Daphne explained that "You had to acquire points. Out of bed by seven forty-five, bed made by eight, room neat by eight-thirty, rounds. Twenty-five points. You could use ten points to go to breakfast unescorted. Fifteen to go to lunch unescorted." Daphne showed me the official hospital records, which included the following prescribed regimen: "Monday, May 24. AM shift. 1. Shower daily. 2. Wash hair daily. 3. Spend 15 minutes with a female peer combing and curling hair and experimenting with make-up. PM. Act out one major feeling per this shift. Process non-verbally with staff. Discussions on how to look more feminine."

After three months of discussing how to look more feminine, curling her hair, experimenting with makeup and coming out of withdrawal from hospital-prescribed drugs, Daphne was informed that she had been "accepted" for an interview to Wilson. "There was a lot of pressure on me to get fully accepted," said Daphne. "It was as if everyone was saying, 'Okay, Daphne, this is your big chance. This is the Yale of the psychiatric wards. Show them your stuff.'" And so she did. Daphne was admitted to the Constance Bultman Wilson Center in Faribault, Minnesota, in June of 1982. The entire time she was there, only one person was turned away, and that was a seven-year-old. Daphne still has the patient profile section of their brochure, which reads, "Co-ed, ages 13–22, at time of admission; from all parts of the U.S. and abroad; most patients have major depression, schizophrenia, manic depressive or borderline conditions; most have had previous hospitalization elsewhere. Average term of treatment 18–24 months. Number of patients: 50. Average number of staff: 200. Campus: 35 acres of wooded bluffs overlooking the Straight River." The name of this river invoked a certain irony for lesbian and gay patients.

At Wilson, all patients had private rooms, although there were sex-segregated, as well as co-ed, wings, or wards. Daphne was placed in an all-male ward, and whenever she became close to another girl, questions about her sexuality arose. In one instance, her friendship with a girl named Bridget became a staff concern. "I don't know if I was in love with her," says Daphne. "I was so far away from thinking about things that way. In a way, I was pretty shocked when they brought it up. The way they did it, I felt like I was being accused of committing a heinous crime. This was more awful than anything I'd done, but I hadn't done anything. They accused us of being physical. We had never been physical, or even talked about being physical. Our reactions, immediately, were to say, 'No way. The idea of being with a woman grosses me out. No way.' I remember specifically sitting in an office with Bridget's doctor, Dr. Klein, and I said, 'The idea of being with a girl turns my stomach,' and he said, 'When my stomach turns, I get excited.' Then Bridget and I were restricted from each other, which meant no eye contact, and no acknowledgment of each other in any way, shape or form."

Most of the children and teens at Wilson were on psychiatric medications like Thorazine, Stelazine, lithium or Prolixin. Daphne's mother did not allow them to medicate her, probably because of the severe withdrawal after the year-long treatment at Michael Reese. Daphne later learned that during one progress interview, the doctors told her mother, " 'We're trying to get Daphne to deal with her sexual identity problems.' My mother said, 'I think she's just gay.' The doctors said, 'Don't worry. We'll take care of that.' And my mother said, 'Don't do that.' " Her mother had been under the impression that Daphne was being treated for being defiant and unmanageable at home, not for possible sexual orientation brought about by a "gender identity disorder." Yet unbeknownst to her mother, the doctors persisted in their treatment, which is reflected in Daphne's medical records: "January 1984: . . . Identity disorder was continued to be evidenced by problems in her sexual identification, friendship patterns, and defining long-term goals and career choices."

After two years and two months at Wilson, and a total of almost four years of involuntary commitment, Daphne turned eighteen, at which point she had the right to walk out of the Wilson Center, which she would certainly do. She was conveniently declared "cured," and "graduated" from Wilson with an almost useless high school diploma, having received mathematics credit, for example, for playing cribbage. Needless to say, as Daphne points out, graduation from a mental institution does not make for a good college or job reference, yet no one prepared her for that reality. In fact, with the encouragement of the Wilson Center, Daphne was given guidance counseling that put her into a junior college law enforcement program. She planned on becoming a police officer until she realized that no police force would ever recruit, much less issue a gun to, a "graduate" from four years of forced psychiatric hospitalization. Nevertheless, through sheer willpower, and perhaps because she was not drugged at Wilson, she managed to graduate from college, and to train as an artist at the Pratt Institute in New York.

"Most people die after they get out," said Daphne. "The recovery from the system is what gets people in the end. Life expectancy of my friends is pretty low. Most of my friends are dead." Daphne is a survivor because she is able to talk about what happened. Gay or straight, most of these children are so demoralized and filled with self-hate that they can barely function.

When I first met Daphne, she was just beginning to speak out. She has now taken her story to the 1995 International Women's Conference in China, where she received a standing ovation. She has testified before the tribunal of the International Lesbian and Gay Rights Association, and her testimony was delivered to the United Nations as an example of condoned human rights abuses.

Daphne Scholinski lives and works as an artist, and her paintings tell the story of a survivor.

Daphne's case came to my attention through Shannon Minter, a young staff attorney and director of the Youth Project at the National Center for Lesbian Rights (NCLR), based in San Francisco. When she first worked for the NCLR in 1992 as a project intern, Minter assumed that mental health professionals and the American Psychiatric Association were allies of the gay community, since homosexuality had been removed from the DSM as a mental disorder. What Minter soon discovered was that Gender Identity Disorder is being used on lesbian and gay adolescents who are gender nonconforming, and that their treatment consists of behaviorism and psychiatric medications in an attempt to alter their gender behavior, in the mistaken belief that this will alter their sexuality. Ironically, the lesbian and gay youth who become visible and vulnerable are the gender nonconformists, while the conformists, who may well outnumber the nonconformists, often fly under the gender radar.

Minter's desk continues to pile up with cases of lesbian and gay youth being committed against their will to psychiatric institutions. Minter receives desperate calls and letters from teens who have been abducted, with their parents' approval, and committed. Treatment for these children can include electric shock to the penis and confinement in isolation rooms. The parents of one young gay man now regret their decision to have their son "treated." He was last seen by his parents in a parking lot in Illinois. They were told that it was best to treat cases like their son's by cutting them off from all contact with the outside world, including contact with those who turn them over for treatment. These parents have been unable to locate or contact the program they turned their son over to. They want him back. The last time they saw him he was straitjacketed by the "escort service" and driven away in a van by specialists in "deprogramming" gay youth.

Then there is the case of the fifteen-year-old girl committed to a facility in New York, the seventeen-year-old boy on the run in South Carolina and the eighteen-year-old girl falsely accused of criminal sexual behavior for a consensual relationship with another girl. In cases in which the youth has actually engaged in sex, the Gender Identity Disorder diagnosis can be combined with a diagnosis of sex offender, since it is illegal for underage youth to have sex with each other in most states. In cases of consensual heterosexual sex between adolescents, the label of sex offender is rarely invoked. As a result of this distortion of the truth, Minter has cases in which young lesbians and gays who have had consensual sex with their peers are being placed in programs alongside adolescent rapists.

One hospital that advertised treatment for "gender identity disorder," and has treated lesbian- and gay-declared youth, was Rivendell, in Utah. Although not alone in its treatment of these young people, and perhaps not the worst, it came to particular attention in 1992 because of Lyn Duff, who at fifteen years old was forcibly brought to Utah from California by her mother, with the help of an "escort service."

Lyn's treatment at Rivendell was behavior modification, psychiatric medication and counseling. Her counselor, Mark, would say: "You need to figure out what it means to be a man. What it means to be a woman." She answered him, "I know what it means to be a woman. What I don't know, I'm still learning. And I don't think I need to be in a hospital to learn that."

Lyn's diagnosis was Oppositional Defiant Disorder, Sexual Identity Disorder, and Gender Identity Disorder. Rivendell expended quite a bit of energy on Lyn's "Gender Identity Disorder." She told me that her counselor read her a story about furry animals, feathered animals and animals that have scales. The furry animals had to accept the fact that they did not have feathers, the feathered animals had to accept the fact that they did not have scales, and so on. This was being read to a fifteen-year-old with an IQ in the upper 160s.

About half of the eighty children and teens at Rivendell were being treated for homosexuality in the guise of Gender Identity Disorder, and the others had been sexually abused, or were labeled perpetrators. One boy, Brendan, was being treated for being gay, but he was straight. He was, however, perceived as gay by the doctors and staff and by those who committed him, because of "feminine" behavior and small body build.

One aspect of Lyn's treatment consisted of being in a girl's group where they would discuss dresses and makeup, and other appropriately feminine topics, attitudes and behaviors. Lyn and a girl named Tammy were also in a special group for sexual "perpetrators" because they had engaged in consensual lesbian sex with their peers before being admitted.

Most of the patients at Rivendell were heavily medicated with drugs like Thorazine, Haldol, Prolixin, Elavil and Stelazine. Some of them were also administered hormones to make them more masculine or more feminine. Lyn remembers being administered hormone pills by a doctor who told her that her hypothalamus was too small, which was affecting her sexuality, and that it had to do with unbalanced neuroendorphins in her brain. Apparently, he thought that if he could make Lyn's hypothalamus larger, she would become more feminine.

Lyn remembers being on a gurney, "and they put these suction cups with wires all over me, on my chest and back, and they showed me these color drawings of people having sex. Women with women. Men with men. People with animals. People with small children." They wanted to measure her biological responses to these pictures, such as heartbeat and rate of breathing, in an attempt to determine what caused her to become sexually excited. "It wasn't the same thing they do with the boys," she said. "The boys would have rubber bands tied around their penises to measure if they enlarged or not when they looked at the pictures." This "diagnostic tool" is called a plethysmograph, which is traditionally used to analyze the sexual response patterns of convicted rapists and child molesters.

One fourteen-year-old named Paul Komiotis, who was also committed to Rivendell, experienced the plethysmograph, but it went further than mere measurement of penile circumference. "They'd put electrodes on our private parts," said Paul, "and show us pictures of men and women. When you got attracted to people of the same sex you got a little electric shock to your penis, strong enough to sting."

Nineteen years old at the time of our interview in March of 1995, Lyn had her own apartment, and she was working as a photojournalist, taking pictures of situations that most people never see, like kids living on the streets. I asked her what she was most proud of right now, and she said, "I'm still alive." "And you're smiling," I said. It's a big smile, with lots of braces. She now does radio news commentary for KPFA radio in San Francisco, and she contributes on a regular basis to National Public Radio on criminal justice and youth issues. She is also on the board of directors at the National Center for Youth Law.

Rivendell is just one hospital system among hundreds which advertises treatment for "oppositional, defiant" youngsters with "identity or personality disorder[s]," and there are almost one hundred of these hospitals in Texas alone. These schools advertise in publications like *Sunset,* an innocuous cuisine and shopping magazine. Many advertise isolated locations and the treatment of "non-compliance," which could mean almost anything, including refusing to act like a lady and wear a dress. The definition in these advertisements of "defiant teenagers on a self-destructive path" is open to an extraordinary range of interpretation, and the diagnosis of Gender Identity Disorder is commonly used in these settings.

The psychological and emotional health of Daphne and Lyn are exceptions to the rule. Minter reflected that "The most disturbing aspect of working on the NCLR's Youth Project was coming face-to-face with the extreme emotional damage that has been inflicted on the young people with whom I have worked— young people who have been institutionalized and labeled mentally ill because of their sexual orientation or gender nonconformity; young people who have run away from home or from a child welfare placement to avoid homophobic abuse; young people who are living on the street, or trading sex for shelter after being discharged, or running away from an institution. No amount of legal advocacy can remedy these kinds of damage."

One of the most frustrating aspects of Minter's work is the lack of rights on the part of these children and teens. In her view, only by carefully monitoring the psychiatric establishment, and making that establishment aware of the sometimes tragic ramifications of their attitudes and diagnoses, can that abuse be prevented.

The abuses of the diagnosis of GID in very young children was made especially clear by Dr. Susan Coates during a lecture she gave in February of 1995 in New York City. Dr. Coates is the director of the St. Luke's-Roosevelt Hospital Childhood Gender Identity Center, where she specializes in the study and treatment of "feminine" boys. She rhetorically asked the audience, "Does the mere existence of a childhood gender identity center further stigmatize children, or does it create a safe haven for them?" Boys are found for her work through channels similar to those once used by Richard Green: solicitations to local psychiatrists, psychologists, social workers, pediatricians and teachers. Referrals for one of her studies "came primarily from local public and Catholic schools that knew of the Childhood Gender Identity unit." It is therefore probable that yes, the existence of the unit, in and of itself, serves to pathologize the nonconforming child along with the child deeply in distress over his body.

Dr. Coates feels trapped in a dilemma: if she changes her gender clinic into a child and family center, she fears that these children will be referred to therapists who use "intense behavior modification." She told the audience, "You would be *shocked,* you would be very shocked, at what goes on even at this age level." She stated that there were units in the United States that had boys referred to them for their interest in "arts and crafts." She added, "Were we in the Bible Belt, we'd have [these referrals] every day." During a break in the proceedings, I approached Dr. Coates to ask her what exactly it was that would shock us about the treatment of these children, the ones who are later sent to her. She was sitting onstage and did not look at me. Staring above the heads of the mingling crowd who remained on the floor, never making eye contact with me, she said, "Behaviorism." I then asked her if these children were being given drugs.

"Yes," she said.

I asked for the names of the drugs, but she did not answer. It seemed to be a deeply emotional moment for her, and only she can know her thoughts and feelings. I then asked if she could at least tell me what kind of drugs were being used. There was another long pause. She never looked down at me, but she answered, "Depression. The children are treated with antidepressives."

In her lecture as well as in her responses to my questions, Dr. Coates confirmed that, not only were young children being subjected to intense behavior modification, they were also being given psychiatric drugs for their gender nonconformance. I am hopeful that, in the interests of the children, Dr. Coates will soon come forward and expose those in the field who are engaging in these practices.

THE ANALYSTS

Although behaviorism, psychotherapy and psychiatric drugs are the primary treatment methods for the gender-nonconforming child, there is also psychoanalysis. In 1982, a five-year-old named Carlos underwent analysis for gender deviance with Dr. Loretta Loeb. He loved the television show *The Flying Nun,* which Dr. Loeb interpreted as representing "his wish to fly, and hence to separate from his phallic mother . . ." His later progress featured a shift "away from a symbiotic attachment to his mother and toward phallic identification with his father, demonstrated by Carlos' sleeping with his father's Navy torpedo pin . . ." Toward the end of his analysis, Carlos asked his mother to put wings on his baseball cap. Dr. Loeb interpreted that request as Carlos' "attempt to renounce his interest in the Flying Nun . . ." Yet, by putting wings on his baseball cap, could Carlos have come up with a creative way to *keep* his attachment to the Flying Nun? If a little "masculine" girl agrees to wear a dress, then she can safely strap on her set of pistols and slip on her cowboy boots without fear of social reprisals. Carlos, by asking for wings on his gender-appropriate baseball cap, satisfies social demands, but is he really attempting to "renounce" the Flying Nun? In the actual television show, only a few people knew about Sally Field's special power to fly, and they tell her that she must keep it a secret. If Carlos learned any lesson about his "femininity," it was to disguise it and keep it as a secret power.

There is an extraordinary passage in Carlos' case history, as recorded by his doctor. Toward the end of his treatment, Carlos sat in her chair, propped his feet upon her desk and "explained that there was a child at school who might appear to be a boy. She dressed like a boy, played like a boy, and had a boy's name. However, she was not a boy; the girl did not have a penis, and that made the difference between boys and girls." He concluded by observing, "You can't tell a book by its cover," a powerful insight from a five-year-old.

Carlos' analysis was very brief, lasting only eight months. The case history that follows, however, features a three-year-old who was in analysis for five years.

STANLEY

THREE YEARS OLD

In 1991, Dr. Calvin H. Haber reported his five-year analysis of a three-year-old child named Stanley, who was brought by his parents to the Psychoanalytic Institute at New York University Medical Center, where he was diagnosed with Gender Identity Disorder of Childhood. Dr. Haber wrote that, had Stanley not been treated, he "would likely have developed into an adult homosexual." Further, he proposed "that psychoanalysis during prelatency can be effective in gender identity disorders, and offers an alternative in some cases to a brittle sense of masculinity and/ or homosexual orientation in the future adult." As the Attending Psychiatrist at Schneider Children's Hospital, certainly Dr. Haber was aware that, by 1991, homosexuality had been declassified as a mental disorder. Yet clearly, the goal of his analysis of this child was to prevent him from growing up gay, something his mother feared.

At first, Stanley's father resisted putting his son into analysis, "insisting that Stanley would outgrow the problem." For the majority of "feminine" boys, this is true, and usually because of intense peer pressure. Dr. Haber cites another reason for the father's resistance: "He was very concerned about finances." Yet the mother prevailed, and it is a disturbing echo of what Dr. Lovaas saw in the mothers who came to him after they had been to the psychoanalysts: enormous guilt, belief they had caused the problem, and willingness to pay any amount of money to take care of it. Dr. Haber wrote, "Four sessions a week with Stanley plus a fifth with either parent or both were met with opposition by the father. Mother feared Stanley might become a homosexual. Father's opposition diminished somewhat when it became financially possible to support the analysis." Dr. Haber does not report telling Stanley's parents that there was no definitive study demonstrating that psychoanalysis would ensure, or even enhance odds, that Stanley would become heterosexual in adulthood.

This is a problem that arises with almost every case that is brought to the attention of a doctor. The parents are worried that their son or daughter will become gay because of gender-nonconforming behavior. As for the children themselves, most of them "deny being disturbed" by their choices, "except that it brings them into conflict with the expectations of their family or peers." The treatment more often addresses the parents' anxiety than the well-being of the child.

The gender identity doctors go along with the parents and agree to treat their children, with the implication that the treat-

ment could prevent adult homosexuality. Richard Green is especially confusing in this regard. He argues for the idea that homosexuality is hereditary, that traditional gender roles have a
biological drive, and that feminine role behavior in boys signals
the presence of a homosexual gene or hormonal abnormality that
leads to homosexuality. He advises that parents should not be
concerned about their role in a boy's femininity, since they are
not to blame if it is biological. (This argument does not account
for the millions of "masculine" homosexual men and "feminine"
lesbian women.) In the next breath, however, Green adds that
"parents have the legal right to seek treatment to modify their
child's cross-gender behavior to standard boy and girl behavior,
even if their only motivation is to prevent homosexuality." The
doctor himself does not seem to believe that changing a child's
gender role behavior will alter future sexuality, yet he is willing to
treat the child as if it will, because the parents have the "legal
right to seek treatment."

In an interview with Kenneth Zucker, who claims his clinic
has treated more gender-disturbed children than any facility in
the world, he told me basically the same thing. "The simple answer is that we do not have any definitive studies that demonstrate" one way or the other that treatment for GID in a child
causes a heterosexual outcome, or that cross-gender play in a
child signals a homosexual adulthood. Yet, again, the parents
come to his clinic for the most part because "they don't want
their kid to be gay." It is this type of convoluted reasoning that
put Stanley and his family into five years of analysis, five times a
week.

Three-year-old Stanley had many classic symptoms of GIDC:
he liked kitchen toys, dolls and carriages. When he was two years
old, he wanted to put on nail polish. He liked Cinderella, Wonder
Woman and Princess Diana. He groomed and dressed dolls. He
also had many childhood ailments, including sore throats, ear-
aches, fevers and allergies. He received frequent allergy shots, and
was on significant amounts of medication, which might explain
why he "avoided sports" and rough-and-tumble play.

The greatest love of Stanley's life had been his grandfather. They spent their days together in walks and conversations. When the grandfather came home one day with a bandage over his eye, Stanley became frightened of bandages, which Dr. Haber interpreted as a "castration reaction." His grandfather was hospitalized for cardiac problems, and after he made some progress, a hospital bed was delivered to Stanley's home for the grandfather's comfort. "Stanley eagerly awaited his return; but his grandfather died the next day . . . Stanley reacted to his beloved grandfather's death by asking to visit him in heaven. When he was told it was impossible, Stanley demanded a rope to climb to heaven. He was furious when he was told that God had taken his grandfather," and he refused to attend church. The depth and power of feeling in this child were remarkable, and his willingness to take on established authority, such as the church, seems extraordinary in one so young.

What else do we learn of this grandfather who inspired such love in Stanley? We learn that he was sixty-eight, retired, that his wife was "a vital working woman" and that he "did light house cleaning while his wife worked." Why is it of such significance that he perhaps washed the dishes and swept the floor? We learn nothing of how he had made a living, probably for over half a century. Haber does not say it directly, but the role reversal of the grandfather's engaging in the traditionally feminine duty of housekeeping, while his "vital" wife worked in the traditionally masculine sphere, seems to implicate them in Stanley's gender identity disorder.

For the first month of analysis, Stanley refused to acknowledge Dr. Haber's existence. He ordered Haber not to look at him, and when Haber spoke, Stanley said, "Shut up." Unlike the profile of some of the other boys, Stanley was quite aggressive. Haber did get his attention by saying the word "grandfather." Whenever Stanley heard the word, he left the room or let out a "loud, anguished scream." But when he returned, he would behave aggressively, telling Haber to "Shut up," or upending the furniture, then ordering the doctor to "straighten everything up."

On one occasion, Stanley was brought to the doctor by his grandmother and his eleven-year-old sister, who both sat in the waiting room. In the office with Haber, Stanley combed a Barbie doll's hair, and asked Haber to help dress the doll. Stanley then took the groomed and dressed Barbie to the waiting room to show to his sister, who reacted only "with a disapproving facial expression." Stanley then returned to Haber's office.

Stanley's sister was gender-role rigid, but she was "correctly" gendered as a girl. She spent her time informing Stanley that boys play with boys, and girls with girls, and certainly that boys were not to play with dolls. Stanley again went to the waiting room, trying to engage his sister, but Haber reported: "This time he returned with a distinct exaggerated wiggle of the hips that mimicked a girl or woman. He told me to shut up and called me ugly when I said he walked like a girl when he was with the girls." Stanley then took over Haber's chair, and Haber asked him if he was pretending to be a boy doctor. Stanley shouted that "this was a girl doctor's office now and that I could get out." Stanley pushed Haber into a closet, left the door open and declared himself to be a girl. Haber then said to Stanley, "Oh, you like girls, so it must be hard to like yourself as a boy." Stanley ended the session by again informing Haber that he was "ugly," an epithet that would last for more than a year.

I suggest that Stanley's behavior was not an expression of his wish to have female anatomy, or to be a girl, but of his desire to feel legitimate in his doll play. Stanley was a sickly boy who did not engage in sports, and he had lost his grandfather, the primary emotional support of his young life. An activity that pleased him was doll play, albeit with the dreaded "Barbie," specifically named in the DSM-IV as an indicator of GID in a boy. He most likely knew that Barbie was a "power toy" for the girls, and he wanted to join them in their play. He was probably lonely.

His sister, however, was adamant that only girls are to play with dolls, and only girls are to play with girls. Yet Stanley "twirled a baton as she did, adopted her favorite color, purple, and preferred her television programs." Clearly, she did not like him encroaching on her domain, and she used gender strictness as a way to shame him and so limit his activities. Stanley also had a fourteen-year-old brother "whose hobby was World War II memorabilia." The brother is described as "the most active in interfering with [Stanley's] cross-dressing," which angered the brother. Stanley's cross-dressing involved wearing "a fake necklace or ring."

The gender-rigid behavior of Stanley's brother and sister probably contributed to Stanley's distress and isolation. Perhaps his siblings could have benefited with some help on their own issues, since Stanley's behavior seems to have been threatening to them. To be traditionally gendered is not, of course, a problem in and of itself, until it includes enforcing that behavior in others, or reacting cruelly toward the gender-nonconformist. Yet the sister sat in the waiting room, and the brother collected his war memorabilia at home, while Stanley was the identified patient.

There was one interchange between Haber and Stanley that seems particularly cruel. Haber told Stanley that, since he liked girls, "it must be hard to like yourself as a boy." This type of reasoning destroys self-esteem, as we have seen with Becky, Jerry and the boys treated at UCLA. Stanley knew that he was a boy, but he did not like to, or could not, engage in traditional "boy" activities. Therefore, because he liked girls and their activities, he could not like himself.

As Stanley matured, he was found to be a gifted child, and beginning at five and a half, at Haber's suggestion, Stanley began to write (by dictation to the doctor) little books about important events in his life. Stanley entitled one book *A Little Lost Lamb,* and another *The Anatomy Book,* in which he "correctly depicted the anatomical differences between the sexes." There was no confusion in this child's mind as to whether he was or was not a boy. He knew he was a boy, but he also knew from the reactions of his family and the doctor that there was something else about him that did not fit the definition of boy.

As with Carlos, all of Stanley's behaviors were interpreted in terms of his atypical gender behavior and his future sexuality.

Wonder Woman and Superwoman were his "phallic" heroines, which he used as "defense against damage, loss of his mother, loneliness, and castration." (We can only wonder how it is interpreted when a girl has a "phallic" heroine, like Superwoman. Is she harboring castration anxiety, or the desire to castrate?)

Stanley was encouraged to share sexual fantasies, and Haber noted during " '69' doll play" that Stanley had peeked into his aunt's and uncle's room while they were making love. Haber said to Stanley "that it apparently had confused him about who was on top and who was on the bottom, and about who was the man and who was the woman." In effect, as the authority figure, Haber instructed Stanley, at the ripe age of five, that a man belongs on top and a woman belongs on the bottom.

During the fifth year of analysis, the now eight-year-old Stanley initiated the end of therapy, telling Haber that he thought he no longer needed to come as often. Haber paints a rosy picture of Stanley, including the fact that his fantasy play no longer included female roles. Haber writes of Stanley's fantasy play on the day they agreed on termination of analysis: "I was assigned to play the President, and he played 'the killer robber.' After killing me and Nancy Reagan, he robbed 'my place.' He then took my attache case to smuggle out of the country. The wish to steal my powerful penis in order to be a fearless boy had emerged, as well as his fantasy that termination equaled death, that if he left me I would die." And there we have it. The now properly gendered Stanley has taken off with the attaché case, smuggling Dr. Haber's powerful penis into foreign countries, leaving behind the mortal remains of the President (aka Dr. Haber) and Nancy Reagan.

Haber summed up Stanley's analysis by explaining that a boy copes with separation and castration anxiety by "moving emotionally and physically away from his mother and toward the father." Since Haber believed Stanley's father to be weak and distant, he viewed himself as Stanley's male role model, the irreplaceable element for achieving masculinity in a boy. This male role model must function as a wedge to separate Stanley from his mother, because the "sight of her reminds him of the threat of object loss and the threat of castration." Haber's final word on Stanley was that his "prognosis and adult outcome is still uncertain," which means he could not guarantee that Stanley would become heterosexual, despite his closing fantasies of stealing Dr. Haber's "powerful penis."

We learn that Stanley's mother responded to stress by throwing temper tantrums that included smashing plates and shouting. Stanley's father responded by ignoring her and distancing himself from the family. The sister responded by twirling her baton and playing with her Barbies, while the brother collected and cataloged his war memorabilia. With the loss of his grandfather, and his deep bereavement, Stanley was left alone to ponder the meaning of life, and to even question and challenge God. Did Stanley need a *male* role model to move toward, "who, like himself, has a penis," or did Stanley need an emotionally mature, nurturing adult in his life? Someone like his grandfather, who just happened to be a man, and a nurturing one at that, whose sense of his own masculinity was not threatened by engaging in "light house cleaning" and daily walks and conversations with a very young child. The relationship between Stanley and his grandfather was significant not because his grandfather had a penis, but because his grandfather loved and nurtured him.

Carlos' and Stanley's cases were not reported in the 1950s from a hamlet in the Bible Belt, but in 1982 from Oregon and in 1991 from New York City. In its unsophisticated forms, psychoanalysis can be an outdated therapy that relies too much upon sexual and genital interpretations of torpedo pins and pens and strings, where the Flying Nun must be renounced and "light house cleaning" could lead to homosexuality or a brittle sense of masculinity. That the penis might be freed from the world of symbolism and take its natural place as a human body part would be a step toward mental health for everyone.

Psychoanalysis has not remained stagnant since Freud, of course, and Richard Green described a departure from classic

Freudian theory in terms of boys. Presented by Anita Bell, this
theory caught my eye for the creative absurdity award: She hypothesizes that a boy experiences anxiety in his first six years
because of the "uncontrollable retractions of his testes." This
anxiety draws him back toward his mother for comfort, which is
not healthy for his sexual development. To counter this movement toward the mother, the father intuitively responds to his
son's needs by playing ball games with him, "whereby the boys
learn to handle and control balls."

In today's world, traditional analysis of little girls seems
equally archaic. Classic Freudian theory describes a girl's psychosexual development as beginning when she becomes aware
"that males have something where she apparently has nothing,"
which arouses "penis envy." The girl then turns on her mother,
"blaming her mother for her lack of a penis," and then turns
toward her father, presumably because he has a penis, as an "object of love. Realizing the impossibility of her aspiration to replace
her mother, she then identifies with her and will later seek out
another more suitable male."

Little girls are no longer taught that, because they do not have
penises, they have "nothing." They know that they have vaginas.
Small children are now more often in preschool situations where
they see each other in the bathroom, and they are often toilet-
trained together. The "trauma" of seeing a penis or a vagina is
perhaps not so great, and might now be rare. Parents are also not
as worried about nudity with their children as they have been in
the past, and so the sight of a naked adult body might no longer
have the forbidden charge it once had.

I learned quite a bit about this when I brought my son at
fourteen months to his first nursery school. I was speaking to the
day care worker and, with a fleeting, half-embarrassed gesture, I
asked her what word they used for his "you know," so I would
know what to call it with him. The woman's smile was patient and
ironic, and I never forgot what she said: "Well, Phyllis. We call it
a penis." A year or so later, after school, I picked up my son and
one of his little friends, who was a girl. She turned her face up to

me, and with an absolute beam of a smile announced, "I have a vagina!" Later that evening, I was bathing my son. He looked at me with a defiant expression and announced that he was going to have a vagina when he grew up. I was shocked and horrified. I told him what a lovely penis he had, and that it was just absolutely terrific. He didn't care. He insisted that he was going to have a vagina. My head was reeling.

I pursued the topic with him as he was putting his stuffed animals in his bed and covering them up with little blankets. I again told him how terrific his penis was, but he was having none of it. I began to panic, envisioning the adoption worker coming to the lesbian household and finding a boy who plans on having a vagina when he grows up. Jesse seemed just as agitated as I was, and I finally asked him the right question: *Why* did he want a vagina instead of a penis? "The girls get to have the babies," he said, and he was none too pleased about that. There was, in fact, a tinge of bitterness in his voice.

The issue of penis envy in girls has been presented as the most powerful component of their childhood development. Yet the power to give birth might far outweigh any envy over the penis in young children, which brings us to a very important situation. Little attention, if any, has been paid to the trauma little boys experience when they learn that they cannot give birth. Rather than becoming enraged at not having a penis, most little girls are now quite puffed up about the fact that they will be able to carry the baby inside their bodies. They often enjoy pointing this out to the little boys. I worked up the courage to ask the father of one of Jesse's playmates if his son had ever thought he could give birth. I was worried that Jesse had gotten this idea because there were so many adult females in his life. I'll always be thankful for his response. "I let him think it for a while," he said. "If a boy can imagine a baby coming out of him, he will be more nurturing." As I talked to this father, I learned that most little boys, until they are informed otherwise, think that they, too, can carry a baby inside their bodies. When they are told that this is not the case, they are often horribly unhappy. When they are told that they have the seed without which the baby could not come to be in the mommy's tummy, it is usually of little consolation.

I recently taught a creative writing class in the uses of personal experience, and I asked the students to describe the first time they remembered being told they could not do something that was very important to them because they were a girl or a boy. Many of the girls remembered resenting that they could not pee standing up, and all of them remembered certain types of sports and professions that were off limits to them. Among the men, seven out of fifteen mentioned giving birth, and four of them had it first on their list, elaborately describing their feelings. One young man, now married and about to have his first child, remembered putting a stuffed animal under his shirt and pretending to be pregnant.

My son finally accepted the fact that he could not carry the baby, but I also taught him that the baby cannot come into the world without his seed. The importance of that role would be clear to the boys if men were truly welcomed in the domestic sphere, but playing house and dolls is off limits to them, or at best, merely permitted.

THE DOMESTIC SPHERE

By looking at what society pathologizes, we can see what society demands of those of us who wish to be considered normal. This concept is especially revealing when looking at gender roles in the domestic sphere. For a diagnosis of Gender Identity Disorder in children, one of the symptoms for little girls is that they "show no interest in dolls or playing 'house' (unless they play the father or another male role)." For boys, their symptoms of the disorder include doll play, and as the case studies show, a deep chord of fear is struck when boys engage in domestic activities, even on the fantasy level.

The case of Robert, reported in 1983 from London, gives a

poignant and precise picture of what can happen to a boy when he transgresses traditional domestic gender roles. Of note in Robert's story is the key participation of a psychiatric social worker who managed the case, treated the other family members, and was co-author of the report. Her name is Virginia Bottomley, and she went on to become England's Secretary of State for Health, during which time she was responsible for dismantling much of the British public health system. In 1995, she was also put in charge of Family Policy for all of the United Kingdom. Constantly embroiled in controversy, Virginia Bottomley is now National Heritage Secretary, a cabinet level position in the British government.

ROBERT

FIVE YEARS OLD

Robert was treated for "effeminate behaviour" at Lister Health Center's Camberwell Child Guidance Unit in London, England. His treatment lasted for twenty-one months, during which time he was seen individually fifty-six times by a male therapist, while his family was treated concurrently by Mrs. Bottomley, who was also the case manager. The family treatment consisted of Mrs. Bottomley conducting forty-eight individual sessions at the clinic: forty with Robert's grandmother, five with his mother and three with his father. She also made eighteen home visits. One of the primary goals of Robert's treatment was to drive a wedge between him and his grandmother, that he might become appropriately gendered for a boy, and it was for this reason that Robert's individual therapist was male.

While Robert was being treated in one room at the health center, his grandmother was being counseled in another room by Mrs. Bottomley. Robert liked his grandmother best, but their closeness was considered by Mrs. Bottomley to be toxic for Robert's budding masculinity. She did not want Robert to have "cosy cups of tea in bed" with his grandmother anymore, and she was concerned that he draped "tea towels" over his head, which was considered cross-dressing.

Robert's first therapist, a male psychiatric registrar, asked Robert why he dressed like a girl, and Robert told him that he did not dress like a girl. The therapist asked him if he thought he was a girl, and Robert told him no, he did not think so. The therapist asked him if he wanted to be a girl, and Robert told him that he did not. In the report, Robert is described as having initially "denied that he cross-dressed" and further, that he "maintained that he preferred boys to girls." The therapists interpreted for Robert what they believed he could not interpret for himself, or would not confess to: he cross-dressed, preferred girls, and engaged in both overt and covert "effeminate behaviour."

The therapist persisted in questioning Robert about the tea towels. Did he not put them on his head, and sometimes tie them around his waist? Yes, he admitted he did do that, which the therapist interpreted to mean that Robert was trying to be a girl.

The therapist continually encouraged him to play war with the toy cowboys and Indians, but Robert was not interested. He liked to take care of the little family dolls. He liked to cook for them and feed them. He liked to bathe them and change them. The therapist discouraged this activity by looking away from the dolls and telling Robert about the excitement of cowboys, Indians and war.

Robert, however, did not want to play war. Robert wanted to play with the family dolls, especially since his own dolls had disappeared from his house after he started coming to the clinic. The "disappeared dolls" were a result of Mrs. Bottomley's therapy sessions with Robert's mother. Perhaps because his own dolls had vanished, Robert now wanted to play only with the family dolls while at the clinic, and no one was very happy about this, except perhaps Robert.

During a subsequent session, Mrs. Bottomley told Grandmother that she should stop Robert from "joining in her domestic chores" and that she should "show disdain if he dressed up."

Also, there were to be no more tea parties. Robert was to be discouraged, once and for all, from being "too good to be true," as his grandmother was fond of describing him. It was simply not good for him, Mrs. Bottomley explained to her, because it was encouraging his "effeminate behaviour."

For six months, Robert refused to play with the cowboys and Indians, no matter what the therapist said or did. When the therapist left the clinic, he was replaced by another psychiatric registrar, Meng Hooi Lim, co-author of the report with Mrs. Bottomley. Mr. Lim also wanted Robert to play with the cowboys and Indians. Robert was probably getting tired of this. He liked to come and play with the family dolls, even if his grandmother no longer laughed when he put on the tea towel, even if they no longer shared a cup of tea and even if she had started to hide her jewelry. Mrs. Bottomley had also helped Grandmother to understand that Robert must never again play with her jewelry, because it was interfering with his masculine development. He had never broken the jewelry or mistreated it in any way. He had liked looking at it, and he had sometimes put it on. It must have looked much more beautiful than anything else in his rough South London neighborhood.

At this point in his therapy, Robert was described as no longer attempting "to deny his feminine interests, playing almost exclusively with the family figures." In an attempt to thwart this activity, and to "discourage feminine behaviour and cultivate masculine interests," Mr. Lim tried to interest Robert in playing war by presenting him with some toy soldiers. Robert, however, proved himself "adept at side-stepping his [therapist's] interventions." Robert held the toy soldiers in his hands, and examined them. As any child who has played with such figures knows, their faces look tired. And what did Robert do, in this particular instance, that was considered deviant? "When the soldiers were brought out, Robert said they were hungry, fed and bathed them . . ." This was not the "correct" response for a little boy toward toy soldiers, although we can imagine that on a real battlefield, a nurturing presence would be elevated and even crucial.

After the soldiers were no longer dirty or hungry, Robert had them stand guard around a play home within which he placed the family figures. He turned the soldiers into protectors, but this was interpreted as problematic, indicating that Robert was not comfortable with masculinity, because he did not put them inside the house. Nevertheless, inside the make-believe home, Robert's family dolls were happily engaged in domestic tasks.

In the real world, however, there was nothing but anger, confusion and recrimination in Robert's home. Everyone was fighting: his mother, his father, his grandmother. Everyone was tired and angry, and they got even angrier when Mrs. Bottomley came to the house; not with Mrs. Bottomley, but with each other. She had pointed out to the grandmother "the high value placed on the feminine role in Robert's family," and therefore implicated such valuing as a reason for Robert's mental disorder. She had "encouraged the father to be more assertive," and suggested that his mother preferred "men to be passive rather than assertive." So in Robert's house, there was war, of a sort: Father was drunk, Mother was furious and there were no more "cosy cups of tea" with Grandmother. This chaos centered on the fact that "Robert was now openly acknowledged to be interested in feminine activities and clothes," as demonstrated by his participation in domestic activities, doll play, and his use of the dreaded tea towel.

After nine months of unsuccessful treatment, tactics changed. Robert was no longer presented with the soldiers, and he was not encouraged to make war between the cowboys and Indians. Since Robert refused to be coerced into playing as he was expected to play, Mr. Lim and Mrs. Bottomley decided to let Robert "indulge" in his "feminine behaviour," which they would then interpret, as if they were psychoanalysts.

When Mr. Lim told Robert that he could play with the cowboys and Indians in any way that he wished, Robert took the cowboys in his hands and put the Indians in Mr. Lim's. For the first time, Mr. Lim did not suggest that they fight, and Robert was probably quite happy about this turn of events. So happy, in fact, was he, that "Robert cooked the food the Indians had hunted."

Robert's play cooking was seen as an attempt to "keep the peace," as if peacekeeping and cooking were inappropriate behaviors for boys.

A primary goal of Mrs. Bottomley's treatment of Grandmother was to get her to pull away from Robert. Mrs. Bottomley told Grandmother that she was much too invested in Robert, and that she needed to release him that he might become a man. At the time, Robert was six years old. Grandmother now went swimming without him, and she was going to go away on a cruise ship. In any event, Robert was not "too good to be true" anymore, and his grandmother now found him difficult and exhausting. His displays of "increasing naughtiness," however, were to no avail, because no matter how bad he was, Grandmother would not repent and become her nurturing self again. This must have been quite painful for Robert, for he would not have had any idea why his grandmother had so suddenly changed her behavior toward him. If nurturing adults suddenly shut down, small children often believe that they have done something wrong, and so have become unlovable.

The grandmother was also encouraged by Mrs. Bottomley to change her relationship with Robert's father, for Robert's sake. To demonstrate this positive change, Mrs. Bottomley noted that Grandmother began to iron the father's shirts and pack his lunch, which seems to have been an attempt at demonstrating, for Robert, appropriate gender deference.

The father's therapy with Mrs. Bottomley is of particular interest. The father had an abusive stepfather, who beat his mother. He had attempted to defend her, and then was put into a juvenile home for hitting the stepfather. He disliked violence and aggression, and Mrs. Bottomley interpreted this as his fear of masculinity. Yet, although she espoused a nonviolent form of masculinity, all of the play therapy with Robert centered on war and dominance, and to this end, Robert slowly began to "improve," as demonstrated by the following scene during the tenth month of his treatment.

Robert set up the cowboys and Indians for a battle, the first time he had done such a thing. Mr. Lim then reported that Robert "procrastinated" in beginning the war.

"Are the Cowboys afraid?" Mr. Lim asked Robert.

"The Indians will take away all the treasure . . . and the Queen, the Queen of Sheba," said Robert.

What was happening in this child's world? What did he see? Finally, Robert managed to get the cowboys to kill the Indians with "a single shot," which was considered a therapeutic breakthrough.

"In this magically safe situation, Robert took the totem pole from the therapist, announcing, 'Now the Cowboys have something to pray to.' " Taking the totem pole and the captured weapons, Robert "laid [them] before the powerful Queen." This, however, was interpreted as a sign that Robert "did not value his masculinity . . ." But was it? The Queen could well have been his grandmother, whom he adored despite her inexplicable, sudden rejection of him as a result of her therapy with Mrs. Bottomley. The Queen could also have simply been a stabilizing power image. What a Queen might represent to a child living in a matriarchal monarchy cannot be so easily dismissed in favor of the clumsy attribution by Lim and Bottomley of Freudian Oedipal theories featuring castration anxiety.

In sessions immediately following the capture of the totem pole, Robert "torture[d] the Indian squaws for having taken 'something' from the Cowboys 'a long time ago.' " Robert was now reported as progressing, "consistent with the ideas of Newman and Stoller," and in this we see the extraordinary reach and influence of the research on feminine boys at UCLA. Here we have these same theories being applied in London's South End by individuals who, by self-report, were not "formally trained in behaviour therapy or psychotherapy."

Nevertheless, Bottomley and Lim believed that Robert was "at risk of developing disturbed sexual orientation or gender identity in adulthood." To back themselves up, they cited a chapter entitled "Perversions and Impulse Neuroses" from a 1945 publication by Otto Fenichel. Robert's perceived "latent hostility" could be linked, they explained, to all sorts of perversions, especially sexual. When I read Fenichel's chapter, I found the range of conditions described quite astounding, especially when they were supposed to apply in some way to Robert. There is, of course, the usual male and female homosexuality, fetishism and transvestism, but there is also exhibitionism, voyeurism, sadomasochism and braid cutting. Apparently, little boys act out their castration anxiety by cutting off little girls' braids. In a more modified form, they simply tug at them. At the time Bottomley and Lim used this book to help them diagnose and interpret Robert's play behavior, the book was thirty years old, and comprised of theories formulated at least a decade before that.

The danger of the availability of the diagnosis of Gender Identity Disorder in childhood is clearly illustrated by Bottomley and Lim. Two completely unqualified individuals embarked on a psychoanalysis of a five-year-old boy who did not display the primary symptom listed for GID in children. They in fact admitted, "[Robert] neither believed nor wished that he was a girl." They further described the child as "relaxed, pleasant and observant," but nevertheless guilty of not engaging in "rough and tumble play." They found him to be physically strong, intelligent, yet having "some" problems with other boys. Their description of him as having begun "cross-dressing when he was two years old" referred to playing with jewelry, and "inventive feminine behaviour" referred to playing with tea towels. Yet the primary focus of their therapy with Robert, and his family, was that he played with dolls, and that his play "centred around domestic activities."

After close to a year of therapy, Robert's grandmother no longer accompanied him to the clinic, and she no longer spoke with Mrs. Bottomley. She had become exhausted by Robert's now aggressive behavior. Grandmother did take Robert with her one last time to bingo, and for that one evening things might have again seemed the same between them. Robert's mother, however, "scolded" his grandmother when they returned, and put a stop to it. Bingo, apparently, thwarts proper masculine development.

In response to Mrs. Bottomley's encouragement, at this time

Robert's father decided to become more assertive. His interpretation of assertion was to take action regarding Robert's collection of pictures and drawings of girls. The father "reacted strongly to Robert's effeminate behaviour, tearing up pictures of girls and becoming angry when Robert played dolls with girls." Father then took Robert to the toy store, and told him to pick out a toy. The pressure must have been extraordinary on Robert, who chose a gun, a choice with which everyone seemed quite pleased.

It was at this juncture that Robert became especially embittered with his grandmother, refusing to kiss her, as he usually did. As part of his development, Robert, who was once "too good to be true," was now pictured as playing his "mother and grandmother against each other" as a method of "rebelling against their authority." While his mother became "dejected" about her deteriorating relationship with her son, Robert's "feminine behaviour had become rare." He was now described as gaining a stronger identification with his father, and his "cross-dressing" via "inventive use of a tea towel had decreased to 'about once a week.'"

Robert stopped cleaning and cooking. That was for girls. Once, he fixed the sink with his father, handing him the tools. That was acceptable behavior because it involved a lot of banging and a wrench. When his mother and father fought, he took his father's side, because he was a boy, and he would always be a boy. He understood that he was not to cook for, feed or bathe tired soldiers or family dolls.

When Robert was six and a half years old, and had been in treatment sixteen months, Mr. Lim and Mrs. Bottomley decided to take a more aggressive tactic because they believed Robert "persisted in feminine play because he still needed to learn how men behaved." To this end, the "female figures were banished on holiday, never to return to the sessions." Robert was now trainable, having been removed from female influences, and he began to explore a series of roles now presented to him. Robert pretended to be "Captain with a whip to make all men submit." Robert could probably see that this pleased Mr. Lim, and so he began to flail the whip at the toy men, until it frightened him to be doing such a thing. "In a moment of panic," Robert handed the whip back to Mr. Lim.

At this point, Lim and Bottomley contend that Robert "learnt to modify his idea of masculinity. He and the therapist took turns to be foreman and factory hand, manager and assistant, pupil and teacher." They were, in effect, practicing power relationships through role play, that Robert might one day take up his masculine duty in society, which clearly was not presented as involving cooperation and equal partnership.

Concurrently, Mrs. Bottomley was trying to work through a "stalemate" between Robert's parents. She decided to use a "contractual" approach, by asking them to agree to specific changes in behavior toward each other as a means of helping Robert to achieve his masculine identity. Robert's mother wanted the father to stop drinking and give her more of his paycheck. Robert's father insisted that it was not his problem with masculinity, but the mother's problem with femininity, that was causing all the trouble, and so he made two requests: that she accept gifts from him graciously, and begin to wear makeup.

Bottomley reported that as a result of her intervention, they learned to "examine and defuse their anger," yet in the nineteenth month of treatment, the mother could no longer tolerate the father. "She could not cope," wrote Bottomley, "with the new man the father had become . . ." Did Mrs. Bottomley really believe that, by encouraging superficial adherence to traditional gender roles, she had created a "new man"? In fact, by forcing the situation, she could have helped to destroy what was left of an already vulnerable relationship, by advising them to basically role-play their lives in a gender-correct charade. Perhaps most crucial is the minimal importance attached to the father's apparent alcoholism, which would certainly be a more profound stressor in their relationship than quibbling over masculine and feminine behaviors.

As his parents' relationship deteriorated, Robert himself was depicted as well on the road to masculine recovery because he now "toyed with his uncle's possessions and shaving utensils." At this point, Mr. Lim told Robert that his therapy would conclude in two months, and that he would no longer need to come to the clinic. Robert responded by telling Mr. Lim a story "of a widow lost alone in the hills, her grown-up son living abroad. When she found her way home, Dracula was there." Robert was then silent, and "the therapist acknowledged Robert's sense of having grown away from his mother and his consequent concern for her." He was now just seven years old, and he was becoming a man.

Soon it was time for Robert to leave therapy. Mr. Lim told Robert that he had done a lot of "play-work," and it was certainly true that play was quite a bit of work at the Camberwell Child Guidance Unit, paid for by the British government. Mr. Lim told Robert, "You have come to learn about boys and girls, what it means for you and your family, what it means for you to be a boy."

Robert then played one last time for Mr. Lim. He became a train conductor, but he was not on the train, he said. The train had gone without him, and in his imagination, he saw himself, running along the tracks, chasing the train, his heart pounding. From far inside the play world where beauty and nurture had been banished as unsuitable, and still chasing the train, Robert shouted into the real world of the therapist's office: "Wait for me! Wait for the little boy . . . I mean, the conductor."

At the end of Robert's therapy, Mrs. Bottomley and Mr. Lim reported that "cross-dressing had ceased although when upset he still showed an interest in feminine activities without indulging in them." This phrase seems so cold when we also listen to the sound of this child shouting in the therapist's office, "Wait for me! Wait for the little boy . . ." When upset, Robert is now portrayed as reverting to deviant feminine behavior, but what that means is never clarified.

Mrs. Bottomley and Mr. Lim followed up on Robert six months after termination. "No feminine activity was observed."

Fifteen months after termination, they reported that Robert and his new boy friends "had been in fights." The impression is that this is a positive sign. They also reported that "The school had not noticed any feminine behaviour . . ." It is rather frightening, and somewhat Orwellian, that someone went to Robert's school and questioned his teachers about any signs of "effeminate behaviour" in the child. Reminiscent of the treatment of Jerry in Florida, the teachers were signaled that should Robert, or any other child, exhibit nonconforming gender behavior, it is a matter for the public health authorities.

Three years after termination, in 1983, Bottomley and Lim reported that Robert was now "taller and had lost his babyish mannerisms." We're certainly relieved to learn that Robert had grown taller after three years, but what does that have to do with his gender identity? Robert was now almost eleven years old, and during a play session in the follow-up, "He involved the therapist in a lively battle in which they repulsed a common enemy from their castle, no women being introduced. He scoffed at the idea of girls joining his gang of six boys when they played at Cowboys and Indians. 'You don't see girls with bows and arrow, do you?' "

Mrs. Bottomley and Mr. Lim concluded, "The parents thought Robert was settled and cheerful. There had been no further incidents of effeminate behaviour."

What exactly did the successful therapy of Robert include? He no longer engaged in activities that could cause him problems in the society of boys, but to avoid bullying, he might have modified his behavior on his own. This is the decision most boys come to. Some children, however, might choose *not* to change something about themselves, despite the responses of other children, because it is simply too important to them. Robert should have been allowed that choice. Rather than being given support in who he was, his (and his family's) therapy with Mrs. Bottomley and Mr. Lim featured an almost complete suppression of nurturing behaviors, encouragement of physical violence and the banishment of girls and females as a toxic presence. This was not the stated goal of Mrs. Bottomley and Mr. Lim, who contend in their report that their aim was to stop Robert's "effeminate behaviour," not to instill in him hypermasculinity. Actions, however, speak louder than words, and the message to Robert was clear: he was banished from the domestic sphere, that he might become a real man.

Although the specter of homosexuality and an assortment of colorful "perversions" such as braid cutting were invoked by Bottomley and Lim, Robert's case was not so much about sexuality as it was about gender roles. Their focus was on what it means to be a boy or to be a girl, and by extension, a man or a woman. To that end, there was a particular emphasis on extinguishing his nurturing activities, such as pretend cooking and caring for the family dolls. As I write this, Robert would now be about twenty-one years old. We can only wonder how his treatment haunts him, what effect it has had on his family life, and what effect it will have on his children.

As a final note, one of the principal architects of the UCLA feminine boy project, Richard Green, now lives in England, where he is the consulting psychiatrist at the Gender Identity Unit at Charing Cross Hospital. At a recent gender conference in California, he told me that treatment is being provided for Gender Identity Disorder in British boys and girls through St. George's Hospital in London, under the direction of Domenico Decegile, and throughout Europe, with specialty clinics for children in Genoa, Italy, and Utrecht in the Netherlands.

TABOO DOMESTIC BEHAVIOR

The psychiatrists and clinical psychologists specializing in Gender Identity Disorder in children insist that they are not trying to inculcate gender stereotypes. Yet when you cut away at the politically correct rhetoric in which they engage, and look at the actual treatment that is given to children diagnosed with GID, the message to the child is anything but flexible in terms of gender role, and the message is particularly strong in the domestic sphere.

In 1981, ten-year-old Kevin was analyzed for standing, walking, sitting and book carrying by William Hay and David Barlow. Diagnosed as "rigidly feminine," Kevin was called "sissy" and "fag" at school, and was afraid of being physically attacked. His tormentors were not treated. Instead, through hypnosis, he renounced the Bionic Woman in favor of Steve Austin, the Six Million Dollar Man. But Kevin was also guilty of nurturing play behavior, because he preferred to "play with girls and toys usually given to female children, such as dolls." Rather than the dreaded Barbie, Kevin's favorite game was "playing with a camper and a family of dolls."

In his *Sissy Boy* book, Richard Green writes of a five-year-old named Richard ("Feminine Boy, Heterosexual Man"). When the parents first brought Richard for treatment, Green asked them, "How far back does his interest in taking the female role go?" We are informed that it went back two and a half years, which would have made Richard two years old. He was, like Robert, found guilty of an American version of inventive tea towel play, but of particular concern was his interest in homemaking, as revealed by this initial dialogue between Dr. Green and Richard's parents:

> Richard Green: What are his favorite toys?
> Mother: Cooking utensils.
> Father: Cooking ware, stoves.
> Mother: Doll furniture.
> R.G.: And when he asks for cooking utensils when he has wanted them, have you gone out and bought them for him?
> Father: Oh, no. His desires are quite *extravagant,* so we haven't always gone out and gotten what he's wanted.

R.G.: The feminine toys he has, you purchased your-selves?

Mother: Yes.

Dr. Green believed that because these parents allowed Richard access to cooking utensils, cooking ware, stoves and doll furniture, they had contributed to his mental disorder. Perhaps if the parents had indulged Richard's "extravagant" cookware desires, the world might have had another five-star chef.

In 1980, Arthur Horton of Winchester, Virginia, who lists no credentials, briefly documented his treatment of "childhood gender role confusion" in a child named David, "a six-year-old black male" in first grade. Horton cites the work of Richard Green and George Rekers at UCLA as the clinical basis for treating David, whose problem was that he only wanted to "play house" with girls. An intervention was arranged at his school, which included interviews with his mother and teacher. According to Horton, David's problems stemmed from the fact that there were no men in his household. Horton instructed the teacher and David's mother "to use social reinforcement and mild reprimands to promote appropriate gender role behavior."

To further assist the deviant David in developing a masculine identity, David and "two other black boys from his classroom, chosen because they exhibited obvious masculine behavior, were seen in a group for a thirty-minute session once a week for six weeks." During this time, Horton would "prompt" and "socially reinforce" masculine behavior by encouraging David to relate to these two boys, and to copy them. What exactly were the "obvious masculine behaviors" of the other boys? We are left to imagine them, but the one thing of which we can be certain is that these behaviors did not include "playing house," with or without girls.

There has been no real change in the relationship gender identity therapists draw between dolls, domestic play and the creation of psychological illness in boys. In 1993, Kenneth Zucker and Richard Green described the mother of a five-year-old boy.

She had been severely depressed during "her own mother's impending death from cancer." At that time, "her son began to play with female dolls, and she recalled that he would play quietly in his own room, talking softly to, and combing the hair of, the dolls." Was this child really displaying a symptom of a disorder? Or was he responding in a tender, nurturing way to the pain he sensed around him? The question arises, what would have been "appropriate" play for this child in this situation?

The nonconforming child has been treated in a variety of settings, including those permeated with rigid gender role training based upon religious practices, by people not necessarily trained in dealing with children on these issues. Yet even the Yale Child Study Center has been involved in such cases. In 1983, "reluctant" parents brought their five-year-old to the Yale Center because his kindergarten teacher told them that their Fred was "well on his way to becoming a homosexual." By the age of four, Fred preferred helping Mom in the kitchen to playing outside. He also dusted and swept. The mother was taught that by allowing Fred to engage in housekeeping, she was contributing to his "gender identity confusion." The father was reprimanded for lowering Fred's self-esteem by returning from work and greeting Fred by teasing, "How's my little girl?" After two months of treatment, Fred renounced Batgirl, no longer insisted on "girl's roles" in school and gave up being "mother's little helper" at home.

Fred's doctor mused that in the future, what was once considered a sign of pathology might simply be seen as the behavior of a child marching to a different drummer. He wrote, "It may soon be 'OK' for boys to avoid rough sports if they want to and cook and help with housework." Will it? Not according to recent research. Little boys remain seriously affected by the taboos on domestic activities, from child care to homemaking, and in our changing times, these taboos are wreaking havoc with families around the world.

A 1990 study conducted by Thomas Weisner at UCLA and Jane Wilson-Mitchell at the Reiss-Davis Child Study Center in Los Angeles revealed that, no matter what social setting a boy is raised in, parents are paranoid at worst, and hesitant at best, about doll play. Weisner and Wilson-Mitchell studied a wide variety of family lifestyle types, all of whom were raising six-year-old children of both sexes. These family structures ranged from two-parent married couples who were low to moderate on countercultural values and high in socioeconomic status, to "avant garde" families with high countercultural values, socioeconomic status and education.

The researchers found that, no matter what the family structure, gender roles were relatively more flexible for girls than for boys. In every area that they investigated, from play and toy preference to occupational aspirations, when girls were treated differently than boys, it was true, across the board, for all family types. Overall, in terms of dress or behavior, "few parents were willing to risk the questioning by others of their child's gender identity." Fear appeared in even the most liberal and "avant garde" family groups, especially if there was a "risk" of a boy being mistaken for a girl.

Not surprisingly, messages to these six-year-olds were clear in terms of play behavior. "Regardless of family life-styles . . . boys were much more likely than girls to be permitted to play with guns, and girls were actively discouraged from gun play. While counterculture parents generally discouraged children of either sex from playing with guns, they were nonetheless more likely to discourage girls than boys. Similarly, while counterculture parents rarely said that they actively discouraged children of either sex from playing with dolls, all parents were more likely to encourage doll play for girls but, at most, only permit it for boys."

How often have we heard educated, professional, moderate and liberal parents express amazement at the apparent spontaneity of their children's sex-typed behavior, especially in terms of dolls and playing house. Every television show we see on the differences between the sexes seems to feature baffled parents who insist that they treat the girls and boys just the same, and that there is some mysterious force at work attracting girls to dolls and boys to guns. That mysterious force is not nature, but a pervasive cultural backdrop fueled by something akin to gender terrorism aimed at children. This force, and the anxiety it promotes, permeates the child's world so powerfully that it creates the illusion of being inborn. As long as doll and house play can be described, in and of themselves, as features of mental illness, or diagnostic tools to detect a disorder in *any* child, then all children are at risk.

When boys are diagnosed with Gender Identity Disorder because they pretend to be "mother" and only play house, is it because they think they must choose one arena over the other? Why would they think otherwise? The domestic sphere is a forbidden zone for the man, and therefore for the boy. When middle-class women began to join the work force in the sixties, and the number of working mothers began to rise, there was the assumption that the husband would participate more fully in household chores, including child care. This belief was fueled by the idea of equality of the sexes, that girls could do whatever boys could do. Feminists assumed that there would be a spillover effect, and that men would become more comfortable in the traditionally feminine domestic role. But there was little or no emphasis on teaching boys that they could do whatever girls could do. While girls edged their way into masculine territory, boys remained trapped by the masculine mystique, and its taboo on female-identified behaviors.

In 1986, Shelley Coverman and Joseph F. Sheley undertook a study to clarify two very different points of view. At the time, many popular articles claimed that men were taking on more traditionally female household roles, but more technical studies, published by social scientists, revealed a different story. Studying households in which both husband and wife worked full-time, researchers found that working men had at best slightly increased their housework between 1965 and 1975 by "two minutes per day." Another research team found that men's overall participation in domestic chores, including child care and shopping, had actually *decreased* by two minutes. Occasionally, a study did surface which showed men performing significantly more housework than they had in the past (2.4 hours in 1972, 5 hours in 1976), but these figures, when compared to women's figures of from 36.8 to 32.6 hours per week, did not indicate a leveling of the domestic burden between husband and wife.

Coverman and Sheley found that, in fact, there were no statistically meaningful differences in the amount of time men spent doing housework between 1965 and 1975. They also found that men were working about one hour less per week outside the home, forty minutes of which they now used for leisure activities. They noted that "despite popular beliefs, there is little indication that class variables (income, education, and professional-managerial employment status) had any bearing on men's involvement in domestic work between 1965 and 1975."

The issue of division of domestic labor is a hot one between working couples, and it is the rare couple that is immune to the tension that can arise around who performs which task. In 1976, *American Psychologist* published a report based on surveys sent out to couples both of whom were professional psychologists. The survey focused on the division of household labor, including child care. "Fifteen anonymous respondents indicated that they had been unable to complete the questionnaire because of the conflict it had stimulated."

The analysis of the data gleaned from the psychologist couples who did manage to return the survey revealed that "the only stereotypically female activity for which professional wives do not bear an absolute majority of responsibility is house-cleaning, but only because outside help is employed rather than because husbands share the responsibility. Outside help, rather than husbands, take responsibility for a large share of the laundry chores as well." These same couples, some of whom could not even complete the questionnaire, so much hostility did it engender between them, belong to the profession that determines gender role norms and disorders in children, and their work still stands largely unchallenged.

In the 1990s, not much has changed in the domestic sphere. When there are reductions in the amount of time women spend doing housework, and they appear to be doing a similar amount of work as the men, it is not that the men are doing more, but that the women are doing less. Men do not view themselves as equal partners in terms of domestic duties, and so they tend to describe themselves as "helping out" when they do housework or child care. It was thought that a man's lower housework participation could be related to whether or not his wife worked outside the home, the idea being that the wife was functioning as a full-time homemaker. According to Marjorie Starrels at the University of Michigan, this is not the case. Several studies have shown that "husbands of employed women spend little or no more time in housework than husbands of nonemployed women."

These lopsided divisions of domestic duties tend to unleash fury, righteous anger, and a sense of betrayal in many wives, yet in none so much as the new mother. Research shows that men become more rigid in their gender behavior after the baby comes, most noticeably in their hesitance or outright refusal to perform child care and domestic tasks. Women are energy-depleted from pregnancy and childbirth, and instead of a deeper commitment to the household, they find that the men often do less. This, of course, presents quite a dilemma to the new mother, who often has to return to work after three months, put the infant in child care and start in on an expanded "second shift."

There have been many explanations for this behavior in men. We often hear from psychologists, pop and clinical, that the man is jealous of the attention his wife is paying to the child. While this might be true in some cases, it is probably way off the mark as a general rule. Far more likely, the man often behaves in a more sex-role-rigid fashion after the baby comes because he is trying to perform his role model task, which has been drummed into him from day one. This could be proven if the researchers separated the first-time fathers into two groups: fathers of boys and fathers of girls. I would predict that the fathers of girls would not exhibit as significant sex-typed behavior changes as the fathers of boys. The fathers of girls might even help out more with household chores and child care. The fathers of boys would probably be found to be highly charged around the issue of their sons, trying to perform correctly the role that will allow their sons to function like men in the world.

The couples depicted in these studies are not from cultural pockets of hyper-rigid sex-typing. They often express "egalitarian attitudes," but they "do not necessarily translate their values into behavior." From what we have seen, we can understand this quite easily.

From the moment a boy first picks up a toy, there is an undercurrent of apprehension. Will he pick up the yellow Tonka truck or the baby doll? Will he pick up the hammer and hit the pegs, or will he pick up the pot and spoon to stir imaginary soup? If a girl picks up the truck or the hammer, we smile. We indulge, even patronize her. We might even encourage her and feel pride in what we interpret as her adventurousness. If the boy picks up the doll, as we have seen from the most recent, wide-ranging study across all family types, he is at best "permitted" to play with it, and at worst, the dolls are grabbed away from him, or "disappear," as they did in Robert's case. If a girl wears a toy hard hat, she might be seen as precocious and assertive, two positive traits in a girl, as long as she has some compensating "feminine" traits. Yet if a boy wears an apron, regardless of any other attributes he might have, he usually experiences either palpable discomfort or pejorative amusement from the adults around him. He is sometimes encouraged to act "like a mother" as entertainment for others. The message to this child is loud and clear: he is a freak, a clown enacting a role that can never be his.

At two years old, a boy will find mysterious the attention adults pay to him for his behavior, but by the time he is five, his behavior will be cause for alarm, and he will understand why. If he persists in wearing the apron, in acting "like a mother," and if he prefers to play house and dolls with girls, he is at risk for treatment by the psychiatric establishment, usually at his parents' request, although sometimes at the suggestion of the nursery school or kindergarten teacher. If his desire to play house is as strong as the sex-typing around him, he could come to express the desire to be a girl, since he will perceive that as the requirement for domestic play. Most children believe two things: first, there are only two ways of being in the world: the boy way, and the girl way, and there are very explicit roles that belong only to boys, or only to girls; and second, you must be one or the other.

A family type not described in the study on families and gender training in six-year-olds was same-sex couples. In terms of division of household tasks and child care after the arrival of a newborn, through birth or adoption, lesbian and gay parenting couples offer psychologists a fascinating opportunity to study gender roles. Charlotte Patterson of the University of Virginia authored a 1995 study on the lesbian baby boom of the mid-1980s. Lesbian couples cannot, of course, separate household tasks by gender as the heterosexual couples did, but rather shared the tasks in a more egalitarian manner. Of particular note among lesbian couples was the fact that the sharing of household tasks did not change after the birth of a child, regardless of the fact that one woman gave birth. In terms of child care, researchers have found "that both biological and nonbiological lesbian mothers were more involved in child care than were heterosexual fathers." It was also found that the nonbiological mother was not as involved in child care as the biological mother; however, she was vastly more involved than the heterosexual father, and this involvement contributed to her overall satisfaction in her relationship with her partner.

Of special importance among the lesbian couples is the fact that "children with mothers who shared child-care tasks evenly and who expressed satisfaction with this arrangement appeared to enjoy the most favorable adjustment." This is not too difficult to understand. The children experience primary nurturing by more than one adult, and therefore there is simply more quality time and energy for the child.

For heterosexual wives, their husbands' involvement in child care has been a pivotal issue for marital satisfaction after the baby arrives. Curiously, among lesbian parenting couples, "relationship satisfaction was unrelated to involvement in child care or satisfaction with involvement in child care." This could be because the division of labor by gender role expectations was never an issue in the first place, and so is irrelevant to relationship satisfaction.

Patterson reviewed the substantial research on the heterosexual first-time mother which explored the role of "violated expectations" about her husband's participation in both child care and household labor after the baby's arrival. These studies, and others like them, consistently found the first-time mothers "doing more child care and feeling more dissatisfied than they had expected." Rather than feeling supported and embarking with her husband on a new adventure, she feels abandoned and betrayed. And what about the husband's marital satisfaction? There do not seem to be many studies in this regard.

In contrast, there have been studies on the nonbiological lesbian mother (the partner of the woman who has given birth). These nonbiological mothers, although not as involved in child care as the biological mothers, were actually happier the more involved they were with child care. Of special significance, the more involved the nonbiological mom was in raising the children, the happier the children themselves were. Would not the children of heterosexual men be just as delighted with a deeper involvement by their fathers, and would those men not experience a deeper happiness with family life in its earliest stages?

There are those who might argue that it is not fair to compare two-mother households to mother-father households, in the belief that we are still talking about two women, and women, regardless of sexuality, are more nurturing. Consider, then, the research of Dr. Dan McPherson on gay parenting couples who became first-time parents, and their heterosexual counterparts. The gay male parenting couples, like the lesbian parenting couples, divided household and child-care tasks in an egalitarian manner, and felt a higher degree of satisfaction with those arrangements than the heterosexual parenting couples. The heterosexual parenting couples in McPherson's study were in "basically sound relationships . . . yet, they do indicate a desire to alter their present parenting roles and responsibilities in a manner that would be more satisfying . . ."

In the lesbian and gay male parenting households, there are no tasks that belong to women or to men. Hammers and spatulas know no gender, nor do diaper changing or lawn mowing. As a result, there seems to be less internal stress on the family. But what is to be done for the vast majority of mother-father households, where gender and task remain, for the most part, fused? Is there any way out of the gender trap, and how responsible is it for the breakdown in families, which is now a worldwide phenomenon?

A recent study by the Population Council, "Families in Focus," showed that families are changing in similar ways, even in different cultures. A 1995 Whirlpool Foundation study by the Families and Work Institute broke the startling news that 18 percent of women were their household's sole provider, and among married women, 66 percent provided half or more of the family income. Women were described as the "new providers," and this study sent shock waves through the world of gender experts, including the groups who espouse a return to traditional sex-typed gender roles in order to strengthen families, with the husband as provider and the wife as homemaker, providing at most a supplementary income.

There is the implication that men have lost their sense of responsibility, and are solely responsible for abandoning their families. Is this really the case? Douglas Besharov, a resident scholar at the American Enterprise Institute who was interviewed by Tamar Lewin for the *New York Times,* believes that working women are the moving force behind the change in the world's family structures. "In the post-industrial age, when the earning power of men and women becomes quite equal, that creates a very different relationship between men and women and makes it easier for women to leave unhappy relationships." Is it simply the men who are abandoning the family, or are women pushing them out, no longer satisfied with the gender role charade, now that 84 percent of American women, including those who are single, earn half or more of the household income?

The fatherhood movement seems blind to this reality, and the men participating in that movement are being set up for a cruel fall. The predominantly white Promise Keepers, who meet fifty thousand strong in ballparks, and the Black followers of Louis Farrakhan's Million Man March have been preached to about their duties and rights as men and fathers. Always, the primary solution posed by these groups, and groups like them, is that to get fathers back into the home, there must be a return to the traditional role of the father as sole, or primary, economic provider. Spokespersons from liberal children's rights groups, such as Lois Salisbury, the executive director of Children NOW in Oakland, California, believe that "A man who is not thriving in the labor market is not necessarily someone who's going to abandon his family, but someone who's not going to commit to the family in the first place. The glue is greatly weakened." In order to get fathers into the home, and keep them there, she suggests that "a stronger emphasis on education, job training and well-paying jobs for young men could help turn the situation around." Echoing Ms. Salisbury's sentiments is Ralph R. Smith of the Annie E. Casey Foundation. Citing the "inextricable connection between work force participation and family formation," Mr. Smith believes that "to address the problem of absent fathers, you also need to address the job problem."

Although these individuals and institutions have the best of intentions, and truly care about children and families, what, then, are they saying is the real role that men are expected to fulfill in the family? Not the equal partnership role that was envisioned in women's and men's consciousness-raising groups, but the *real* role. When push comes to shove, and across the political spectrum, a man is primarily viewed within the family organization as the economic provider, a sort of human money tree. Good jobs are needed by everyone, male and female, but trumpeting a call to give young men jobs, so they will be able to take their places in their family, is reinforcing rather than relieving the situation.

No one would ever suggest that mothers need more schooling or money or jobs in order to be legitimate mothers. The mother is assumed to have a God-given right to be there. The father is viewed as having to earn the right to be there. How much money will be enough? If he loses his job, should he leave? If he gets sick, or becomes disabled, is there no place for him? If there is a national economic crisis, should he hit the road? Is he no longer a worthy man? For so many men, those are the implicit, sometimes explicit conditions for their presence in the home. These words might not be spoken aloud, and if suspected, they might be hotly denied, but the message is loud and clear. Many men leave the home because they cannot fulfill their primary role of money tree, and since they have been locked out of the "feminine" domestic role of their family life, no other presence in the family is allowed.

If we were told that a mother abandoned her family because she could not find a decent job, and if she could just find a decent job, she would come home and be a mother again, we would look at the speaker as if he or she had lost their mind. A mother is someone who is expected to be there, no matter what. This is not true for fathers. When will fathers get the message that no matter what happens, no matter how much money they make, their presence is legitimate? They cannot get the message if it is never sent, and if we do not break down the gender barriers of domesticity for boys, they will never believe this, because it will not be true.

A boy is *never* taught that he is *supposed* to play house or dolls, the two activities that would prepare him to take a full role in his home, and the two activities that are expected of girls. Some boys are taught that they can do these roles if they want to, even though it is primarily girls who like to play house and dolls. This is a weak and confusing message. If the best we can do is to "permit" boys these activities, even in our most liberal, counter-cultural families, then the best they will ever be able to do as men is "help out."

The breakdown in traditional gender roles has been blamed for the crisis in fatherhood, but those roles are the culprit, not the solution, to the deterioration of the family. We are living in a nostalgic fantasy that says, if Dad comes back, everything will be okay, but Dad was never the miracle worker we pretended he was and then demanded he be.

Women are not going to be leaving the work force anytime soon. In fact, their positions will only strengthen and expand over time. If men are to keep up, they need to be trained as full partners in both the economic and domestic arenas of their family lives. Boys need to be expected to baby-sit, and they need to be shown how to hold, diaper and feed a baby, not just how to play with it. Most important, they need to be taught to recognize their nurturing feelings as something to be proud of, not something to hide.

We are seeing signs of a social evolution in this direction. Twenty percent of preschool children are now cared for by their fathers while their mothers work outside the home, and fathers now head 14 percent of single-parent households, up from 10 percent in 1980. Perceptions of fatherhood are evolving even in the most macho of arenas. In 1993, David Williams was the starting right tackle for the Houston Oilers. He chose to miss a football game so that he could be present for his child's birth. The coaches called him a "wimp," and fined him $125,000. He was accused of letting down his team and hundreds of thousands of fans, but when word of this broke in the news, the Oilers were deluged by fan sentiment in favor of Williams, and he was never fined. "My family comes first," said Williams. "That's the way I've always been, and that's the way I always will be, long after I'm finished being a football player."

When I began to question my own notions of gender, I noticed things that had been invisible to me, especially around the topic of men as nurturers. I was walking through Noe Valley in San Francisco, a neighborhood populated with families of all varieties with young children. Two men in their mid-twenties were up ahead, standing on the corner, and one of them was gently pushing a stroller back and forth. As I noticed them, I thought for a moment that, being where I was, this could possibly be a gay couple with their new baby. The men were dressed in nondescript clothing, sneakers and baseball caps, an outfit quite common with gay dads out for a Sunday stroll.

I stopped and said hello, remarking on the sleeping baby, and as I walked away, something about my interaction must have tipped them off that I thought they might be a couple. They then got very boisterous with each other, punching each other in the arm and giving each other small jabs. The one pushing the carriage then shoved it in front of him so that it rolled for a few feet by itself before he caught up to it. Both men pretended that they were not looking at the carriage, even as it rolled away on its own. During all this, they glanced nervously over their shoulders toward me as I continued up the street. What struck me most forcefully was that they thought it necessary to cover up their nurturing behavior of gently pushing the baby carriage because they associated that behavior with a perception, on my part, that they might be a gay couple.

Yet another, quite different experience, seemed to me the epitome of the devaluation of a man as a primary nurturer, despite all evidence to the contrary. The mother of one of the children at my son's school was dying. We'll call the child Jack. Jack's father loved his wife, and cared for her at home until she died. He worked full-time through her illness, and still showed up, with a smile on his face, for all of his son's school events. He dressed and fed the boy, made his lunches, took him to the doctor and shored him up in every way possible for the coming emotional impact of the loss of his mother. Upon Jack's mother's death, a well-meaning parent asked another parent if this father would be "keeping" Jack.

The question was not meant to be cruel, and in years past, it was a question that might not have been asked. Instead, Jack would have automatically been sent to a female relative, probably on the deceased mother's side. There would not have been any discussion about it. If the father had hesitated in turning his son or daughter over to a female, well-meaning friends and relatives would have intervened and convinced him that he must relinquish the child, for the child's own good.

If Jack's father had died, would anyone ever ask if his mother would be keeping him? Would anyone suggest she give him up, for his own good? The relationship between Jack and his father has nothing to do with his father's economic status, and everything to do with the emotional, psychological and spiritual bonds between parent and child. Jack's father did not give him up. Why would he? Not only did Jack need him, but perhaps, he needed Jack.

Men need their children just as women do, because it is often through a child that we experience our deepest connections with the world. By breaking the taboo on boys in the domestic sphere, by removing doll and house play as an official symptom of mental disorder in *any* boy, we will be taking a step toward strengthening our families and the bonds between women and men.

APPEARANCE

Human appearance signifies powerfully, sending messages through the clothes we wear and our bodies themselves. Appearance influences every aspect of life, from jury deliberations to courtship rituals, yet nothing is so profoundly affected by appearance as the perception of masculinity and femininity. As soon as we think we are seeing a male or a female, even if we are looking at exactly the same piece of clothing, or an identical texture and shade of skin, meaning is immediately skewed. If we see a child in a baseball cap, we run through a series of cues in our mind to determine the child's sex. Our interpretation of the cap will be connected to whether it is on the head of a boy or a girl, depending upon the customs and gender mores of our culture or subculture. The sarong on a male Pacific Islander will not signify in the same way to a resident of Samoa and a resident of New York City. What is masculine in one world might be feminine in another. What has sexual connotations in one place might have religious connotations somewhere else. Beneath the clothing, the body itself has powerful cues of masculine and feminine. Hair color, the shape of the lips, the size of the eyes, the length of a toe, all have meanings almost mythological.

We are often judged, fabricated and constructed by others based upon nothing but our image, by what people see on the surface. The Madonnas, Michael Jacksons and David Bowies of the world take control of what others see. They have a genius for creating and re-creating themselves. They have a profound understanding of the power of appearance, from their clothing to their bodies, reshaping themselves at will, as if the human being were an infinitely plastic creature. The touchstone for their transformations is always gender, and a shifting of the masculine and feminine, some signals utterly clear, others deliberately mixed. While most of us are at the mercy of gender cues, these individuals take power in society by playing with the cues and crossing the gender barrier.

If the transformations of Madonna, Jackson or Bowie are too quick and too often, there comes a time when it seems impossible for them to change into something truly new. Their new image breaks down, and seems like a cartoon, a pretense, a surface, "not real." But was it ever "real"?

By watching these morphing icons, we witness a strange irony which contains the two ultimate questions of identity, built upon the masculine and the feminine: Is identity so plastic that it can endure powerful transformations and still hold together? Is the "character" created by Madonna, Jackson or Bowie, a product of style, or is style a product of the character they have created?

If we ourselves believe the gender mythology, our clothing and our bodies will be the source of our identities, the arbiter of what is "real." But is anything about clothing, or the body, objectively real? Is it just a matter of style, style that has come to signify so powerfully that it does not express content, but creates it? Do style and the shape of our bodies determine who we believe ourselves to be, and who others believe we are?

OUTFITS, COSTUMES, UNIFORMS AND DISGUISES

Originally, pink was a boy's color and blue was for girls. Before World War I, blue signified "delicate and dainty," and pink represented "a stronger, more decided color." It would be virtually impossible in 1995 to find an article of boy's clothing in pink, because it would be considered "unnatural." Colors have extraordinary power, but the meaning of those colors is subject to change, as are styles and cuts of clothing.

In the early 1970s, without exaggeration, there were editorials and news stories that literally predicted the end of civilization as we know it if women were allowed to wear pantsuits. At the time, I worked as the secretary to the president of Data General Corporation, and I was the first in my office to don the pantsuit. The day was chaotic as everyone walked past my desk to take a look, but I particularly remember the personnel administrator strolling up to me and stopping to chat. I knew that he was testing to see if I would still have the appropriate deference and attitude for an executive secretary, despite the fact that I was wearing "men's" pants. I did, and continued to work there.

I understood, even then, that the clothes I chose for the sake of comfort, and to minimize sexual harassment in the workplace, were threatening not just to most of the men, but to most of the women. The clothes were tied into a Gordian knot with identity. From where did these rules come?

There have always been informal societal norms in clothing, but actual rules for what a person was allowed to wear were clearly delineated in the sumptuary laws (related to the word "consumption") of medieval and Renaissance times. In *Vested Interests,* Dr. Marjorie Garber, Director of the Center for Literary and Cultural Studies at Harvard, explains that these laws "sought to restrict the wearing of certain furs, fabrics, and styles to members of particular social and economic classes, ranks, or 'states.' " The ultimate aim of these laws was to "mark out as visible and

141

above all *legible* distinctions of wealth and rank within a society undergoing changes that threatened to blur or even obliterate such distinctions . . . as a person's social station, social role, gender and other indicators of identity in the world." The rules regulating clothing were a tool of social control, governing, above all, property rights, wealth and the status these conferred. In modern Western society, if you have the money, you can have access to the fabrics, the jewels, the furs. These rules have evolved to guard, for the most part, only gender.

In some Middle Eastern countries, if a woman wears a garment meant for a man, or refuses to wear the garments designated for women, she can be sentenced to death. Lest we think modern Western society is immune from such extremes, as late as the 1960s in the United States and some European countries, an individual could be arrested for not wearing at least two or three articles of gender-appropriate clothing.

Ever since the pantsuit, the notion of appropriate female attire has been evolving. However, the road has been long and bumpy. A 1992 *Washington Post* article by Amanda Spake, "Dressing for Power," reported that in the nineteenth century, "stylish feminine attire consisted first and foremost of a corset, laced so tightly a woman could scarcely breathe. Over that were layers of chemises, petticoats and crinolines, then a long dress with trains made of yards of silk or wool. Buttons, ribbons, bows, a bonnet and perhaps furs and feathers were added to make the costume 'prettier.' This outfit might weigh as much as thirty pounds. Women's shoulders, chests and necks were bare and they wore no underpants—[which were] considered immodestly imitative of male garments." Clearly, there would be no hanging upside down from the monkey bars by any little girl in that society.

The effects of these articles of clothing upon women's bodies was by no means benign. Ribs were deformed, back muscles atrophied, and chronic respiratory problems were common. Spake noted that after corsets were abandoned in the 1920s, they were replaced with "the garter belt, the long line bra and the girdle. These later two items . . . were required for the no-hips, no-thighs, no-stomach, no-butt look touted as 'sexy' by the early 1950's." These undergarments were worn throughout the sixties, often by barely pubescent girls who weighed no more than eighty-five pounds, sometimes causing digestive tract problems and breathing impairment. Girdles certainly did not cultivate any tendencies toward "rough-and-tumble play" in girls.

Only during World War II did women temporarily put these clothes aside in favor of overalls and shirts, more practical for taking up positions in the stateside industrial work force. To attract women into these jobs, media campaigns began to glamorize the working woman, and emphasize that she could maintain her femininity even though she was "doing a man-sized job." She could achieve this by "tuck[ing] flowers and ribbons" in her hair and "try[ing] to keep our faces looking pretty as you please." This campaign is all the more remarkable when you realize that women were performing heavy labor jobs like welding and iron work.

As the war came to a close, the government had practical social and economic reasons for getting women out of the work force and back into the home. There would not be enough jobs available for the returning GIs if women continued to work, which would trigger widespread unemployment and possible insurrection by military-trained men who would return to a world where the gender codes, and therefore identity, had been broken. Yet getting women to resume subservient domestic roles would not be that easy. A 1944 government survey found that 61 to 85 percent of women did not want to leave the work force and go back to housework. Through an aggressive media campaign, patriotic duty and the naturalness of a dependent role were presented to women as the reasons to leave the work force. Dutifully, they took up their girdles, spike heels and skirts, but there were renegades who had learned the truth about the so-called naturalness of roles. That knowledge would sow the seeds of the women's movement in the mid-1960s, when the feminine mystique was challenged and middle-class women reentered the work force.

By the mid-1970s, these women began moving up through the hierarchy to positions of greater responsibility, but when a woman's career inevitably hit the glass ceiling, she found that there was a connection to her clothing. Women employed in corporate settings who wore feminine clothing were not considered equal to men, and they tended not to be promoted. The solution was to create "a professional uniform for women—a dark colored, skirted suit, similar to the recognized suit men wear for business." Women who adopted this "uniform" tended to be promoted and given responsibility. Today, if you watch C-SPAN, you can see on the floor of the House and the Senate one or two bright splashes of red among the sea of dark blue. Post–Nancy Reagan, red has become the accepted power color of choice among female politicians, although the color might not be as useful in the corporate world.

If women are taking over some items of male clothing that they might enter the world of male-dominated power, men have long cross-dressed as a rite of initiation. For example, *Newsweek* published a photograph of heterosexual sailors on the deck of a warship, dressed as female hookers. This was described as "a rite of passage on crossing the equator for the first time" and characterized as a typical warship ritual. No further explanation was given of its meaning.

There are many powerful fraternities, such as Harvard's Hasty Pudding Theatricals (formed in 1770) and the San Francisco-based Bohemian Club, whose membership, which includes the heads of world governments, appear in theatricals in women's clothing, or "drag." The word "drag" comes from a Shakespearean stage direction. During Shakespeare's time, women and girls were not permitted to take the stage. Young men and older boys played the parts of girls and women, and these parts would be designated with the word DRAG, which means, "dressed as a girl."

Angela Padilla was the second female president of Harvard's Hasty Pudding Club, which is connected, "legally and spiritually," to the Hasty Pudding Theatricals. While the club itself is co-ed, all of the actors in the Theatricals are male. A brilliant, high-femme, assertive corporate attorney, Angela Padilla was adamant when I questioned why the performers are all men: "It is all male, it has always been all male, and it will always be all male . . . I used to wonder whether it should be co-ed or not, because my politics wanted me to think it should be co-ed. But the fact of the matter is that it is a tradition that it is all male, perhaps because it's funnier when men dress up as women than when women dress up as men. It's not as much of a gender bender when women do it. We can even wear ties and jackets, and nobody would laugh at us on the street. But if a man went out in the clothes that I wore to work today, if a man wore a skirt, it's really scandalous." When I asked her if all the men who cross-dressed in Hasty Pudding were heterosexual, she said, "Totally straight. Beefcake."

To cross-dress, whether across class or gender boundaries, means to challenge the identity that society has dictated, to declare that you are not quite what has been determined by powers outside of yourself. Cross-dressers often feel cut off from a vital part of themselves, and so look to the props of the opposite sex as a technique for establishing contact with the full self. The reasons for cross-dressing are wildly complex and vary greatly from individual to individual, but to paint with a broad stroke, men generally want to experience beauty and sensuality, and women generally want to experience power and authority.

When I looked through Angela Padilla's scrapbook of her Harvard Hasty Pudding Club days, I noted that she wore very dramatic full-length gowns to club events. I asked her if she had ever entertained the idea of cross-dressing for herself. It was not possible, she explained, because she was too small. Although she did confess that she would have loved being able to look "butch," she simply had never found masculine clothes that looked good on her body type. This is a common problem for women attempting to cross-dress. They often end up looking like boys, which is usually not the desired effect. I asked Angela, if she thought she could have an empowering male image, would she consider wearing a suit? She answered, "Definitely."

When a woman attempts drag (or should it be "drab" for "dressed as a boy?"), if she is small of stature and appears boylike, she will not command respect. In *Vested Interests,* Marjorie Garber describes resources available to help women overcome this problem, such as the advice in John T. Molloy's *Dress for Success,* which is directed toward small, young men who want to be taken seriously. "The best shirt for the small man is the solid white; the best shoes are traditional wingtips; the best coats are heavy and luxurious, such as camel hair. They should only wear rich-looking attire, and they should be neat to the point of being precise." Books and pamphlets are one thing, but a real-life workshop for women interested in transforming into convincing men for a day is now available. If anything can give a woman a moment of gender shock, it is moving through the world as a man.

DIANE TORR'S "DRAG KING WORKSHOP"

Diane Torr is a performance artist who lives with her husband and daughter in New York City. She conducts a "Drag King Workshop" throughout the United States, Europe and Canada. Torr guarantees that you will learn the "basic male behavioral patterns. How to walk, sit, talk and lie down—like a man. How do men use space? How do they pick up an object? How do they assume the importance that they feel is their birthright—handed down to them from Adam?" She emphasizes that perfecting a male alter ego will be of tremendous value to the average woman in terms of "career advancement, or even in something as simple as getting your full share of a seat on the subway!" You are then instructed to think carefully about the kind of man you would like to become. You must bring to the workshop the clothing you will need for your male persona, plus "hair gel, wide bandage to bind breasts (if needed), and fake penis (the most convincing is a piece of tubular bandage, stuffed with cotton wool and sewn at either end—don't make it too large!!)."

When I interviewed Torr in New York, she said she was always amused at what a woman thinks appropriate for the size of "her penis." Torr cautions them "that it is meant to be a penis at rest, and that it is best to be humble." The Drag King Workshop experience is not merely a fantasy play within safe confines. Torr's workshop culminates in the ultimate challenge: ". . . a visit to a public space, where we will test our new identities."

Washington Post staff writer Paula Span participated in one of Torr's New York workshops in October of 1993, and she reported on the event, describing the women who arrived at the Lexington Avenue apartment as showing a nearly "anthropological interest in how the other half lives. They're smart and artsy, ranging in age from twenties to forties."

Torr's reasons for cross-dressing are quite clear: she wishes to experience, and have her workshop participants experience, "male authority and territory and entitlement." For Torr, it is not about wanting to be a man, but about learning to question what has been internalized as a woman. If nothing else, Torr's workshop is probably the most mind-bending assertiveness training experience a woman could ever have.

In terms of sitting on a bus or in a subway car, Torr is fond of pointing out that women cross their legs and arms, and sit with only one buttock on the seat. In contrast, she has observed that when a man is on public transportation, he sits with his legs open and his arms out to the sides, even when conditions are crowded. Most significantly, each of his buttocks is firmly planted on the seat. He takes his space.

In terms of interacting with the material world, there is a

lesson in how to grab a glass of beer. You are instructed to basically take firm possession of that glass, to in a sense make all objects of the world an extension of yourself.

The physical transformation is awkward and entertaining for most women, especially in the particulars of approximating the male anatomy. Breast binding has to be done in a very systematic manner. Torr explained that flappers used this method in the twenties when, oddly enough, it was chic for a woman to have a boylike body, although she still usually wore a dress. Taking wide Ace bandages, Torr instructs her pupils to "start at the bottom, cover the nipples, work your way up, quite tight, but not so tight you can't breathe."

From London to Boston, to Amsterdam and New York, the most fun anatomical adventure is the creation of the penis, or what Torr refers to as the "arts and crafts section of the workshop." Julie Wheelwright, writing for a London newspaper about an Amsterdam workshop, reported Torr calling out to her charges: "Does everyone have a penis? Does everyone know how to put it on?" In New York, Paula Span wrote that as she was humming an old Lou Reed song, someone dressing in the back room called out, "Diane. How are we supposed to attach our penises?" to which Diane responded, "With safety pins." The women learned that the side the penis hangs on was not of concern only to them, but also to a tailor, who will ask a man if he "dresses right" or "dresses left," so that extra material can be left near that leg to accommodate his penis. Joy Press, a reporter for *The Guardian* and another workshop participant, reported, "My penis slips every so often—I knew I should have pinned it on." My favorite story of the "arts and crafts portion of the workshop" was reported by Caroline Knapp of the *Boston Phoenix.* As Knapp was busily transforming herself into a man, one participant suddenly exclaimed, "Oh, no! I just went to the bathroom and my penis fell into the toilet."

Each of the women in Torr's workshops take on personas of men they would like to be. Sometimes, however, they are unable to achieve the effect because of their body type and because of their nature, and they become a man they did not expect to become. One woman realized that if she left in one earring, she could become a convincing gay man, able to pass as a man in a gay bar. Another woman accommodated her long hair by becoming a rock-and-roller, while another became a computer nerd. Knapp described a woman who used her husband's "shoes, jacket, pants, and tie (oh, and underwear). But when Johnny [the makeup artist] added a moustache and five-o'clock shadow, her name became Eddie . . . A somewhat sleazy public-interest lawyer . . ." The woman saw her reflection in a mirror and exclaimed in astonishment, "Look at me! I'm an asshole!" She had become the kind of man she hated: egotistical, pretentious and arty. Knapp concluded that the woman "was absolutely right," and then she added, "Actually, a lot of us turned into assholes."

This phenomenon could be a result of Torr's rules, and her own male persona. Torr takes on the identity of a department store manager, father of four, and ardent gun lover from Jim Thorpe, Pennsylvania. During a performance in New York City, she brought her persona to the stage, and he offered several rules to the man-in-training: (1) Walk into a room and through the world with a sense of ownership. (2) Don't smile. Smiling opens you up to exploitation. Women smile, but men do not. It's a question of maintaining respect. (3) Stop apologizing. You are a man in a man's world, and you are right. (4) Speak slowly. This emphasizes how important everything is that you have to say. Torr concluded her performance with crucial advice: "If you find yourself in an ISS (Informal Social Situation), and you're obliged to dance, don't."

Torr carefully constructs the field trip part of the workshop, where the women test their male identities in the world. Bright lights are avoided, because it is easier in those situations for people to "read" her students. A cross-dresser always wants to avoid being "read," which means that someone has detected that you are wearing the clothing of the sex to which you were not born. Torr has taken her participants to block parties and clubs, including a place called Billy's Topless Bar. The success the women experience in not being "read" varies, but one workshop cannot be expected to erase a lifetime of movements and ways of being.

Torr admitted that it is much easier to become a stereotype when you have only one lesson. In Europe, however, she has conducted six-week intensive workshops, and the results for those participants were startling. They had more of an opportunity to develop a male persona in depth, to really explore the character they chose. There was time for the woman to develop, if she wished, a persona that was more mature and not so into the easy out of the unsmiling "asshole." "It's like being a spy," Torr said. "Not just how does this man walk down the street, but how does this man feed the ducks?"

In the six-week setting, the workshop participant is able to create a narrative for her male persona, that is, she can give "him" a past and a present with a decidedly masculine slant, a concept common to most cross-dressing how-to books. In order to bring the male persona to life, "he" is given a name. Names are powerful signifiers in terms of gender, behavior and expectations.

A 1981 study out of Tulane University, led by S. Gary Garwood, tested for a "relationship between child-naming practices and the perpetuation of traditional sex-role expectations of masculine and feminine behaviors." They found that names rated as most desirable, for both males and females, were the names that were rated as more sex-typed, and that those names occurred most frequently in the population. They also found that names were powerful tools in the shaping of a child's psychology. If parents wanted to raise their children with more flexible attitudes, they advised them to avoid sex-typed naming, because it creates a self-fulfilling prophecy. They explained that the child's name elicits certain responses from the world, and contributes to internalizing a sex-typed identity in the child. In addition, Garwood also found that teachers graded identical essays lower for students identified as Elmer or Bertha than for those identified as David or Karen.

In 1995, two researchers presented a paper at the Forty-Second Annual Meeting of the American Name Society. Carol Lee

Johnson and Helen Petrie conducted a study in Britain that indicated "the more feminine the name, the more feminine the girl." They found that the most "ultra-feminine" name was Sophie, or Sophia. They also identified the most "unisex" names as Lee, Robin, Terry, Ashley and Leslie, and they noted that in Britain, "one in four women uses a neutral nickname such as 'Jack' or 'Jackie' for 'Jacqueline.' " Johnson and Petrie hypothesized that these sex-neutral nicknames reflect a woman's desire "to shed traditional roles."

There is something truly unnerving about the undeniable power of names and clothes. Yet the question remains: Does Torr's Drag King Workshop serve to set free the trapped "half" of a woman, or does it demand the construction of an identity that is unnatural? If we believe that the construction of a masculine identity by a woman is unnatural, then we might also ask: Is the construction of a "masculine identity" just as unnatural for men?

MISS VERA'S FINISHING SCHOOL FOR BOYS WHO WANT TO BE GIRLS

Nothing took me more by surprise than finding out that from 1 to 10 percent of adult males worldwide cross-dress, and that 90 percent of them are heterosexual and often married. Located in an apartment in the Chelsea district of Manhattan, Miss Vera's Finishing School for Boys Who Want to Be Girls has operated since January 1992, and most of the students are straight.

Visiting Miss Vera was like stepping into a pink candy egg. A banner bearing the school's name and a specially designed coat of arms featuring a high heel, a fleur-de-lis and a stylized butterfly festooned the wall. On one side of the coat of arms was the word "Cherchez," and on the other, "La Femme." A stained glass replica of the coat of arms hung in the window. Upon the walls were several large vanity-style mirrors in dark wood frames. I was invited to sit upon a comfortable flowered sofa wedged between two period chairs covered in velvet. The couch faced a raised, stagelike area, covered with an imitation black and white animal skin rug. To the left of the stage there was a gold-painted reproduction of the famous bust of Nefertiti. Beyond the wardrobe and accessory closet, in the cosmetic area, was a display of flowing women's wigs, in all colors, on Styrofoam heads. Near the cosmetic area was a director's chair with extra long legs, in pink of course, in which the student sits during the makeup and hair transformation. There was a wall of books, and above a doorway, a clock with two shapely legs in black toreador pants and high heels clicked off the seconds as Miss Vera served tea.

Miss Vera herself was elegantly dressed in a black tunic top, and she wore a chain that ended in an ornate medallion. As she spoke, her hand movements were expressive, revealing highly polished nails, and she made constant eye contact as we chatted. Dark hair framed a round face, and there was an unmistakable twinkle in her eyes. She considers herself a female libertarian, and she has testified in Washington, D.C., before the Senate Judiciary Committee on freedom of expression.

Miss Vera explained that the academy was not formed to cater to men, but to educate. The clothes are props which make it easier for the student to get in touch with parts of himself that he cannot usually access. She feels that many of the men have had the feminine beaten out of them, and they are often very fearful when they come to her. One student, who named his "femme self" Patricia, experiences his sensuality every time he dresses. "Before that," said Miss Vera, "every time he started to feel sexy, it was connected with this feeling or idea of wanting to be a girl, so he closed down to it. Eventually, he had totally closed his sexuality down. It wasn't until he started dressing up and allowing himself that avenue that he started to feel sexy."

The idea that a man does not want his male body because he wants to use traditionally feminine garb permeates the clinical literature on cross-dressers. As a result, Miss Vera feels that "there are people who opt for surgery and hormones sooner than I'd recommend . . . It just becomes dangerous when people haven't dealt with the feelings and are left with the same baggage on the other side, and don't know how to deal with it . . . A lot of times they have such a strong sense that they want to live as a female, and a lot of times, it's just a fantasy. It's really strong, but it's just a fantasy."

The typical student enrolls through the mail, and must complete Homework Assignment Number One: create a herstory, in which he is to describe his femme self. She encourages them to really develop this self, and try to go beyond sheer superficial re-creations of what they think it is to be a woman. The enrollment application must then be returned, along with a twenty-dollar fee, in a pink envelope. If a student is unable to make the trip to New York City, there is always Miss Vera's 900 number: 1-900-884-VERA.

Enrollment application completed, the student arrives at the academy with a candle in the shape of a female. Sometimes they bring their own clothes. Incense burns and music plays, all female voices, from the operas of Mozart, to Eartha Kitt. The pieces are selected to complement the mood of the activity. For example, during makeup class, the music might become Billie Holiday, to speed up the process but keep it thematic. Each class begins with a dedication ritual, performed before a small statue of a goddess. When asked which goddess it was, Miss Vera replied, "I don't know who she is, but anyway she's pretty, and we've painted her gold." During the ritual, the student recites the finishing school's goals: "I dedicate myself to releasing all of the juicy female energy inside of me. I place my trust in Miss Vera and the Deans of the Academy, and I thank myself for giving myself this gift."

"This puts them in the right frame of mind," Miss Vera explained, "because a lot of times they have to deal with the baggage they're bringing in. Sometimes they're feeling guilty, or they might be into this fantasy of being forced to do this, and I don't want to participate in that. I like to start them off with the right frame of mind. Some of them have been to the S&M houses, and there, they encourage that trip." Many men give themselves permission to dress in feminine attire only under the conditions of ritualized humiliation.

"It's really important for me," said Miss Vera, "that the student is able to get in touch with that really precious part of himself. For everyone who comes here, it is a connection with sensuality and sexuality. Sometimes it's more blatant, or explicit. Sometimes it's more buried." Many of the men who arrive at the academy are unable to even raise their arms above their heads in order to put on a dress. "They have never stretched in that way. They're so grounded, they're practically hammered into the ground."

There is a potpourri of courses available at the academy: Home Economics (learning to be a good hostess), Ballet I and Tutu (good for learning to walk in high heels), Scullery Maid Training (heavy cleaning), Ports de Bras (how to move your arms and hands), and Elocution and Voice Training. Miss Vera explained, "Initially when they come, they start answering me with 'Uh-huh,' 'Nope,' 'Yup.' They grunt. And I say, 'Yes, Miss Vera. Say "yes" and "no." Let's try to be more refined.' " There is a voice instructor, a ballet instructor, makeup artists, and photographers who will record your transformation. There is even a class called the Cinch Course ("wasp-waist corset training").

Shopping sprees are a favorite activity. "I found the perfect place to take the girls shopping. I've taken them all over the place: SoHo, Saks Fifth Avenue. But then I went to the Lower East Side to Orchard Street and I found a Plus Size shop. I thought, nice for the girls. I sent the students there, and was worried it might be too conservative a place. It turned out that on Orchard Street, practically all the women wear wigs," an Orthodox Jewish custom. One student who especially enjoyed Orchard Street was "Charlene." In his other life, Charlene is a rancher. "He brought these antelope steaks for the weekend," said Miss Vera, "and for his Home Economics class, he marinated them. Antelope is actually pretty tender, I've learned."

Much of Miss Vera's Finishing School is spirited fun. One of the favored activities at the academy is the pajama party, which offers an opportunity for students who are in town for a weekend course to meet each other. "The deans are all here, and we just socialize and have fun. We wear great lingerie, and eat delicious food. I cross-dressed this chef whose female role model was Cher."

Many of these cross-dressers are married, but Miss Vera is careful about how a student shares his femme self with his partner. One student brought his wife to the academy, and they all went out together for his birthday. Miss Vera has found that although the wife may be supportive, she might be uncomfortable going out alone with him in drag, and so they all go out together. This is a new part of the academy, dealing with the wives, and she has to be careful that the wife really wants to be there.

Miss Vera recalled a couple in their sixties who came from Ireland. "She looked like she was at a tea party. She was wearing pink, but I don't think she realized that was our academy color. He was kind of built stocky, looked like he would be smoking a cigar, but I don't know if he actually was. We went out, and she was really nervous. She went anyway, and she hung in there, but it inhibited him somewhat, because he was caught between being her husband and his femme self. So I realized from that point on, I really have to interview the wife very carefully. It was a little more difficult with this couple, since they had come from Ireland, and I hadn't had a chance to talk to both of them on the phone. In the new brochure it says if a partner wants to accompany, then the partner has to write a letter so that I'm sure the wife or partner really wants to be there."

Of all the advantages to supporting one's husband in his cross-dressing activities, none is more salient to Miss Vera than the following: "It's exciting because so many of the students really get turned on when they're doing female clothing. I'll ask them, 'When do you get your most reliable erection? When you're dressed, or when you're not dressed?' And they *always* say, 'When I'm dressed.' And I thought, gosh, if I were married to a cross-dresser, and that's when he really gets hard, I'd want to be there."

Studies have tended to brand the wives of cross-dressers as dysfunctional to one degree or another, with such traits as dependency and lack of self-esteem. In 1989, Dr. George R. Brown, Director of Psychiatric Research at the Mountain Home Veterans Administration Medical Center in Johnson City, Tennessee, reported that these wives had "significant obesity." This conclusion was based upon seven women, and the results of this study have not been replicated. In 1994, Dr. Brown conducted another study, but this time he surveyed 106 wives of cross-dressers between the ages of nineteen and sixty-nine. He found that they measured between 54 and 72 inches in height and weighed between 90 and 280 pounds, with a mean weight of 142 pounds, hardly earning the label "significant obesity," and instead proving the extraordinary spectrum these women represent. The 106 women "were from 25 states and one Canadian province, the middle southwest (all major Texas cities, Arizona, Louisiana), the mid-Atlantic and the northeast regions of the United States were broadly represented. The overrepresentation of Texas (38% of the group)" occurred due to recruitment at the Texas "T" Party in San Antonio, a club for the wives of cross-dressers.

Dr. Brown reported: "Since only a small minority of cross-dressing men or their partners seek mental health treatment, this study group may approximate the sociodemographic features of most women involved in committed relationships with cross-dressing men . . . One is struck by the tenacity and longevity of these unconventional relationships and the fact that over two-thirds of the women never seriously considered divorce or separation because of their partner's cross-dressing (in spite of receiving strong advice from family and/or friends to do so)." Citing other evidence in the field, Dr. Brown concluded that women who are married to cross-dressers are "an unremarkable group of women who unexpectedly found themselves in a marriage with a transvestite husband."

In *From Masculine to Feminine and All Points in Between* by

Jennifer Anne Stevens (the textbook used by Miss Vera at the academy), a section on "Significant Others" addresses when and how the cross-dresser should reveal his activities. They are advised against sharing the information unnecessarily with elderly parents, and it is suggested that they plant "a well-planned series of hints" before final disclosure to their wives. Clearly, the book's author is an adept amateur psychologist. By laying out the hints in advance, when the wife reconstructs how this could be true, and how she could have missed it, she will be able to find "signs" along the way that will help her to create a "narrative" that makes sense of the present.

Many of these men believe their desire to wear feminine clothing will disappear after they are married because they are heterosexual. As with many of the gender psychologists, they believe that the wish to wear feminine clothing is indicative of a nonheterosexual orientation. They are surprised and confused when marriage, however happy, however sexually fulfilling, does not erase their fascination with the forbidden clothes.

The typical feelings of a wife upon learning of her husband's activities include isolation, betrayal at the secret having been kept from her (often for years) and resentment at the time and money her husband spends on his cross-dressing activities, which sometimes give rise to a certain competitiveness between the man and his wife as to who projects a more feminine image. Wives often become confused about their own sexual orientation, wondering if perhaps, in some way, their husband's cross-dressing makes them lesbian.

Studying these wives, Sallie Hunt found that women married to men who become transsexual and opt for hormone and/or genital reassignment do not experience confusion about their own sexual identities as often as the wife of the cross-dresser. She hypothesizes that "transvestism involves greater ambiguity than transsexualism . . . The transvestite self-identifies as male even while crossdressed . . . there is little structure to the transvestite's development of self whereas the transsexual's transition is fairly predictable. The transsexual experience is simply that of a male becoming female. Transsexualism recognizes two rather distinct genders. Transvestism does not." Hunt's point is well taken, and the situation of the wives poses a crucial question regarding sexuality: Do we identify who we are sexually by whom we are attracted to, or by something that is strictly within ourselves?

To soften the experience of confusion in a wife, *From Masculine to Feminine* advises the cross-dresser to slowly bring her into the network of spouses of cross-dressers at such events as Fantasia Fair, which is held in Provincetown, Massachusetts, each fall, or the Texas "T" Party in San Antonio, Texas, which is a virtual hotbed of cross-dressers and their wives. The support offered to the wives, and the wives' own assertiveness in how they wish to be treated, accounts for much of the stability of these marriages. There are several groups offering this assistance, from the Tiffany Club Wives Support Group in Wayland, Massachusetts, to the Delta Omega Chapter of Tri-Ess in Garland, Texas, to the Chi Delta Mu Chapter of Tri-Ess in Morristown, New Jersey.

One spouse published an amazing letter entitled "Your Wife's Rights," which was reproduced in *From Masculine to Feminine*. These rights included: "Don't call me roommate (no matter how you're dressed); never let me forget you are my husband (don't get carried away with your mystical 'girl within'); don't compete with me (in terms of femininity); don't tell me TVism is normal whenever I might express misgivings about your dressing up as a woman. I threw that word out of my vocabulary years ago when I found out that it no longer had any real meaning in a world where no two people are alike; don't speak to me of hormones; don't tell the children you're their auntie if they ever happen to see you dressed. They know you pretty well and won't be the least bit fooled. Let me do any explaining which has to be done if such an emergency ever arises; try lounging around the house in male clothes once in a while; don't always expect me to help you dress; listen to my advice when I make suggestions as to your makeup or hairdo or carriage. I want you to look your best whether you're dressed as a man or as a woman; don't wear my clothes without my permission!; play fair with me when it comes to our social life.

158

I don't object to your TV friends or to going to TV parties so I expect you to accept my straight friends and attend their parties with no complaining about it; stick to the budget when you buy your feminine clothes; try paying as much attention to your male clothes as you do your feminine attire; and stop making excuses for being a TV! If I manage to live with your transvestism, you should be able to bear up under it quite well. You might be surprised to know that, from a wife's point of view, a lot worse monsters live in this world than TVs, and I'm glad you are not a drunkard, or a junkie, or a compulsive gambler, any of whose problems makes you pale into insignificance by comparison. All I really ask of you is that you relax, be yourself, and be in love with me."

This is an extraordinary document, written by and for women who have taken control of the situation they find themselves in, however unusual it is. If the wives of cross-dressers can form social groups in places as conservative as San Antonio, Texas, and Wayland, Massachusetts, and if an elderly woman from Ireland has the guts to accompany her husband to Miss Vera's Finishing School in New York City, anything seems possible.

As I was leaving the academy, Miss Vera confided her personal goal: "I want to change the world, and I'd like to do it with costumes." When asked what she thought of those in the mental health profession who would consider her students to be suffering from mental disorders, her eyes twinkled and she said, "At the academy, we don't believe in gender dysphoria. We believe in gender euphoria."

STEFAN LYNCH

The fear of creating a homosexual by allowing cross-gender dressing and role play remains powerful, and in that regard, I offer the story of a young man named Stefan Lynch. When I met Stefan, he was twenty-three years old, tall, handsome, with brown hair and green eyes. He grew up one block from the Clarke Institute of Psychiatry at the University of Toronto, where Susan Bradley and Kenneth Zucker created a clinic for "gender identity problems of children and adolescents." Bradley and Zucker felt the need to create the clinic in the mid-1970s because of the growing influence of "the gay crowd," which they felt was beginning to interfere with their treatment of gender-deviant children and adolescents.

Beginning in 1975, "any child who presented to the Intake Department with a *suspected* [italics added] gender problem, or who was described as manifesting cross-sexed behaviour, was referred to our clinic." The criteria for "suspecting" a gender problem, and details of what constituted "cross-sexed behaviour," were not discussed. The Clarke Institute has become one of the two largest clinics in North America for treating Gender Identity Disorder in children, the other being Susan Coates' clinic in New York City. Zucker likes to emphasize the fact that, because of Canadian national health insurance, his clinic treats children from every demographic group, not just those with access to health care insurance.

One of the Clarke Institute's goals was to "Identify the factors which will allow prediction of the probable outcome of a patient's gender and sexual orientation upon reaching adulthood." As we have seen, cross-dressing and cross-sex role play in a child, coupled with the parents' indifference or permissiveness regarding their child's behavior, were and are considered primary predictors of a child's future adult behavior.

Stefan remembers hearing about the Clarke Institute's work "with children whose gender identities didn't match their biological sex," and how they were "curing" these children. One day, when Stefan was fourteen years old, his curiosity got the better of him, and he decided to go inside the institute. "It was friendly, muted, welcoming," he said, "but the locked doors and security people gave me the sense they were trying to keep people in. It wasn't until later that I realized they were trying to change these little sissy boys and butch girls into what they were supposed to be."

In 1980, when Stefan was eight years old, his family gave a writer named Joe Gant permission to live with them for three weeks. Gant was writing the first book on lesbian and gay parents and their children, and five families were profiled. Stefan's mother, Gail, was lesbian, and his father, Michael, was gay. The book's contents and title were a betrayal of the family's trust. *Whose Child Cries* portrayed Stefan as nervous, fat, effeminate, neurotic and nonathletic. Gant was especially focused on Stefan's lack of interest in girls, although he was only eight years old. "I was training to get a lifeguard certificate," said Stefan. "I was an excellent student, and I was athletic every day," said Stefan. "I played all the time at recess. I had boy friends and girl friends, but mostly boy friends, and I was absolutely not afraid of 'rough and tumble' play." In 1989, Stefan became a tennis all-American, and won the National Small College Athletic Association's tournament, but the writer did not want to see that potential. He saw what he expected to see.

Stefan describes his mother, Gail, as a private person, "the constant, solid presence" in his life. "She's ridiculously average and normal . . . very, very mainstream." When Stefan was eight, his mom's partner for the next seven years was Pat Bond, the late actress who toured the country in a one-woman show about Gertrude Stein. When his mom moved with Bond to the West Coast, Stefan divided his time between his father's Canadian residence and his mother's home in San Francisco. From his mother he received "unending love. I was always her number one priority. She was the person who always made me feel needed and wanted." From his father he experienced a joie de vivre that has not yet been matched.

Michael Lynch was a professor of English literature at the University of Toronto. He was also a full-time gay rights activist, the type of individual who was making "the gay crowd" visible and problematic for the Clarke Institute down the street. At the university, Michael Lynch taught "all the gay nineteenth century authors: Willa Cather, Melville, Whitman, Oscar Wilde," and at home, he produced some of Toronto's most elaborate drag parties, in which Stefan participated.

"I did drag all the time," said Stefan, "starting from five years old. I probably did my first Bette Davis at six, with the whole complete getup. I still have my cigarette holder somewhere in the basement. My friends would come over for my dad's parties, and we'd be the troubleshooters." They would empty ashtrays and do cleanup, and all of the boys would be in drag. "I don't remember thinking twice about doing it," said Stefan, "but I was disappointed the first time. People did not take me seriously enough, and I was trying very hard to do an accurate Bette Davis."

One of Stefan's favorite memories is the "Clutch and Earring" party. "There were prizes for the best clutch/earring combination. I actually won for best earrings. I was probably eleven. I had cut a tennis ball in half. And at that party, there was an opera singer who performed Gilbert and Sullivan, and arias from *Carmen,* while my dad played the piano. Our house had a little balcony overlooking the living room. He stood up in the balcony and threw confetti down. I had so much fun growing up."

Stefan, and every single one of the little boys who for years participated in the drag parties, grew up straight. Stefan laughed and asked if I had ever heard of the mental disorder known as ego-dystonic homosexuality, wherein a gay person is deemed mentally ill because he or she is uncomfortable with their sexuality. "Well," said Stefan, "I'm ego-dystonic heterosexual. I grew up in this wonderful gay community, and observed all the culture. Then I got tricked. I grew up straight, and technically, I wasn't a part of it anymore."

Stefan is the executive director of COLAGE (Children of Lesbians and Gays Everywhere), an international support group headquartered in San Francisco. Stefan's mother still lives in San Francisco, but he lost his father to AIDS. When Stefan speaks of his father, his voice is heavy with emotion. He loved him deeply. Like his father, Stefan is an activist, and he cherishes the gender freedom his parents gave him, despite his so-called ego-dystonic heterosexuality. We can only imagine the reaction of the Clarke Institute psychologists if they had known what was going on with those little boys just one block away.

We have seen that clothes and names help to create masculine and feminine identities that we take to be real and essential, but which are constructions, artificial and made. It is difficult to see beyond the trappings of a part to the person underneath. It would require a new way of seeing, perhaps a new way of being, for that to be possible. Even if clothes and names no longer influenced who and what we thought a person to be, we would have to overcome another formidable obstacle: we have been trained to perceive the surface appearance of the body itself as an indication of the true nature of the human being beneath the skin.

THE BODY AS EVIDENCE

Though we pride ourselves on being a culture of substance, every child and adult is subject to judgment because of the shape of their face, their height, their hair or muscle mass. Working with U.S. government grants in the early twentieth century, researchers claimed that people with "low brows" were stupid and criminally inclined, whereas people with "high brows" were intelligent and morally upright. In the 1950s, eugenics studies were undertaken at Ivy League universities which required all freshmen to strip and have themselves measured and photographed. These studies were meant to prove that the shape and stature of the body itself were Darwinian factors of elite intelligence and social power.

There are many studies in longitudinal archives from the 1920s and 1940s which follow a group of people over an extended period of time, sometimes a lifetime. These studies document painstaking measurements of the bodies not only of Ivy

Leaguers but also of those incarcerated for crimes. The identification of a "criminal body" would be of great use to law enforcement, while the identification of a "superior body" would be of great use to social engineers.

These studies of the past are a source of embarrassment for most of the scientific community. However, the drive behind the studies—*that the body's appearance is evidence of the true nature of a human being*—is alive and well. From birth, the body itself, before any behavior whatsoever has been undertaken, is perceived as evidence of character and intelligence, as well as masculinity and femininity.

Since the 1870s, when Charles Darwin wrote that men chose their wives largely based on "external appearance," many studies have investigated other beliefs and qualities attributed to the perception of attractiveness. The list is astounding, including everything from fertility to jury decisions.

In 1986, Michael Cunningham at Elmhurst College in Illinois conducted a study in which men were shown photographs of fifty women, whom they rated for attractiveness. They were then asked which of these women they felt altruistically inclined toward, and which women they would "select for dating, sexual behavior, and childrearing." They were also asked to predict the behaviors of the women based upon their appearance.

"Females with greater eye height, smaller nose area, greater cheekbone width and a wider smile were seen as brighter than their counterparts." Attractiveness, therefore, was a sign of intelligence.

"The females with greater eye height and width, smaller nose area, wider cheekbones, higher eyebrows, wider pupils, and wider smiles were perceived to be more sociable." Attractiveness, therefore, was a sign of social skills, which is important for many men's business aspirations.

"Females with greater eye height, smaller nose area, and wider smiles were seen as more assertive, whereas those with smaller eye height, larger nose width, greater chin length, narrower cheekbones, and lower eyebrows were seen as more modest. Those with large eye height and width, shorter chins, wider cheekbones, narrower cheeks, higher eyebrows, wider pupils, and wider smiles were seen as more likely to be fertile and have many children, but also more likely to have an extramarital affair." Attractiveness was now a sign of assertiveness, fertility and infidelity.

Attractiveness in a woman, which is inextricably bound to notions of "femininity," was also a determining factor in whether the man would perform some type of self-sacrificial or risk-taking act which involved a woman. These events included the man's rescuing a woman from drowning, from a burning building, or throwing himself atop a grenade; loaning a woman $10,000 to start a business, donating blood or even a kidney. It's rather chilling to think that one's chances of survival might in any way be contingent on eye spacing, yet that is exactly what this study demonstrated.

From Darwin in 1871 to Illinois in 1986, physical attractiveness, and hence "femininity," has been shown to be a decisive stereotyping factor in the assessment of women by men. (Women tend to judge men more by their provider capabilities.) The consequences of this phenomenon affect not just the outcome of beauty pageants, but everything from the perception of fertility to probable infidelity, not to mention the destinies of that woman's child.

A particularly disturbing study was conducted in 1979 by Judith Langlois and Chris Downs at the University of Texas at Austin. Sixty-four children, three and five years old, were selected for the study, after being sorted for "attractiveness" and "unattractiveness." The researchers decided to investigate whether or not there was a connection between unattractiveness in a child and that child's aggressive and antisocial behavior with other children.

Rather than testing for a perception problem among those who were judging the children which would lead them to believe the unattractive child was aggressive and antisocial, this study sought to prove that "attractive children are friendly and behave prosocially." Seeking to establish a real connection between physical appearance and behavior, adult raters sorted the children by their physical characteristics, and then paired them in same-sex dyads, sometimes in attractive pairs, sometimes in mixed pairs. The researchers found that the unattractive children were more aggressive, had higher activity levels and more sex-stereotyped play behaviors.

"Negative evaluations of unattractive children seem to be a reflection of the actual tendency for these children to be aggressive," they reported. "The higher activity level of unattractive children may lead them to be associated with more disturbances and become perceived as 'troublemakers.' " Not only were unattractive children perceived as more aggressive, but they were declared at risk for being labeled as troublemakers.

The power of sex-typed judgment on the basis of appearance encompasses employment considerations and even therapeutic decisions made by mental health professionals. Physical unattractiveness in women has accounted for significantly longer stays in psychiatric hospitals when they were matched with attractive women with the same degree of psychopathology. The unattractive, or unfeminine, women were "expected to do more evil things," and received less sympathy if fortune did not favor them. One particular result of this study was truly shocking: ". . . the more unattractive the subject is, the more likely she is to receive a diagnosis indicative of severe maladjustment (schizophrenia)."

Appearance judgments of this type are not confined to adults. Physically attractive children are given more referrals for special educational opportunities than their unattractive or moderately attractive classmates. Even sentencing to jail terms or probation has been linked to the defendant's appearance, as was found in a study by Gloria Leventhal and Ronald Krate at the Center for Probation Studies at William Paterson College.

Are we doomed to forever judge even a child on the shape of the body, to attribute and predict traits and behaviors and to set up self-fulfilling prophecies based upon nothing but appearance? The work of Dr. Sandra L. Bem, then at Stanford and presently at

Cornell, sheds significant light on this problem, and reveals that as the concepts of masculinity and femininity evolve, the attributes we project onto others because of their physical appearance become less stereotyped.

In 1974, Bem created a new measurement of sex-role characteristics which is still in use. The development of the Bem Sex Role Inventory (BSRI) is a widely acknowledged turning point in the psychological study of gender. Bem questioned the assumption, in psychology and society, that masculinity and femininity were the opposite ends of a single continuum, or pole. This "bipolar" concept of gender meant that an individual was either masculine or feminine, but could not be both. This is the basis for sex-typing and seeing the world as a "sex-typed" individual, or one who strongly adheres to strictly masculine and feminine roles. The BSRI revealed that sex-typed individuals were "seriously limited in the range of behaviors available to them as they moved from situation to situation." The rigidity of sex-typed individuals could seriously impair their ability to function appropriately in a situation, because they suppress any characteristics within themselves that they consider to be against their purely masculine or feminine identities.

In effect, Bem successfully challenged the very basis of psychological assessment, which was built upon the assumption that sex-typed individuals represented mental health. Sex-typed individuals were found, instead, to be laboring under tremendous social and psychological deficits.

In 1981, in terms of appearance, Dr. Bem and Dr. Susan M. Andersen (then at Stanford and presently at New York University) conducted an experiment in which twenty-four male and twenty-four female undergraduates engaged in four different "getting acquainted" telephone conversations with both males and females. They were told that the person they were speaking to was supposedly attractive or unattractive. The results of the study were revealing. Those who tested as sex-typed on the BSRI interacted more positively with the allegedly attractive person, and indifferently or negatively with the allegedly unattractive person, despite the fact that they could not see the individual on the other end of the phone line.

The ruse that the person on the other end of the line was attractive or unattractive was enough to significantly alter the sex-typed individual's behavior. The crucial gender stereotypes of masculine and feminine appearance operated even when the person was not visible, creating a self-fulfilling prophecy: attractive people are treated better by sex-typed individuals, and so they act more socially toward them. The conclusion held by the sex-typed individual, based on the self-fulfilling prophecy set up by their own perceptions, is that attractive children and adults are innately good because of how they look, and unattractive children and adults are innately aggressive, or tend to be troublemakers, because of how they look, and their behavior proves it. In contrast, the individual who ascribed to both "masculine" and "feminine" characteristics did not attribute traits to others based on alleged attractiveness or unattractiveness, and did not set into motion the self-fulfilling prophecy of "beauty equals goodness." (There is, of course, the archetype of the beautiful and evil "femme fatale" figure, but her power rests in the fact that she is an aberration.)

In 1991, researchers at Auburn University, led by Dr. Malcolm D. Gynther, conducted a study on heterosexual men and their perceptions of female attractiveness, as well as femininity. Two hundred and forty-nine men rated twenty-two photographs of young women, and seventy-nine of these men were given three tests: the Macho Scale, the Survey of Heterosexual Interactions and the Bem Sex Role Inventory.

The Macho Scale was developed in 1977 by Wayne J. Villemez at the Florida Atlantic University and John C. Touhey at the University of California at Santa Cruz. The Macho Scale measures sex-role orientation and authoritarianism in males. Representative items from the Macho Scale are: "Women who try to be independent of their families are just hurting themselves" and "I would not want to be one of a couple where the male was considerably shorter than the female."

The Survey of Heterosexual Interactions is used to analyze the behavioral problem of heterosocial avoidance, which means the level of discomfort that a heterosexual male experiences in the presence of women. A representative question on the survey is: "You are at a dance. You see a very attractive woman whom you do not know. She is standing *alone* and you would like to dance with her. You would: be unable to ask her in every case, be able to ask her in some cases, be able to ask her in every case."

What was shown in Gynther's 1991 study, using these three measurement tools, confirmed the researchers' predictions, and confirmed the sex-typed analysis that Bem and Andersen had shown a decade earlier: the men who scored high on the Macho Scale, and were therefore sex-typed individuals, rated all of the women far more harshly than those who scored low on the Macho Scale.

A 1987 study at the University of Georgia examined the relationships between physical attractiveness, sex role orientation and the evaluation of adults and children. One hundred and forty participants rated twelve slides of six adults and six children, male and female. The researchers had already sorted the slides according to physical attractiveness. The participants were given various scenarios depicting social transgressions attributed to the individuals pictured. They were then asked about the probability that the adult or child had transgressed similarly in the past, or would transgress similarly in the future. The study showed that sex-typed persons were deeply influenced by physical appearance in assessing individuals, but the results of this experiment are especially poignant in the assessment of children. "When evaluating children, sex-typed males and females rated the highly attractive children as less likely than the moderately attractive [and the unattractive] to commit a similar transgression in the future." Again, those who were not sex-typed, but described themselves as having a variety of "masculine" and "feminine" traits, "were not influenced by the physical appearance of the child."

This is a powerful argument for the encouragement of gender independence. As young Carlos told his analyst, "You can't tell a book by its cover," but to truly understand this, we must be capable of seeing beyond the surface characteristics of a person's body. Only then can we be free of supersitious, mistaken assumptions about each other, and even ourselves.

THE BODY, GENDER IDENTITY AND SEXUALITY

In all the studies of appearance, I found one group to be consistently penalized because of beauty. According to the Langlois study mentioned earlier, "attractive boys were generally disliked by acquainted peers. In the context of day-to-day interactions, the 'prettier' and less active boys may be perceived more negatively and as less desirable as friends, when children, particularly other boys, actually play with the toys and engage in the active rough-and-tumble games characteristic of these ages."

How can we understand this? Sex-typing among young children is very rigid, as they struggle to find their identities and conform to the expectations of the adults around them. Adults teach children that their most important source of identity is that they are a girl or a boy, and in terms of appearance, girls are supposed to be pretty and soft, and boys are supposed to be rugged and tough. One father I knew was thrilled when his son got a scar from stitches on his forehead. His son was "pretty," and the father thought the scar would help the boy socially, and make him appear more "manly."

If a boy is too pretty, he can be a source of confusion. Something is perceived as "wrong." He does not fit the sex-typed male stereotype, especially if he combs his hair neatly, or color-coordinates his clothes. A pretty boy will often make the sex-typed nursery school teacher very uncomfortable, especially if that boy exhibits interest in "girl" activities, and that teacher's discomfort would be picked up on by the other children. We can excuse this assessment when it is made by small children who are being raised with rigid sex-typed identities, but can we be quite as forgiving of teachers? If nursery and grammar school teachers should be held to a higher standard of perception, how are we to respond to prominent neuropsychiatrists and clinical psychologists who persist in hypothesizing a connection between a child's physical appearance and gender disorder?

As early as 1965, Robert Stoller made the following observation of the boys brought to the UCLA clinic: "We have noticed that they often have pretty faces, with fine hair, lovely complexions, graceful movements, and—especially—big, piercing, liquid eyes." In the 1970s, Richard Green asked parents to reconstruct their memories of their baby as an infant. Since the children were brought to the clinic because they were perceived as inappropriately feminine, the parents were likely to remember any detail which might tend to make them less culpable for their son's behavior. The parents were presented with a list of questions which included describing their baby, and what he was like as an infant. The size of the baby's eyes was targeted: If the eyes were "ordinary," they were connected to "never mistaken for a girl." If the eyes were large, they were connected to "perhaps occasionally mistaken for a girl." If the eyes were attractive, "perhaps with long lashes," they were connected to "occasionally mistaken for a girl." If the eyes were big, and "girl-like," they were connected to being "frequently mistaken for a girl." And finally, if the eyes were big, with long lashes, they were said to be "just like a girl," and "Everyone says the child should have been a girl."

As recently as 1993, an appearance study was undertaken by Kenneth Zucker at the Clarke Institute in Toronto on seventeen eight-year-old boys diagnosed with Gender Identity Disorder and seventeen clinical control boys. They were rated on a five-adjective scale: attractive, beautiful, cute, handsome and pretty. ("Clinical control boys" refers to children brought to the clinic for psychiatric reasons other than Gender Identity Disorder.) When the results of the test were tallied, the researchers were confused as to why the boys diagnosed with Gender Identity Disorder were rated significantly more "handsome" than the clinical control boys. "Handsome," they had reasoned, could only be applied to "masculine" boys, and so their expectation that GID-diagnosed boys would look like girls was not met. Zucker then questioned the use of the word "handsome," which he conjectures was actually being used with a feminine intent by the raters, despite the fact that "handsome" is rarely used to describe females. It is typical of this field that when a study does not produce the expected results, the results are considered unreliable, and the study is redesigned. If this particular study of physical attractiveness of boys with GID is repeated, it will probably be designed so that the GID-diagnosed boys will come out as "prefeminine." To that end, Zucker has suggested that "regardless of the role of objective facial properties," the mothers and sometimes the boys themselves have deliberately fashioned their hair to a "softer, cute look."

In 1995, the Clarke Institute undertook a study of physical attractiveness in girls diagnosed with GID. The girls were of varying ages, with a mean age of six years six months. There were three groups, with twelve girls in each group: the girls diagnosed with Gender Identity Disorder, the clinical control girls, and the normal control girls. When the Clarke Institute forms a normal control group of children, they place advertisements in local newspapers for children who have never been treated for psychological problems (although two of the normal control girls in this study were the sisters of boys with Gender Identity Disorder). The clinical control girls were under the care of a child protective agency, having experienced sexual and/or physical abuse, as well as emotional neglect. There is something very chilling about using these particular girls as a control group in a study on physical attractiveness. Surely the public funds used to support this study would be better spent in therapy and support services for these abused girls, rather than assessing the length of their eyelashes or the shape of their mouths.

The rating scale for girls is an interesting contrast to the rating scale for boys. The girls were scored as "attractive, beautiful, cute, pretty and ugly." The boys' rating scale had no pejorative term like "ugly," unless the word "pretty" was intended as pejorative when applied to a boy. As predicted, the girls with Gender Identity Disorder "were rated as significantly less attractive than the normal control girls." They even found that the girls referred to the clinic for perceived Gender Identity Disorder ("gender-referred girls") who were also "ugly" had greater behavior problem scores. The fact that these girls were not interested in "feminine" hairstyles, clothing and attitudes was not taken into consideration, but could be an important factor in the "objective" judgment of their faces. The raters knew that they were supposed to be rating "girls," and these particular girls seemed dedicated to not appearing "girlish." The aim of this study was to demonstrate that the child's appearance was *driving* her behavioral gender disorder. "Masculinity" in a girl's face is therefore toxic to her feminine development.

Little vignettes were included in this study, the most disturbing of which concerned a four-year-old girl who entered a preschool and was thought to be a boy. "Her [white] teacher was convinced, based on her appearance, that her parents had erred in identifying her on the school registration form as a girl. Because this girl came from a non-Western [East Indian] culture, her teacher was unable to determine her actual sex based on her given name. She was unable to ask the girl about her sex because she did not speak English. The teacher reported that she took this little girl to the washroom and pulled down her blue jeans 'to check.' " The researcher stated, "The sequence of events led to the clinical referral." Make no mistake about it: The researchers were not reporting this anecdote in order to expose a neurotically sex-typed teacher who could not endure spending one day in the preschool room with a child whose sex was not clear. The child was the identified patient, not the teacher. The researchers presented this vignette only to illustrate the social chaos caused by the child, and that "six of the twelve gender-referred girls in the present study were systematically misidentified by peers or strangers as boys at the time of the assessment."

This study was described in very scientific terms. The viewing of the girls' photographs was done in a darkened room illuminated only by a small light so that the rater could see his or her coding sheet. The researchers take care to tell us that the rater sat "about 9 feet [2.7 m]" from the screen. These details are an attempt to give the illusion that some sort of real, objective science is occurring.

As a result of this "scientific" study, the researchers concluded that it "would also appear warranted to analyze infant photographs of girls with gender identity disorder" to determine whether or not "premasculine infant girls have facial properties more commonly associated with infant boys." The results would probably be published in newspapers around the world, and anxious parents would be studying their infants for signs of a disorder for which there is not one single objective test.

There is an obvious and crucial question that is overlooked with these physical attractiveness studies of GID in children. Are feminine-appearing tomboys who engage in athletic, high-energy activities as frequently referred for Gender Identity Disorder, or are they simply considered spirited? Are masculine-appearing boys who engage in quiet, low-energy activities, like doll play or arts and crafts, as frequently referred for Gender Identity Disorder, or are they considered intelligent and artistic? Are girls and boys who "look like" girls and boys assumed to be in a developmental stage regarding gender issues? Do parents and teachers believe there is no cause for alarm, and that they will "grow out of it" or add to their behavioral repertoire as time passes?

The "pretty" boy or the "ugly" girl, however, are disturbing. They are treated suspiciously, as if they harbor some secret gender perversion within their bodies. Suspected of being premasculine or prefeminine, these children threaten the identities of the sex-typed individuals who judge them, and on the basis of their physical appearance, all sorts of hypotheses and myths are expounded. If the body is evidence, these boys and girls are genetic suspects, and viewed as out of synch with the bipolar gender system which is connected to heterosexuality. The search for a "homosexual body," based upon appearance, however, was dismissed as early as 1940 by Wortis, and in 1945 by Margaret Mead, the noted American anthropologist. Neither Wortis nor Mead found any anthropomorphic differences between the homosexual and heterosexual. Yet the obsession remains, and public funding to find this elusive "gay body" continues.

In 1981, Dr. Muriel Wilson Perkins conducted a study which declared that "the homosexual woman has statistically narrower hips, increased arm and leg girths, less subcutaneous fat, and more muscle than controls [presumably heterosexual women]." In other words, the homosexual woman physically resembles a man. Dr. Perkins undertook this study to refute the work of Meyer-Bahlburg in 1979, who concluded that there were statistically insignificant group differences in body build between heterosexual and homosexual women, if these differences existed at all.

Keeping in mind that there are 2.54 centimeters in one inch, the leg girth differences reported by Dr. Perkins were 34.5 cm for the "presumably heterosexual women" and 35.1 cm for the homosexual women. Do we really want the National Institute of Mental Health to bankroll a study so that a quarter of an inch difference in leg girth can be reported? Not only is it statistically not particularly impressive, but if a different group of lesbians from another part of the country had been measured, the results could well go the other way. To make matters worse, Dr. Perkins did not even have a contemporary control group of heterosexual women. Instead, she used two preexisting studies, one performed between the years 1950 and 1965, the other performed between 1960 and 1968, on what she describes as "presumably heterosexual women," which means that there were probably some lesbians mixed into the group, since the women were not asked questions concerning their sexuality. Perkins herself did not conduct these studies, and she did not reveal the regions from which these women came, but it is safe to assume they were not all from Dallas, or even Texas, the location of all the lesbian women in her study. The demographics of the groups being compared were not matched.

To simply invalidate her government-sponsored work, some of the body size statistics against which Dr. Perkins measures her lesbian sample were compiled as early as 1950, over a quarter of a century before she measured the Dallas women. Any anthropologist, or person involved with measuring the size of human beings, will tell you that *all* people are getting larger.

In 1985, Mary Amanda Dew, at Harvard University, undertook a very interesting project. She asked twenty-five women who worked as secretaries at Johns Hopkins University Hospital if they would agree to participate. (Johns Hopkins was an ironic choice, since they are the source of so many studies on gender and sexuality.) Twenty-two of the secretaries agreed to participate. Dew had photographs taken of the women, about whom she knew nothing. She told the female and male raters to assign attributes to the women based only on these photos.

The attributes included whether or not the woman was pretty, statements about her wardrobe, hair, potential alcoholism, whether or not she was married and whether or not she was gay. The raters were told that, of the twenty-two women, eleven of them were, indeed, homosexual, and they should try to pick those women out of the crowd. (None of the Johns Hopkins women was known to be gay.)

The test results indicated that if the woman was "considered to be homosexual, she was also viewed as being less extraverted and generally less attractive. She was also seen as not dressing as well, not having as pretty a face, not having as attractive a hairstyle, and not being as desirable to meet as a woman not considered to be a homosexual." When the raters were informed that none of the women in the study was known to be homosexual, they seemed "genuinely surprised." Dr. Dew also found that "conservative females were likely to choose as homosexuals those women to whom they had given the worst evaluations concerning physical appearance, where more liberal females were less likely to do so."

Many studies point to a connection between severely sex-typed individuals and conservative ideology. A 1990 study at the State University of New York at Cortland found that "more conservative" individuals made connections between a person's face and their sexuality, and that these individuals believed that homosexuals could be identified by "how they look." Homosexual men, of course, were "feminine," and lesbian women were "masculine." Hence the tremendous mainstream fascination with the 1990s revelations of the feminine gay woman, now known as the "lipstick lesbian," and the masculine gay man, particularly the athlete, such as Olympic gold medalist Greg Louganis.

Sex-typed individuals have pronounced discomfort with these two groups of homosexuals, since they are not so easily identifiable and make it possible for just about anyone, including themselves, to be stigmatized as gay. Yet despite the revelation that feminine lesbians and masculine gays exist, the physical appearance meter is so strong that it defies ideological markers. Although studies indicate that conservative individuals are more likely to be sex-typed than liberal individuals, liberals are not immune to sex-typing others by appearance, as in the case of the hearings on the nomination of Attorney General Janet Reno, whom *Newsweek* described as "Annie Oakley meets Harry Truman."

During Reno's confirmation hearings for Attorney General, a strange alliance was forged between John B. Thompson, a right-wing defeated political opponent of Reno, and the Washington, D.C., chapter of Queer Nation, the street-activist, media-savvy arm of the gay rights movement. There was no evidence that Reno was lesbian, but based upon the fact that she was unmarried, without children, "masculine" in physical appearance, and had a relative lack of interest in fashion, the assumption was made.

Supposed indicators of Reno's sexuality entailed such things as her height (over six feet), and that she walked in long, determined strides. John B. Thompson actually sued Reno for criminal battery when, after months of attack and confrontation over her sexuality, which did not cost her the election, she touched him on the shoulder and said, "I'm only interested in virile men. That's why I'm not attracted to you." Meanwhile, the Queer Nation chapter sent out a press release "outing" Reno, stating that she was "more likely than not" lesbian. The fact that she "looked like a lesbian" was not within the official press release of any group, but was a common response to Reno's image, not only by heterosexuals, but by gay men and lesbians as well. As a prosecutor in Dade County, Attorney General Janet Reno would probably not have been able to hide a lesbian lifestyle, or much of anything, for that matter, including the fact that she's also not particularly interested in housework, which did not help her femininity score on the gender meter.

Judging upon the basis of physical appearance crosses ideologies, yet those who are more inclined toward sex-typing, whether they are gay or straight, liberal or conservative, are at risk for categorizing others, and themselves, with voodoo-based knowledge. Many gay men believe that a "pretty" man must be homosexual, or at least a closet case, regardless of what they themselves look like. Many lesbians view the most athletic women, women with assertive body language, or women with short cropped hair, as lesbian or closeted, regardless of their lifestyle or statements to the contrary. There is room for everyone to grow in terms of judgment issues, regardless of sexual orientation. Physical appearance as an indicator of sexuality is an equal opportunity distortion.

SEEING MALE,
SEEING FEMALE

In 1975, the Baby X study showed that those who believed they were holding a boy baby "noted the strength of the grasp response or the lack of hair," and those who believed the baby to be a girl "remarked about the baby's roundness, softness, and fragility." However, when the participants were holding a boy, they were told it was a girl; and when they were holding a girl, they were told it was a boy. Their judgments about the babies were based solely on sex-typed expectations, and not on reality.

But what happens when we must guess the sex of the child? How do we decide which sex we are seeing? A 1977 study conducted at Michigan State University found that "adults are biased to assume male gender when an infant's actual sex is unknown. On the other hand, a cute infant with a wide face across the upper cheek bones most likely will be perceived to be a female."

What do we see when we attribute sex, and how many cues are necessary for us to be sure? We know that very small children attribute sex based upon length of hair and style and color of clothing, rather than activities. But what does it take for adults to determine a person's sex? To answer that question, Dr. Suzanne Kessler, a professor of psychology at the State University of New York at Purchase, and her colleagues designed the Overlay Study, which would become a famous study on gender cues and the perception of sex.

The Overlay Study featured a series of "overlays" on plastic sheets, and on each sheet there was a drawing of one physical characteristic, or a piece of clothing. For example, an overlay might feature long hair, short hair, wide hips, narrow hips, breasts, flat chest, body hair, a penis or a vagina. The human figure representation upon which the overlays were placed had facial features that were not gender-specific. Nine hundred and sixty participants were asked three questions: Was the figure male or female, how confident were they of that determination, and how many cues about the figure would they need to change the figure into the other sex.

Kessler found that the presence of a penis always overrides any other cues, including long head hair, breasts, hips and no body hair. These "female" cues cannot overpower the attribution of male. When the figure had a vagina, no breasts, no hips, body hair and short head hair, the figure was again seen as male, despite the fact that it had a vagina. Kessler concluded that there seemed to be no cues that were definitely female, while many were definitely male, accurate or not.

When there are not enough cues visible for us to make a determination of an individual's sex, we can be disturbed, fascinated or both. Yet many individuals have ambiguous secondary female and male characteristics. These individuals are usually not transvestites or people otherwise engaged in actively playing with gender roles. They are simply not stereotypically, by appearance, of one sex or the other. These people are everywhere, and many of them have told me of unusual experiences, such as being stopped by security guards as they enter public sex-segregated bathrooms, or being followed through department stores by other shoppers who cannot make up their minds if they are seeing a female or male purchasing lingerie or ties.

Perhaps one of the most common problems of this kind is with female facial hair. Facial hair on a woman, particularly a moustache, is very common, and an entire industry has grown up around disguising the hair. As an alternative to laundry bleach, Jolen Bleach Company was the first to create a "cosmetic bleach" that is used almost solely on female moustaches. Evelyn Kosack, the chairman of Jolen, told me that the company produces over a million units a year. A bottle of this moustache bleach can last for years, so there are easily millions of women carefully disguising very normal facial hair because they are afraid it will make them appear to be male.

In the course of my research, I interviewed a woman whose life was ruled by the fact that she had an inherited condition that caused extreme facial hair growth. It affected everything from her personal relationships to her chances on the job market, and so she was constantly waxing and bleaching in an attempt to control the hair. If you open any Yellow Pages, you will find extensive listings for electrolysis and hair removal that cater to women. Sadly, there is often an element of shame involved, and many women are highly secretive, telling no one of their treatments.

For men whose hair is beginning to thin, there are now extensive Yellow Page listings for hair replacement. Yul Brynner and Telly Savalas are no longer in fashion, and Rogaine hair replacement commercials are featured on many sports programs. Men fear they will not be viewed as virile, or worse, as effeminate, because they are balding.

That so much could happen to a human being because of *hair* reinforces why so many studies are done about human appearance, but the most revealing "hair" story that I came across was reported in 1995. It concerned the so-called "werewolf gene," and how this gene could shed light on hair growth, with an aim to curing baldness. This rare condition of excessive hairiness is called congenital generalized hypertrichosis: "Many victims of the condition have spent their lives performing in circuses. Dr. Pragna Patel says that affected people have been displayed as 'hair men,' 'dog men,' 'human werewolves' and even 'human Skye terriers.' " In the news report, several doctors commented on the "cause" of the condition. One biologist hypothesized, "Because the mutation makes people as hairy as some animals, it might actually be rewakening [sic] ancestral traits." Every other part of this person's body was normal, but because of the extreme hair growth, this biologist believes "ancestral traits," presumably primitive, animalistic and sexual, could be "rewakened." Because hairiness is seen as masculine and virile, too much hairiness is seen as a throwback to an earlier evolutionary time when we were closer to the animals. In this dramatic example, physical appearance is linked to an inner state of being based upon gender stereotypes of masculinity.

Hair protects the body from the elements, and functions as a cooling system. It has nothing to do with fertility or the call of the wild. Depending upon the part of the world your ancestors came from, your body will have thick tufts of hair, even if you are female, or be absolutely hairless, even if you are male.

Margaret Mead asked a question in 1945 that is still relevant today: "If the tribe sets hairiness up as a desirable male characteristic, will the less hairy become confused about their sex role, while if the tribemen think that hairiness is simply a brutish characteristic, the very hairy may be almost sexually ostracized and the most hairless will not thereby be regarded as less male?"

Mead was a particular specialist in the Balinese. The typical male is almost hairless, and his breasts "are considerably more developed than are a Westerner's," while the Balinese female typically has "narrow hips and small high breasts." If the male and female of the Balinese are placed alongside the male and female of Western Europe, Mead explains that the male will appear "feminine" and the female will look "boyish." Mead surmised that the man, and perhaps the woman, would be sexually suspect, and the woman would not be thought capable of bearing children, and certainly not of breast-feeding them. These would, of course, be inaccurate assumptions, but projecting from one cultural point of view onto another, they might seem so true that biological arguments of all kinds would be made.

Mead believed that, based upon nothing more than their bodily appearance, the Balinese might be thought of as more bisexual and less sexually differentiated than Western Europeans. Yet some of the factors used to interpret the Balinese male as lacking in masculinity "do not really affect his masculinity at all: his height, girth, hairiness, and the like." From the Balinese to the northern Europeans, from the Andamanese Pygmies to the Nubian giants, the range of human body types, exhibited in both males and females, renders "certain of the criteria for masculinity and femininity inoperative."

Nowhere is the masculine stereotype of hair played out with such obsession as in Robert Bly's *Iron John*. He contends that "a man's moustache may stand for his pubic hair," and so act as a facial sign of his genitals. As proof of this, he tells the story of a friend who grew a moustache, but then found his mother would not look at him until he shaved it off. For Bly, hair represents sexual energy. He contends that "humans traditionally wear long hair, as do the animals they hunt," and therefore hair stands for the "life of wild animals." If a boy does not hunt and kill animals, Bly explains that he will never be at peace with his mythological hunting past, and "will still be bringing a deer back to Detroit on the top of his car when he is fifty." This hunting of the hairy animal, while sporting as much body hair as possible, is for Bly the route through which the male learns about God. He goes on to explain that beyond hunting and closeness to animals, hair "suggests all forms of animal hot-bloodedness." Hairiness is a sign of "passionate impulsiveness, spontaneity, explosive emotions, leonine fierceness, tigerish jealousy." Hair "suggests excess. The hairiness of Enkidu, the Babylonian Wild Man, or Pan, the goat-man, suggests that hair stands for what is beyond the boundaries of all middle-of-the-road civilization."

Robert Bly is a wonderful poet, but he seems to have moved from metaphor, to simile, to fact, claiming that body hair is a literal sign of wildness, the uncivilized past, and our connection to the animals. What would a harelip mean to Bly, or a missing finger? Is there a meaning to blondness? Is the blackest of skin some kind of sign?

Bly takes an image from his poetic imagination and presents it as truth in the real world, a real world where women are so horrified by the "meaning" of their moustaches that there are entire industries built around its disguise and removal, a real world where men cover their baldness with toupees, perform elaborate "comb overs" or implant hair plugs in their scalps, that their masculinity, and hence virility, not be questioned.

Bipolar categories, whether they are labeled masculine and feminine or instrumental and expressive, are an obstacle to experiencing our true identities. They tangle us up in myths and mirrors. They send us on wild-goose chases after the truth, and they leave us completely unprepared for the last stages of our lives, when the clothing fades and the body ages. Who are we when the discernible cues of masculine and feminine crumble? What then happens to our sense of what is "real" and who we are?

By releasing ourselves from the bipolar trap and claiming gender independence, we have the opportunity to affirm those parts of ourselves we have denied, but need. Gender independence does not mean that women will be wearing jockstraps, that men will be wearing dresses, or that everyone will be in trousers. It could mean that men will reveal their beauty and flexibility, and that women will reveal their intelligence and rationality. When the dust settles, there will probably be just as many high heels and Brooks Brothers jackets, because gender independence is an inside job, not a fashion statement. Gender independence can affect outward appearances, but it is an expression of the inner world, not a response to the outer. The hallmark of gender independence is flexibility, the trait most crucial to psychological well-being in the postmodern world, and the key to strong, intimate relationships between equals.

SCIENCE

Is having a male or female body the most powerful predictor of how we will act and what we will feel? This question is at the heart of the gender riddle. We might be willing to allow some leeway in behavioral similarities between men and women. We might even be willing to admit that independence is just as possible for a female as a male, and that nurturance is just as possible for a male as a female. Yet we might also believe that men are naturally independent because they have male bodies, whereas women are naturally nurturing because they have female bodies. Therefore we would reason that a woman must learn to be independent and a man must learn to be nurturing; that these traits, while possible for either sex, do not come naturally if we do not have the correct body.

Whether it is an argument about the brain, or hormones, or genes, almost all of the scientific gender research focuses on finding the innate, objective *differences* between the male and female bodies, and then interpreting the meaning of whatever differences appear to have been found. Because the United States government declared the 1990s to be the Decade of the Brain, and also set into motion the Federal Human Genome Project, whose goal it is to map out the estimated 100,000 genes in the human body, tremendous financial resources have been poured into biological gender research. The results of these studies are invariably debated and politicized in arguments about everything from female fighter pilots to paternity leave.

Biological gender studies are being performed inside and outside of academia, and one assumes they must get dramatic results and media attention to continue their funding. The economic realities of our research system explain why the similarities between the sexes are rarely studied. Differences between men and women, not similarities, get attention. Underlying this search for differences is a belief that many scientists bring with them into the laboratory before a single test has been performed: "masculine" and "feminine" behavior in males and females is rooted in biology.

A recent *New York Times* report on the scientific study of carrots offers us some perspective on scientific research in general. Entitled, "Health Factor in Vegetables Still Elusive," Jane E. Brody concluded that scientists cannot agree on whether or not carrots are good for us. If scientists cannot agree on carrots, how can they possibly make definitive statements about the biological causes of behavior, or about the human brain, the most complicated organism on the planet?

In 1973, a study entitled "Blood group genes and Negro-white ability differences" disproved a 1972 hypothesis of William Shockley. Shockley believed that "blood group genes more characteristic of European than African populations would tend to be associated with good performance on cognitive tests within the U.S. Negro population." Although old ideas die hard, and there are some who still search for proof of race-driven genetic superiorities and inferiorities, this type of research has been discredited, and it is doubtful that public funding would any longer support it.

Yet our understanding of gender has not evolved enough for us to question the basis of gender research, in which it is perfectly acceptable to clump human beings into the two colossal categories of male and female and then to make generalizations about all men and all women. Rather than making scientific judgments based on ancestry and the color of skin, we take for granted that we can assign innate attributes based upon primary and secondary sex characteristics. This type of reasoning can lead us to draw false conclusions based upon stereotypes. For example, a girl who excels in math might be suspected of having a "male" brain, whereas a boy who plays with dolls might be suspected of having a "female" brain.

On the surface, biological gender research can be compelling, but as we look more carefully, we find it to be riddled with assumptions that will one day seem as quaint as the belief that the earth was flat.

ARE BOYS AND GIRLS DIFFERENT?

The single most important fact in the biological comparisons of the sexes is that there are greater differences between *men as a group,* and between *women as a group,* than there are between men and women. According to Dr. Anne Fausto-Sterling, a developmental geneticist and professor of medical science at Brown University, and author of the landmark book *Myths of Gender,* many brain studies show no sex differences at all, and the ones that do show differences do so through elaborate manipulation of statistics. For instance, it was widely reported that there was a difference in volume between males and females in INAH-3, a region of the brain within the human hypothalamus. When Fausto-Sterling closely analyzed the data, she found instead that "we are dealing with a region that varies in volume by more than ten-fold *within* each sex." She also noted that there was enormous overlap between men and women.

In terms of brain size, women's brains were believed to be smaller than men's brains, and this was taken as a sign of their inferior intelligence. To answer criticism of the "bigger is better" theory, the researchers divided the brain size by body weight. There was a surprise in store for them, however, when by that method of calculation, women's brains turned out to be proportionately bigger than men's. Because of this, that method of calculation was dropped. Fausto-Sterling also cites a study of four thousand males and females which found that "the average male/ female difference in brain weight for all ages is 9.8 percent." In this case, when height, weight and brain size were factored, "the difference in adults virtually disappeared."

Scientists studying fetal brains (from miscarriages) and newborns (from stillbirths) have not reliably detected any of the supposed sex differences. They are also beginning to report that, when at rest, the brains of men and women are indistinguishable from each other. It is only when the brain is awake and involved with its environment that they find there to be two exceptions: the "ancient and primitive regions . . . involved with action" seem to have more activity in men, and "the newer and more complex" areas "involved in symbolic action" seem to have more activity in women. These two regions exist in both men and women, and so the same potential for use is present.

The connection to social roles is obvious: the male-dominated activity area is action-oriented, the female-dominated area is symbolically oriented. This is the only research in the area of the brain that does not seem to have the high level of overlap between individual women and men (yet there is still overlap). While some might say that this is proof of innate differences in brain function between the sexes, this might also profoundly demonstrate the power of masculine and feminine gender role training.

While men and women do have the same brain capacities, those resources are not necessarily being tapped. Scientists might

190

well be measuring the results of behavior on the brain, not the brain structure dictating behavior. There are many examples of behavior changing the structure of the brain, the simplest being the brain of the alcoholic, which changes in color, flexibility, shape and capacity as drinking escalates. (Notably, it takes about eight years for the brain of the recovering alcoholic to realign its nodes, and so ceasing a behavior can also affect the brain's structure.) A UCLA study by Dr. Lewis Baxter found that behavioral therapy for the treatment of obsessive-compulsive disorders, such as the repeated washing of the hands, produced the same types of changes in the brain that are observed with successful drug therapy. Dr. Lisa F. Berkman of Yale found that, in cardiac patients, emotional support and social ties have a direct effect on the brain that may lower blood pressure and relax the heart.

The problems of categorizing humanity into the two overlapping, enormous clumps of male and female were addressed by Sharon Begley in her 1995 *Newsweek* cover story: "The New Science of the Brain: Why Men and Women Think Differently." The author of an article does not choose the headline, and ironically, although part of Begley's story did report on studies claiming to show differences in men's and women's brains, significant points were also made to the contrary. Begley concluded that the "overlap between men's and women's scores on just about every psychological test is huge. Any randomly chosen woman might do better at a 'male' skill than a man and vice versa." She also cited a Yale study which found that, in one particular experiment, 42 percent of the women's brains "worked like the men's." Ironically, in *Myths of Gender,* Fausto-Sterling cites another *Newsweek* cover story that ran in 1981. Entitled "The Sexes: How They Differ and Why," it concluded, "Perhaps the most arresting implication of the research up to now is not that there are undeniable differences between males and females but that their differences are so small relative to the possibilities open to them." Oftentimes, the headlines we read on the biology of gender lead us to believe that absolute differences between men's and women's brains and bodies have at last been confirmed. Yet, as in the case of these two *Newsweek* cover stories, when we read the article in its entirety, we find that there is powerful evidence to the contrary.

In her 1995 article, Begley tackled one of the biggest media attention-getters in the biology of the sexes: research on the corpus callosum, which connects the left and right brain. This research was performed at UCLA by Laura Allen and Roger Gorski, who claimed that the corpus callosum in women was larger and therefore, they postulated, more complex than men's. Begley observed, "This brought neuroscientists as close as they ever get to jumping up and down in public. It fit their cherished idea that, in male brains, the right and the left side barely know what the other is doing, while in women there's practically nonstop left-right neural chitchat . . . There is just one problem with these tidy explanations. A bigger corpus callosum matters only if it has more neurons, the cells that carry communications. After all, fat phone cables carry more conversations only if they contain more wires. But despite years of searching, scientists cannot say for sure that women's corpus callosum has more neurons."

These types of studies give the impression that all men have one brain structure and all women another, but that is not true. There is a gradation of brain structures in men as there is in women, even in the corpus callosum, and the differences are more significant among men, and among women, than between men and women.

Men's and women's bodies are different because of reproductive design. Differences based on reproductivity, however, do not generalize to the ability to shoot a gun or wash a baby. Primary and secondary sex characteristics, such as body hair, wombs and testes, do not establish spatial or verbal abilities. Yet researchers continue to troll for sex differences and bankable headlines.

Dr. Ruben C. Gur, a neuropsychologist and director of the brain behavior laboratory at the University of Pennsylvania, offered the following anecdote as evidence that women's and men's brains were different in terms of verbal memory: "If you rattle off fifteen items to get at the supermarket, women are more likely to remember the most. That's some of the wifely frustration when the husband comes back and has forgotten some of them. It may be endemic to his sex." No consideration is given to the possibility that the husband might not be accustomed to remembering these items because he is generally not the one who does the grocery shopping. If he had been asked to remember fifteen items he needed at the hardware store in order to finish a carpentry project, I wonder if he would fare any better.

While most of these studies of men and women do not take into account the effect of lifelong gender role training, a 1994 study at Fresno State University in California exploded one of the most popular myths that informs the research assumptions of many neuroscientists. Dr. Matthew Sharps tested the hypothesis that, because of brain structure, men have superior spatial cognition, an ability associated with map reading skills. Spatial cognition refers to the "thought processes regarding location, orientation and manipulation of objects and images in space."

Dr. Sharps redesigned the test that assesses this ability by asking the questions in a neutral manner, or using traditionally female skill areas, such as handicrafts, to frame the questions. He found that: "Where spatial abilities of traditionally male occupation information showed up in the instructions, male performance went up significantly, and female performance either stayed stable or dropped. When no such information was provided—when the subjects had no way of knowing they were doing a 'spatial' or 'male' task—no significant sex difference was observed." Dr. Sharps concluded that if you think you will not be good at something, you probably won't be.

Since sex-typed gender behavior would tend to stimulate one area of the brain more than another, denying the parts of ourselves that don't fit in with the gender myths is literally taking a toll on our neural structure. Through gender independence, there is the amazing possibility that, if our behavior became more flexible in terms of notions of appropriate masculine and feminine roles, we could literally affect the structure of our brains, and even the flow of our hormones, which are tied into behavior and psychological response, not just reproduction.

According to Begley, Melissa Hines, a neuropsychologist at UCLA who has been searching the callosum for sex differences, admitted "That some of the women's brains looked like the men's is true of all these sex studies . . . Girls play with boys' toys more than boys play with girls', for instance. Males for whatever reason are more exclusively channeled into one way of behaving." If playing with "boys' toys" will cause a certain part of a girl's brain, identified by scientists with males, to develop more, then this is evidence of the impact of gender role behavior on the shaping of the human brain.

Sex-typing in children has a profound impact upon the brain, and upon mental functioning. In 1993, Patricia J. Bauer of the Institute of Child Development at the University of Minnesota performed a study on twenty-five-month-old children. During the preliminary test session, both boys and girls played equally with all of the toys (or "props"). Later, the toys were used to model sex-stereotypic activities, like changing a diaper and making breakfast (feminine), shaving a teddy bear and building a house (masculine), and going on a treasure hunt or having a birthday party (neutral). Before any sex-stereotypic sequences were performed, both the boys and girls played equally with all of the toys.

The toys themselves could not be responsible for any differences in toy selection. When the sex-stereotypic sequences were performed, such as changing a diaper and shaving the teddy bear, identical, fifteen-inch, jointed teddy bears were used, as well as identical infant washcloths, differing only in color (one was yellow and one was green). Any differences in behavior between boys and girls would have nothing to do with an attraction to the toys or objects themselves.

Three different play sequences, one feminine, one masculine and one neutral, were enacted. Since twenty-five-month-olds have limited language skills, no verbal instructions were given. Later, when the children were asked to perform the tasks they had watched, the researchers found that the little girls could remember all three sequences with equal skill. Boys, however, remembered male-stereotypic and gender-neutral task sequences more clearly than female-stereotypic task sequences. "Results indicate that, at least for boys, use of gender schemata is evident by 25 months of age." The researchers concluded that toddler boys "are more highly stereotyped than their female peers. Consistent with this suggestion, boys demonstrate same-sex stereotype toy preferences somewhat earlier than girls, and they avoid opposite-sex toys more than do girls . . . Thus, at the time they are beginning to label persons as belonging to one gender group or the other, young boys at least are selectively processing information 'appropriate' for their own gender group." So powerful are the social forces that shape the typical male child, that by the age of twenty-five months, his mental ability to remember a female sex-stereotypic action sequence is impaired.

A 1982 study of third- and fourth-grade children, conducted by Kay Bussey at Stanford and David Perry of Florida Atlantic University, found that "although there is no difference between boys' and girls' acceptance of same-sex behavior, boys tend to reject opposite-sex behavior more than girls." The boys made a conscious decision not to perform what was perceived to be a "girl" behavior, not because they preferred same-sex models, but because they avoided anything that might identify them as engaging in a "girl" activity. In 1994, a *New York Times*/CBS poll found that teenage boys consider themselves superior to girls, and that girls know it. To engage in "girl" activities would taint their maleness and diminish their status. While the girls considered themselves equal to boys, boys believed that even most girls thought boys were "better than themselves." Why would they think otherwise? The boys have been trained this way from day one.

Ironically, journalist Michael D'Antonio, writing for the *Los Angeles Times Magazine* in December of 1994, observed that there was a growing body of scientific research that finds boys, because of their biology, to be more psychologically at risk than girls. In "The Fragile Sex," D'Antonio reported that emotionally disturbed boys outnumber girls four to one, and twice as many boys are diagnosed with learning disabilities, particularly ADD, or Attention Deficit Disorder. Dr. John Ratey, a Harvard psychiatrist, hypothesized that the reason boys are more often diagnosed with these disabilities has to do with the style of learning that has been inculcated in them. Most schools now favor cooperative learning and social skills, but boys' games and models are often hierarchical, with one individual on top and everyone else subservient to the leader. While there are certainly children of both sexes who suffer from hyperactivity and the inability to concentrate, many boys are probably being diagnosed with a neurological disability that is really a learned behavioral disability caused by the masculine sex-typing of boys.

One of the favored treatments for ADD is Ritalin, and D'Antonio reported that this stimulant "may be enough to quiet a boy down and keep him on track in school." He also reported that despite side effects of loss of appetite, sleep disturbances and slowed growth rates when used for an extended period of time, there has been a 300 percent increase in Ritalin production since 1990. Paul McHugh, the chair of the psychiatry department at Johns Hopkins Medical School, has gone on record against the drug: "Ritalin will slow almost any kid down. And a lot of kids who supposedly have neurologically based ADD can't sit still in school but they can watch TV for two hours. That tells me that we're too impressed by our biological discoveries and using them to explain things without taking into account other factors." McHugh sums it up: "How boys are treated has a much greater effect on their behavior than brain structure."

In a review of the literature in 1992, Dr. Barbara Mead of the University of Tennessee noted, a trend from 'hierarchies to networking.' Since boys' play is characterized by hierarchical arrangements, perhaps this aspect of play socialization should no longer be considered advantageous." Crucially, experts predict that a cooperative leadership model (a characteristic of the play of girls) rather than an authoritarian management model (characteristic of the dominance issues and hierarchical system of boys' play) will prevail in the 1990s." If boys are being trained to fulfill the demands of a hierarchical model that society is moving away from, when they become men they will be mystified to find themselves locked out of many positions and opportunities.

The world of sex-based biology is in a state of upheaval. What has been taken as an absolute, and taught in medical schools until very recently, is that all fetuses start out female, and that in order to become a male, the Y chromosome must be added. In 1994, Dr. Giovanna Camerino of the University of Pavia in Italy found new evidence that "suggests that there may be genes for femaleness just as there are genes for maleness." Science writer Natalie Angier reported that "Other scientists welcomed the new research and said they hoped it would help quash the old chestnut that the fetus is inherently female . . . In the new paradigm of sex determination that is emerging, the fetus is roughly female to begin with—just as a child's drawing vaguely resembles the work of Matisse. Whether making it a boy or a girl, the final flourishes demand an artist's touch."

This concept of all fetuses being "female" until the Y chromosome is added to make a male has been presented in psychobiology courses with the implication that the male is a more complex, and therefore more highly developed, life-form than the female. Radical feminists fought back with their own interpretation: the male is a corrupted form of female, they claimed, as evidenced by his inability to bear children! Neither of these interpretations has held up over time. Many "scientific" deductions were made, however, based on the presumption of primitive femaleness and developed maleness, encompassing everything from intelligence to hand-eye coordination.

However, the big bang award for the explosion of gender myths has to go to recent revelations on testosterone. In June of 1995, Natalie Angier reported a biological story for the *New York Times* that did not appear in the science section, but on the front page: testosterone does not cause aggression. The culprit is *too little testosterone*. Angier asked her readers if they were "ready to give the so-called male hormone a break and retire all testosterone cliches with a single pound of Iron John's drum."

It is well known that all women have testosterone as well as estrogen, and all men have estrogen as well as testosterone. There are some men, however, who do not have enough testosterone, and when Dr. Christina Wang of UCLA treated those men with testosterone replacement therapy, they became optimistic and friendly. To think of testosterone as the "friendly" hormone is a far cry from what we have been led to believe over the last half a century since testosterone was first discovered. Now the scientists are hypothesizing that estrogen might be the cause of aggression. Why does it have to be one or the other? Because the bipolar gender system demands it.

In a sense, this is not the first time the estrogen theory has been raised. Premenstrual syndrome (PMS) almost made it into the DSM as a mental disorder of women, instead of a biologic rhythm, when lawyers of women who had killed their husbands, or performed other violently antisocial acts, began to use PMS as a criminal defense like temporary insanity. Connecting a surge in hormones to murderous impulses that leave women irresponsible for their actions would have allowed men to challenge women as not particularly qualified to lead a corporation, or a country. Feminists, in particular, objected vehemently to its inclusion in the DSM, and they won, pointing out that PMS does not even exist in some populations, such as the Japanese, which is thought to be due to their diet.

That the male of a species is always the aggressor is another myth taken for granted by almost everyone, yet Dr. Marcy F. Lawton of the University of Alabama in Huntsville vividly debunked this belief in 1994. She reported that a group of scientists were studying the pinyon jay birds, and they kept trying to determine which of the males was the alpha bird, the one in charge of both the males and females, identifiable by his aggressive behavior. No matter what the scientists did, the male birds were resolutely peaceful and noncompetitive. When they attempted to get the birds to compete with each other for food, the worst thing one male would do to another who got to the food first was "give it a dirty look." When the birds eventually performed "extreme acts of aggression . . . locking talons in combat and stabbing at one another with their beaks; feathers flying while the furiously entangled pairs fell to the ground," the vicious warriors turned out to be the females, not the males. The scientists observed that the aggression was occurring "just as the females were reaching hormonal readiness for breeding." They wrote the behavior off to "pre-breeding syndrome," a form of PMS for hormonally disturbed birds. They then "returned to their search for the elusive alpha male," whom they never found, since it was an *alpha female* who controlled the dominance hierarchy among these jays.

What we believe is what we look for, and what we believe is what we see. Many scientists come to experiments with the aim to prove the differences between the sexes, and so they often see what they expect to see. When they see something unexpected, particularly profound similarities, they question how the experiment was set up, and redesign it to get the expected results, or reinterpret the results so that their theories remain intact. For example, a 1995 ABC news special, *Boys and Girls Are Different,* began with a videotape of an experiment with one-year-old children who were placed behind a mesh gate, their mothers visible to them on the other side. Some of the children rattled the gate to try and get to their mothers, while others sat and cried. A male announcer's voice explained, "Watch these babies try to reach their mothers. The boys get aggressive. The girls cry for help." As a concluding segment for the television show, a camera crew went to the original study site and the researchers re-created the experiment. The results, recorded live by the cameras, were not as expected. *All* of the boys sat and cried, and *all* of the girls aggressively rattled the gate to get to their mothers. On that day, with that particular group, the test results were entirely opposed to the original results, yet it was not then postulated that girls are aggressive, while boys sit and cry. Instead, it was suggested that aggressive girls and crying boys are not representative of the norm.

As with race-based hypotheses obsessed with "white blood genes" in African Americans, when women excel at "male" activities, they are suspected of harboring some secret maleness, and when men excel at "female" activities, their maleness is suspect. This assumption of the biological basis for behavior, and the division of human beings into two discrete camps, is reflected in the research and diagnosis of Gender Identity Disorder in children.

As early as 1968, UCLA's Robert Stoller believed there to be a "basic biological contribution" to gender "deviance" in children. Since that time, gender-nonconforming children have been suspected of harboring a biological drive for their "cross-sex" play behaviors, as evidenced, for example, by "beauty" in boys or "ugliness" in girls. Stoller believed that the physical appearance of these children elicits certain responses from their families, which allows their disorder to flourish.

According to Dr. Susan Coates, almost all those working in the field of GID in children share the conviction that a biological drive will be found. That conviction is based upon the notion that boys and girls are innately different, and that "masculine" or "feminine" behavior is biologically driven. Attempts to create objective tests to diagnose GID in children have been far-ranging yet completely subjective, from the Sex-Typed Animal Preference Test which presumably delineates which animals should stir the affections of boys or girls, to the play behavior ratio method, wherein the child who plays 70 percent of the time with the "wrong" toys is suspected of gender disturbance and referred for further testing. George Rekers, who developed this diagnostic ratio, warns that the 70 percent threshold could produce "false negatives." Therefore, even if the child does *not* play 70 percent of the time with the "wrong" toys, Rekers advises, as if he were conducting an objective blood test, that the child could still be "positive" for Gender Identity Disorder.

One of the riddles of GID in children concerns the fact that for every girl, five boys are referred for treatment. Dr. Coates has asked if that is because society values men over women, "or is it that [girls'] pain is not recognized?" (Girls should count their blessings that they are not as often diagnosed with GID.) Kenneth Zucker and Richard Green have postulated that the reason for the higher referral rate of boys "may be that the true prevalence of psychosexual disorders is greater in males, perhaps owing to a differential biologic vulnerability." They argue that the development of a male fetus is more " 'complex' and thus more susceptible to errors that may affect postnatal psychosexual genesis." Dr. Giovanna Camerino's new evidence of a gene for femaleness clearly challenges the belief that the development of a male fetus is more "complex." GID boys cannot be explained as mutations, or undeveloped creatures biologically in between male and female, any more than GID girls can be shown as biologically partly male. If a child is intersexed, and literally has a combination of male and female physical sex characteristics, that child cannot even be diagnosed with GID, according to the DSM-IV. Regardless, no boy in any of the UCLA or Clarke Institute studies had biological female sex characteristics.

Why, then, are more boys referred for GID, and why do they hold on to their "Feminine" play patterns, despite intense adverse reactions from both peers and adults? It could simply be that, although they are engaging in stereotypically feminine behaviors, they have nevertheless been raised as boys, and taught to hold their ground. The therapy itself of the GID boy tries to toughen him up, make him more assertive, or more "playful" with gender (i.e., more masculine). This can have the effect of sending his behavior "underground," yet paradoxically, it could also teach him to assert his right to his preferred, "feminine" activities, with even more determination. Why, then, do most girls "grow out of" their "tomboy phase"? Probably because, although they are engaged in "masculine" activities, they were nevertheless raised as girls, and girls are taught to compromise, acquiesce, and nurture others. Their "therapy" would feature this type of gender training.

The continuing search for the biologic drive to GID resembles the search for the nonexistent alpha male of the pinyon jays. Dr. Coates now contends that boys with GID are temperamentally oversensitive and hyperreceptive to external stimulation. "A mother may report, for example, that her child will spontaneously remark on good odors, such as cookies baking in the oven, but that he will gag when a garbage truck passes. Similarly, these boys are frequently drawn to bright vivid colors but will sometimes have strong aversions to dark colors to the point where, for example, some will refuse to wear black. Another child will be described as enjoying music and will demonstrate musical talent but will also cry at unexpected loud sounds . . . Many boys with GID refuse to wear a new shirt unless the tag is cut out, but by the same token they will derive obvious enjoyment from the feeling of soft textures next to their skin."

Does this mean that these boys are more like girls, or that "normal" boys do not notice the smell of baking cookies, enjoy the smell of garbage, hate bright colors, wear only black, exhibit tone deafness, and have thick, insensitive skin? Dr. David Schwartz has challenged these contentions. A psychoanalyst in private practice, and a board member of the journal *Gender and Psychoanalysis,* Schwartz has worked in a range of clinical settings, from outpatient clinics to intensive psychiatric care units. He was also a research associate at the New York State Psychiatric Institute, where he investigated aspects of depression and borderline syndromes. Schwartz believes that Coates focuses on the biologic theory of GID as a way of helping parents cope with their nonconforming child. In other words, a biologic source tells the parents that they are not to blame for their child's behavior—Nature is.

"Coates says that 'boys with GID are more like girls in that they typically avoid rough-and-tumble play,' " said Schwartz, and that " 'the aversion to rough-and-tumble play likely reflects a hormonal influence operative in prenatal development, though such a hormonal influence has not been documented to date.' " This statement is very powerful, and very convincing to the average parent, yet there is absolutely no evidence that the gender play of these boys is in any way influenced by hormones. Coates herself has noted that "there is a much smaller difference between boys and girls in rough-and-tumble play prior to the achievement of gender categorization as compared to afterward."

The hormone argument of GID specialists always cites the observation that girls with CAH (Congenital Adrenal Hyperplasia) are believed to play more often with "boy" toys (although not to the exclusion of "girl" toys). Yet they ignore the fact that these little girls are born with "masculinized" genitals that are, to varying degrees, "virilized." The clitoris can be as enlarged as a penis, and there can even be enlargement that gives the appearance of a scrotum. The most developed CAH child will have "a fully formed penis and an empty scrotum." The parents are certainly aware of their child's "maleness," and they generally approve surgery on their children in order to make them appear more girllike. They are also aware that, as their child reaches puberty, they will have to be on hormones for the rest of their lives to prevent the appearance of secondary male characteristics like body hair or a deepened voice. This greatly affects the manner in which they interact with their child.

And what of the children themselves? In a 1994 study of thirty CAH children, "twenty-one had corrective surgery up to age three years and one at age nine years." These children were well aware that there was something penislike between their legs, and as Kessler and her colleagues demonstrated with the overlay study, in our society, the penis is the most powerful of gender cues, overriding all others. That these girls play with "boy" toys is no surprise, and to use them as the basis of a scientific argument on the biological naturalness of male and female sex roles does these children, and their families, a disservice.

Coates also proposes that GID boys have a "constitutional" and "genetic predisposition" toward the disorder, and are in particular more prone toward SAD (Separation Anxiety Disorder). She proposes that SAD is the underlying cause of femininity in a boy. This type of reasoning could result in eliminating GID of childhood as a primary diagnosis and inserting gender-noncon- forming behavior in the DSM as a manifestation of separation anxiety. But if we tried to apply this diagnosis to girls, would their basketball playing then be considered symptomatic of paternal separation anxiety?

That children are taken to a clinic for treatment of a gender- based mental disorder is probably, in and of itself, a source of panic and contention within their families. The stress on the fami- lies could produce anxiety symptoms in the child, and so it seems unfair to assume that separation anxiety is caused by the child's body, and not the child's situation. In any event, many of the boys are described as separating easily from their mothers, and do not exhibit "a shy, inhibited temperament." Fred, a five-year-old treated at the Yale Child Study Center who was reported to have "strikingly long" eyelashes and skin "like porcelain" was also de- scribed as "articulate and cooperative." Further, Fred "readily separated from his parents and eagerly explored the playroom." Stanley, our three-year-old who went through five years of psy- choanalysis, was certainly not shy about his opinions, referring to his analyst as "ugly" for almost a year, telling him to "shut up" and locking him in a closet. Five-year-old Carlos, who was partial to the Flying Nun, went so far as to take over his analyst's chair, put his feet up on her desk and give her a lecture on the illusion of appearances. That any of these children could be so demon- strative, yet have a biologic, genetic condition that triggers severe separation anxiety and then produces "effeminate" behavior, makes no sense.

The only striking "contributing factor" displayed by both boys and girls diagnosed with GID concerns hand-eye coordina- tion, but this has nothing to do with hormonal "imbalances," or inspiring little boys to mimic adult women or little girls to mimic adult men. It has everything to do with these boys not being talented, and the girls excelling, at "masculine" athletics. As the girls, in particular, practice their athletic skills, their "gender deviance" becomes more pronounced. (In the 1970s, parents were advised by some doctors that girls were at risk for developing Gender Identity Disorder if they participated in competitive athletics.)

Sports scientists have discovered that the most important factor in the development of gross motor skills is *practice*. As the GID-diagnosed girl persists in playing sports, her abilities naturally and rapidly develop, just as any child's would, but she is described in the psychiatric literature as having "unusual physical skills" in athletics. To this end, Rekers explains that the diagnosis of GID can be "assessed" by comparing the child with his same-sex, same-aged peers "in such skills as distance in throwing the football, distance in socking a playground ball, distance and accuracy in kicking a kickball, percentages of baskets made from the free throw line, and accuracy and distance in throwing a softball." I would hate to think that a child's diagnosis of mental health would depend on basketball shots made, or not made, from the free throw line.

Coates' hypothesis of underlying hormonal and genetic factors in nonconforming behavior can sound scientific and impressively objective, but when carefully examined, her theory makes as much sense as Rekers' basketball shots, or 70/30 gender play diagnostics. Dr. David Schwartz asks, "Isn't it time to admit that the search for biological determinants of gender has met with failure?" and he joins those who are calling for a moratorium on gender science.

The general reproductive differences in the bodies of girls and boys have not been shown to cause "masculine" and "feminine" behaviors, although the behaviors that girls and boys are encouraged to perform can make parts of their brains more responsive, or cause their motor skills, both fine and gross, to develop along different paths. As girls have been encouraged to perform athletically, however, the level of women's team sports on college playing fields has risen dramatically. For example, as women gain access to quality training, the gaps between male and female runners have narrowed significantly. "In 1934 . . . the women's time for the 100-meter run was 13.5 percent lower than the men's, but by 1974 the difference had decreased to 9.1 percent." In 1992, both *Nature* magazine and the *New York Times* reported that, by the year 2050, it is possible "that sex differences in all running events [will] disappear."

That proper training makes all the difference was again dramatically demonstrated in a 1996 "strength study" by the Army Research Institute of Environmental Medicine. At the beginning of training, "women could lift a 40-pound box to a height of 52 inches 106 times in 10 minutes. Six months later, they could lift the box an average of 140 times." Before the study, "women could average 16 squats using 100-pound barbells. At the end of the study, the average number of repetitions was 62." The most startling improvement was in backpacking, where women's speed increased to "4.4 miles per hour, a 33 percent improvement."

Shifts in the performance of boys have also been evolving. As boys have been encouraged to verbally communicate, verbal skill differences between the sexes have been fading. Experts predict that as girls begin to take the same number of math classes as boys, the mathematical skill differences between the sexes will also fade. Eventually, no longer will girls and boys be thought of as more naturally right- or left-brained.

Dr. Roger Sperry, a well-known neurobiologist, has said, "The more we learn, the more we recognize the unique complexity of any one individual intellect and the stronger the conclusion becomes that the individuality inherent in our brain networks makes that of fingerprints or facial features gross and simple by comparison." Rather than conceptualizing the brain as a hardwired, printed circuit board, Fausto-Sterling and others like her encourage us to understand that the brain, in constant, complicated interaction with its environment, is creating a unique network in each individual. As Fausto-Sterling eloquently writes, "[The brain] resembles more the weaving of an untutored artisan who, starting out with a general plan in mind, modifies it in the course of his or her work, using the available materials and dyes, while covering up or making creative use of mistakes in pattern."

The variations in the bodies and brains *among children* are complex, and a tribute to the biodiversity of nature. While boys and girls are not different based upon the fact that they are boys and girls, it should not be argued that children are all "the same." No two boys, and no two girls, no boy and girl, are exactly alike. They each have gifts and abilities that develop from their uniqueness, and they deserve the space and time to explore and transform, regardless of being born male or female.

SEXUALITY

Heterosexuality and homosexuality are complicated phenomena, and no gene has been found for either behavior. Just as in the studies of the brains of men and women, the overlap between the brains of straights and gays is greater than any perceived differences. Again, as with the studies of men's and women's brains, the headlines tell us one thing, while the articles or studies themselves tell us another. Recently, Dr. Sandra Witelson of McMaster University in Hamilton, Ontario, reported that the isthmus (a passageway between the left and right sides of the brain) was bigger in gay men than in heterosexual men. The local headline read: BRAIN STRUCTURE MAY BE GAY CLUE. Yet, in the final paragraph of the newspaper story, Witelson herself noted that "some of the gay men had a thinner isthmus than some of the heterosexual men, so an individual's isthmus size cannot reveal his sexual orientation." Dr. Paul Billings, an internist and human geneticist in Palo Alto, California, has dubbed reports of a gay gene as "a new fish story," recalling that in the 1920s, thalassophilia (a love of the sea) was reported by an eminent American geneticist to be an inherited trait on the X chromosome. In retrospect, this story seems quaint, almost charming in its naïveté. Yet the power of genetic reductionism that Billings saw reflected in the public's willingness to believe such a "fish story" is anything but benign, and could unwittingly have profound social consequences, hearkening back to the eugenics theories of early social engineers.

From body type and cosmetic appearance, to affectional relationships in childhood and the roles of the masculine and feminine mystiques, there is no one path to form anyone's sexuality. A certain combination of natal traits in one social setting may lead to completely different learning experiences in another, and to the development of very different sexual responses. In any event, not all homosexuals feel, think or even make love in the same way, any more than there is a cookie-cutter mold for thought processes or lovemaking among heterosexuals. While research into the causes of heterosexuality is low-key, tremendous interest and public funding are poured into the search for the homosexual brain.

One of the most high-profile individuals working in this field of neurobiology is research anatomist Laura Allen, who works with Roger Gorski at the University of California at Los Angeles. The laboratory is located in a monolithic structure with a brick facade, and the hallways are so complex that, upon entering the building, maps are given out at the information desk. The building's interior feels reminiscent of the mazes negotiated by the little rats, filled with hormones and cheese, that are used to theorize about human behavior. The door to the Department of Neuroendocrinology has been redecorated by the staff with a movie poster of Arnold Schwarzenegger as Terminator II. A pumped-up *"Hasta la vista,* baby" Arnold now sports the words "Department of Neuroendocrinology" over his motorcycle handlebars.

Dr. Laura Allen grew up in the Mojave Desert, where her parents taught high school. She spent the first eighteen years of her life there, and then went directly to UCLA, where she has been ever since. She lives in a suburb of Los Angeles with her husband and two children. Dr. Allen is conventionally feminine in her presentation. Her voice is quiet, almost inaudible, not a whisper, but close. You feel that she is telling you a secret when she speaks. Much of her work has focused on finding sex differences between men and women in the corpus callosum, which links the right and left parts of the brain. She personally believes that the female of the sex is harder to understand for evolutionary reasons, because female brains were designed to consider more factors involved with childbirth. She also believes that "men do not like smart women," and that "they in fact resent them"; and that "men and women still want the same things from each other. Women want money, and men want youth and beauty."

In her search to find the differences between the brains of men and women, much of her time has been spent dissecting rats. For the past fifteen years, the Gorski laboratory, where Allen is a senior researcher, has been studying the "preoptic nucleus" in rats, because they found that the male's is larger than the female's. Gorski himself has said that they still do not know what the function of a rat's preoptic nucleus is, but they continue to pursue the study, speculating that it has something to do with sexual behavior, perhaps because of the size difference. The peculiar thing about this interest in the preoptic nucleus of the rat, whose function is still unknown, is that according to Gorski, there is "nothing like it . . . in humans." (Studying human behavior based upon rat behavior has always been a source of controversy, because unlike rats, one of the most profound developmental drives in human beings is language.)

Dr. Allen has expanded her interest from the study of differences between the sexes to the dissection of the brains of gay men, straight women and straight men. She believes that the anterior commissure, which also connects the right and left sides of the brain (or perhaps keeps them separated), has a more complicated fiber tract in women. This finding complements her belief that women's brains are designed to consider more factors than men's brains. She also believes that gay men and straight women have larger anterior commissures than straight men, and therefore that gay men's brains are more femalelike.

As a student, Dr. Allen became interested in how the brain is connected to sexual orientation when Roger Gorski showed her a picture of rats that had been injected with hormones. "They were behaving in reverse," she said. "The female rat, given testosterone early in life, was exhibiting mounting behavior, and the castrated male rat was exhibiting lordosis." Lordosis, in rats, is when the female flexes her back in a U-shape, "presenting" herself to the male for penetration. "And I thought," said Dr. Allen, "what about homosexuals? Is there a correlation between brain structure and homosexuality?"

Lesbians have *never* been shown to have increased testosterone, nor gay men increased estrogen. Lesbians and gay men have, in fact, typical female and male hormonal distributions. Needless to say, gay men are rarely, if ever, castrated. Comparing the lesbian and gay population to testosterone-injected female rats and castrated male rats seems problematic, at the very least, and demonstrates a profound confusion on the part of Dr. Allen and her colleagues as to what it means to be lesbian or gay.

I asked Dr. Allen where her interest in sexual orientation came from, and she said she had never talked to anyone about their sexual orientation, and had never known anyone who was homosexual. This, she believes, is why she is "really an objective scientist" in terms of studying sexual orientation. I doubt Margaret Mead would agree that knowing nothing about a population aids in studying their genesis and culture.

In terms of the "lesbian" rats who mount other rats when exposed to large, perhaps toxic quantities of hormones, and the castrated rats who allow themselves to be mounted, Dr. William Byne and Dr. Bruce Parsons of Columbia University had this to say: "If we apply such reasoning to our own species, then we would be forced to conclude that there is only one homosexual when two individuals of the same sex are engaged in sexual intercourse, and that the homosexual is obvious from the position he or she assumes. Thus, in these rodent models, 'homosexuality' is defined by the particular behavior displayed and not the sex of the partner, whereas in humans, sexual orientation is defined on the basis of sexual fantasies and the sex of the preferred sex partner." Byne's and Parsons' point is crucial. So often when mounting behavior is discussed in animals, the homosexual behavior is only ascribed to the animal who is not acting in accordance with the bipolar gender role expectations of the researchers. What about the female recipient of the sexual attentions of the mounting female? What about the aggressive attentions of the male mounting the male?

I asked Dr. Allen if she plans to examine "lesbian brains," and she explained that "lesbian brains" are very difficult to get, as there is often nothing in the medical records indicating a woman's lesbianism. Dr. Allen does, however, have a hypothesis as to what a "lesbian brain" might look like: "More malelike in structure if the hormonal hypothesis holds up. I would suspect this just based on pure science . . . Based upon an endocrine hypothesis, it would be more like the male brain." This hunch is contrary to the 1979 review of psychoendocrine data on lesbians compiled by Dr. Meyer-Bahlburg at Columbia, which clearly concluded that prenatal or postpubertal hormone levels do not determine the development of sexual orientation. Byne and Parsons, in fact, cite a later 1984 Meyer-Bahlburg review of the literature, in which three studies suggested lower testosterone levels in male homosexuals, twenty studies found no differences and two studies reported that the male homosexuals had *higher* testosterone levels.

When I pressed Dr. Allen on these issues, she did admit that "somebody has been doing cognitive studies, and they find that lesbians have even more feminine patterns of cognitive skills in some cases. I think actually two different groups have been finding that, and they don't know what to make of this, which is interesting." In the sex-typed view of the world, feminine lesbians make no sense, as if lesbians were somehow faux men. Lesbians were raised as girls, and many are highly woman-identified. That lesbians test high in "feminine patterns" of cognition should not be surprising. Only with bipolar gender role expectations is one caught off guard, not knowing "what to make of" it.

In terms of homosexuality, Dr. Allen explained, "I just don't see any evolutionary purpose to homosexuality. It has nothing to do with making more people." I explained to her that gay men and lesbians have been contributing to the gene pool since time immemorial. There are no differences between the reproductive systems of homosexuals and heterosexuals, and therefore homosexuality and reproductivity are not mutually exclusive. Historically, most lesbians and gays married heterosexually and had children. In postmodern society, the trend is toward insemination, surrogate mothers and arranged parenting situations. In terms of making more people, that might not be such an important evolutionary factor at this point in time for the human species. She listened thoughtfully, and then remarked, because I am lesbian, "I guess you don't like being thought of as a mutation."

Dr. Allen remains convinced of her pure scientific objectivity because she does not have a visceral repugnance or hatred toward gay people. "I think I analyze the world a little differently," Dr. Allen said. "I'm left-handed and they say people who are left-handed are less homophobic. That's kind of an anecdote. Bill Clinton is left-handed, and he's doing a lot for gay people." I mentioned that Ronald Reagan, George Bush and Gerald Ford are all left-handed.

"Ronald Reagan is left-handed?" Dr. Allen was amazed. "It's just a very loose anecdote," she said. "And of course, a lot of gays and lesbians are left-handed. A higher percentage are, which is interesting." The idea that a left-handed person has a higher chance of being gay has been studied by several individuals, and a summation of the studies, and a further study, was conducted at the Clarke Institute, which found there to be "absolutely no evidence to support the hypothesis." Further, although there are studies showing more gays to be left-handed, "there were many no affect studies" which showed gays to be left-handed at the same rate as straights.

When individuals begin to study gay issues, they are often suspected of being gay, and so I asked Dr. Allen if anyone had ever inquired if she were lesbian. "Nobody has ever asked me that, but I did get a call from a congressperson the other day, and he said, 'We were at a party the other day, and a woman at the party said that everybody doing this work is homosexual.' And I laughed, and I never say this . . . my husband was there, my kids were screaming . . . 'Well, I'm not.' He said, 'Well, I could tell by your voice.' And I said, 'Well, you can't always tell by people's voices.' " The conventional wisdom is that a homosexual scientist must have a political agenda, and that agenda affects his or her objectivity. In terms of homosexuality studies, the only individuals considered objective are heterosexuals or homosexuals who agree with the results of their heterosexual colleagues. This is unfortunate, but it is something faced by African American researchers disputing race-based intelligence theories, and female researchers disputing sex-based theories of inferiority in females.

UCLA is only one of many laboratories involved in the publicly funded search for the gay body, and in 1993, Byne and Parsons decided to perform a thorough examination of the biologic theories which focus on homosexuality. In terms of the anterior commissure (AC) study by Allen and Gorski that found there to be larger ACs in women and gay men than in straight men, Byne revealed, "This study requires replication as the only other laboratory to examine the AC for sex differences found a tendency for it to be larger in men than in women . . . Even if the recent study by Allen and Gorski proves replicable, the size of the AC alone would tell us nothing about an individual's sexual orientation because the overlap of AC size between homosexual and heterosexual men was tremendous (i.e., the size of the AC of 27 of 30 homosexual men fell within the range established by 30 heterosexual men)." Significantly, the brains of the gay men which Allen and Gorski dissected belonged to men who died of AIDS. The medical treatment they received, and the nature of the disease itself, caused 90 percent of their brains to show significant atrophy, according to Dr. Allen. Obviously, this would affect their size.

If homosexuality were genetic, then it stands to reason that the genes would be passed on, and that the children of gays would have a higher incidence of homosexuality. This is clearly not the case. In 1995, researchers from Northwestern University reported on the sons of gay men who had reached at least seventeen years of age. They found that more than 90 percent of the sons whose sexual orientations could be rated were heterosexual. The study was intended to prove that "any environmental influence of gay fathers on their sons' sexual orientation is not large." Studies on the children of lesbians have yielded similar results. How could there be 100 percent gay fathers and only 10 percent gay sons, and a similar result constantly appearing for lesbian mothers and their children, if homosexuality were genetically based? Shouldn't the percentages be significantly higher?

The results of a "gay gene" study conducted by Dean Hamer at the National Cancer Institute came under scrutiny in July of 1995. Hamer's 1993 report found gay brothers to share a piece of genetic information at the tip of the X chromosome. Many gay human rights activists greeted this information with open arms, believing that if homosexuality could be proven a biological condition, equal rights would have to be extended to gays. Hamer's work has been questioned, however, since a former collaborator claims that Hamer failed to include information in his study that would have weakened his results. Efforts to replicate Hamer's study have failed. Hamer, himself, has never claimed to have found a "gay gene." That is a label the media have applied to his work. "Genes play a role," said Hamer, "and there's probably more than one of them—and other factors as well."

Those other factors might well include genetic information that sets up motor functions like hand-eye coordination. If so many boys with poor hand-eye coordination are perceived and treated as if they are gay, or "feminine," and then do indeed become gay, they might all be found to have a "gay gene" that is actually a marker for motor skills and has no direct correlation whatsoever with sexuality. The same consideration of the hypothalamus studies should be made. The hypothalamus in gay men and straight women has been viewed as smaller than the hypothalamus in straight men. The hypothalamus is also the body's thermostat, which sends signals throughout the body to alter its blood flow so that body heat will be safely regulated. We know that "pretty," smaller boys are often trained that they are "feminine" and "prehomosexual." If there were a difference in the size of the hypothalamus in many gay men, might it be because the hypothalamus is the appropriate size for regulating heat in a smaller body? Overall muscle mass, height, weight and bone structure of the gay men in the hypothalamus studies were not considered.

In terms of genetics, it has been shown that different genes can trigger the same diseases in different ethnic groups. In 1995, Dr. Theodore Kurtz, of the University of California in San Francisco, found that a common genetic marker associated with high blood pressure in African Americans had no such association in Mexican Americans or Caucasians. The gene that seems to be a genetic marker for high blood pressure in Mexican Americans and Caucasians has no such connection for African Americans.

The exact location of a gene on the chromosome is known for very few genes, and the complete contents of that gene, which is known as the DNA sequence, is known for even fewer. The aim of the Federal Human Genome Project is to catalog the estimated 100,000 genes that have been evolving since life began about three billion years ago. Yet to simply label gene number one as having a particular function is simplistic and, ultimately, dangerous. All 100,000 genes, and each gene's DNA sequence, could be arranged in a mind-boggling number of combinations. Further, "estimates suggest that there is enough DNA in each of our cells to contain information for from ten thousand to fifty thousand different proteins." If we then consider the likelihood that the interaction of the genes in particular sequences could alter the meaning of their codes, then the idea of a hard-wired "gene map" seems particularly primitive.

To look at one isolated gene and believe it to be a cause of homosexuality sets up grave dangers in reasoning, not only in the public's mind, but in the minds of scientists. In one particular study, gay men who had a genetic marker thought to be linked to homosexuality had heterosexual brothers with the same genetic marker. This would seem to prove that the genetic marker the scientists were looking at is not connected to sexuality. Dr. Allen, however, told me that the heterosexual men who had the same genetic marker as their gay brothers might not really be straight. Rather, they might be "lying" about their homosexuality. This is hardly objective science.

Many gay human rights activists have embraced the idea of biological homosexuality as a means of attaining human rights, but this is a tragic miscalculation. Right-wing politicians, frightened that the biological argument will indeed make gay rights more easily attainable, are now referring to homosexuality as an unfortunate "handicap" comparable to alcoholism. Lesbian and gay people will not earn a place at the table on the basis of biological homosexuality. No one is invited to sit down and make decisions that affect society as a whole when they are actively alcoholic, and certainly no one will be welcomed if they are a "mutation."

Most important, that a child might be found to have a certain gene at birth should not be an indication to us that he or she will grow up straight or gay, any more than a child's play behavior is a beacon of future sexuality. Although all recent studies have shown that "homosexual men and women have typical gender identity," the issue of recalled childhood play preferences remains a hot one. Studies claim that gay men remember playing with dolls and lesbians remember playing with trucks. To understand this phenomenon, we must look at the nature of memory, which was eloquently addressed by Dr. Robyn M. Dawes in his book *House of Cards: Psychology and Psychotherapy Built on Myth.* "Memory is basically a *reconstructive* process," he wrote, "as we demonstrated in laboratory experiments as far back as 1930 by Sir Frederick Bartlett. We attempt to 'make sense' out of our recall of bits and pieces of our past . . . in terms of what we 'know' to be true of the world today, by 'filling in the gaps.' Moreover, the general ideas that we evolve after filling in some gaps will influence our search for the other traces that we end up recalling."

This process is called *hindsight bias,* in which we not only conclude that we "knew it all along," but are unable to recall what we actually believed before an outcome was known. From Dawes' research, it would follow that the family of a homosexual would delve into the past to look for signs that would explain the present. The signs that would be searched for would be stereotypic feminine behavior in men and stereotypic masculine behavior in women, and those signs would take precedence over all other behaviors, even if other behaviors were more prevalent.

For example, because of the reaction of astonished relatives to what Santa had delivered to a little boy, a gay friend clearly remembers getting an Easy-Bake Oven for Christmas. Yet, that same Christmas, he also received a Rock 'Em Sock 'Em boxing toy, which he remembers "only because I tripped on it and broke it Christmas night." His other early childhood behaviors, of which he could have little or no memory, might well have been of the male gender-typical variety, but they would not take on the same importance of any gender-atypical behavior. Because of this, making sense of the present by reconstructing the past blurs cause and effect, so that knowledge could as easily come from our stereotypic misconceptions as from true insight.

I had a personal experience of this when I visited the Barbie Hall of Fame in Palo Alto, California. For twenty-five years, I recollected with great clarity having had no interest whatsoever in Barbie, and immediately giving my Christmas Barbies to my twin sister. Loving Barbie did not fit into my self-perception as an independent, feminist woman who rejected objectification by men.

Upon entering the Barbie Hall of Fame, I saw a wall display of neatly boxed Barbie outfits, and began to have a memory. I asked Evelyn Burkhalter, the Hall of Fame's owner, if Barbie had ever had a gold suit, and she showed me a gold brocade cocktail outfit: a shimmering, sophisticated number with a short skirt and

smart jacket. I had an instantaneous, vivid mental image, as well
as tactile memory, of playing with Barbie at eight or nine years
old, and specifically of that gold brocade suit: putting it on her,
carefully adjusting the skirt and fixing her hair for an exciting
evening on the town. The truth was, I loved Barbie.

My own epiphany of sorts in the Barbie Hall of Fame forever
humbled me to the selective powers of memory. As the developmentalist George Vaillant has framed it: Once a caterpillar becomes a butterfly, it does not remember being a caterpillar; it
remembers being a little butterfly.

The prolific British novelist Fay Weldon, whose favorite topic is
love and obsession between men and women, came through town
on her latest book tour, and I asked her if she thought there was
any biological basis to male and female gender behavior. She
paused, and then said that courtship seems to bring the high heels
out in a woman, but that she'd best not expect to be wearing
them when the relationship got under way. I would add that there
is, to date, no word on a gene for high heels.

Looking at one gene, or one part of the brain, can never tell
us much about a human being. No one comes into the world as a
prepackaged frozen dinner to be popped into the microwave. The
brain is phenomenally complex. By adulthood, it is "crisscrossed
with more than 100 billion neurons . . ." and "all told the brain
has more than 100 trillion connections." Oliver Sacks explained it
best when he wrote of the hundreds of tiny, minutely differentiated areas in the brain, each area holding, transmitting, exchang-
ing and vibrating with simultaneous critical information. "The
miracle," he wrote, "is how they all cooperate, are integrated
together, in the creation of a self." This, he says, is the ultimate
question in neuroscience, "and it cannot be answered, even in
principle, without a global theory of brain function, one capable
of showing the interactions of every level, from the micropatterns
of individual neuronal responses to the grand macropatterns of an
actual lived life."

218

Dr. Sacks is not a brain mechanic, but a true physician. He sees the integrity of the whole system, and approaches the human being with a spiritual reverence, a reverence which should serve as a model for all neuroscientists. There are certainly genetic rules that guide our learning, but experience, in all its quantum variations, is the hand that molds the clay.

ALL GIRL, ALL BOY?

Nature has an amazing biodiversity. In 1994, the male Dayak fruit bat, captured in a Malaysian game reserve, was found to have milk-producing breasts. Perfectly normal male domesticated goats, "with normal testes and the proven ability to inseminate females, surprise their owners by spontaneously growing udders and secreting milk." No one would think to surgically remove the breasts of the male Dayak fruit bat or the udders of the male goat so that the other bats and goats could relate to them more easily. Yet if a human being is born whose body does not fit into the strict categories of male and female, pediatric cosmetic plastic surgery is usually performed without hesitation, whether or not it is medically necessary.

Our understanding of gender rests on the solid assumption that there are two sexes, male and female, and that these are the only two types of human bodies walking the earth. In 1993, Dr. Anne Fausto-Sterling exploded that myth in her article "The Five Sexes: Why Male and Female Are Not Enough," which appeared in *The Sciences* and was reprinted in modified form on the Op-Ed page of the *New York Times* as "How Many Sexes Are There?" Her research has prompted huge response—both validating and derisive—as the scientific community grapples with its own denial and paradigms. There were those who went so far as to declare Fausto-Sterling "deranged," a word once used to describe the doctor who suggested surgeons wash their hands before operating, that patients might not so easily die of infection.

Rather than exhibiting derangement, Fausto-Sterling was simply viewing, from a new angle, what is known in the medical literature as "intersex." "Biologically speaking," she wrote, "there are many gradations running from female to male; and depending on how one calls the shots, one can argue that along that spectrum lie at least five sexes—and perhaps even more . . . The standard medical literature uses the term 'intersex' as a catch-all for three major subgroups with some mixture of male and female characteristics: the so-called true hermaphrodites, whom I call herms, who possess one testis and one ovary (the sperm- and egg-producing vessels, or gonads); the male pseudohermaphrodites (the 'merms'), who have testes and some aspects of the female genitalia but no ovaries; and the female pseudohermaphrodites (the 'ferms'), who have ovaries and some aspects of the male genitalia but lack testes. Each of these categories is in itself complex; the percentage of male and female characteristics can vary enormously among members of the same subgroup." The number five, however, has been following Fausto-Sterling from place to place, and at a 1995 conference in New York, she began by setting the record straight: five was an arbitrary number; the actual diversity is far greater.

What seemed so preposterously radical to many in the medical community was Fausto-Sterling's proposition that, rather than being "experiments of nature," a polite term for freaks, these individuals are members of sexes just as viable as male and female, and that they have been made invisible by the medical procedures performed upon their bodies as infants since the 1960s onward. Although some children require surgery for life-threatening conditions, the rationale for most of the surgery is that it will help the child and the child's family avoid stigmatization, and assist assimilation into the two-sex world. Fausto-Sterling challenged this long-held belief: "Modern investigators tend to overlook a substantial body of case histories, most of them compiled between 1930 and 1960, before surgical intervention became rampant. Almost without exception, those reports describe children who grew up knowing they were intersexual (though they did not advertise it) and adjusted to their unusual status . . . there is not a psychotic or a suicide in the lot." Fausto-Sterling went on to suggest that, except in terms of life-threatening conditions, surgical intervention after birth was simply preventing the natural, and real, human physical diversity to become visible.

The hermaphrodite, today, is treated at birth as a "social emergency." Bo Laurent, a Ph.D. candidate at the Institute for the Advanced Study of Human Sexuality and an intersexuality specialist, explained that the binary sex system assumes concordance between the sex chromosomes, gonads, genitals, secondary sex characteristics, gender identity and role. Hermaphroditic children, however, do not fit into the system for two reasons: either their genes, gonads or genitals don't "match," or the child has ambiguous genitals in which the clitoris is "too big" or the penis is "too small" or the "wrong shape." Physicians assert that intersex is a very rare condition, but as a result of her research, Laurent estimates that the frequency of intersex births for every 1,000 live births is 1.7. "That's over four hundred thousand in the United States. Everyone knows someone, but no one is talking," she said.

In working with members of the intersex population, Laurent has become convinced that after years of medical management, beginning in the 1960s, some important changes are needed. After declaring the child's birth a social emergency, the doctors are taught that their primary duty is to assure the parents that the child is "really" male or female, and that they will uncover the "true" sex of the child. The sex chosen by the doctors is enforced by radical plastic surgery. The child is then presented to the parents as strictly "girl" or "boy," and they are assured that the child will be heterosexual, a primary concern.

The criteria for sex assignment indicates that penile length outweighs all other factors. The male must be able to stand to pee, and should be able to penetrate females. The females must not have a phallus, should be fertile and should be penetrated by males. Based on these criteria, 90 percent of the children are assigned female. According to Laurent, they are given clitorectomy (more politely, clitoroplasty) and vaginal construction or expansion, since some of them do not have vaginas. Ten percent are assigned male, and receive plastic surgery of the penis.

The problems with these surgeries are legion. In the child assigned as male, when there is a micropenis, the child sits to pee because the urethra's opening is often located very high up, beneath the penis, rather than at the tip. To make it possible for the child to stand to pee, an artificial urethra is extended through his penis so that the urine will come out of the tip. This surgery is one of the easiest to become infected. Included with this type of reconstructive surgery is the attempt to lengthen the penis through extensive skin grafts. Laurent acknowledges that some intersex children have birth conditions that could lead to urinary infections or painful nocturnal erections, and she believes surgery is justified in those cases. Medical intervention such as cortisone treatments for electrolyte imbalances is also critical. The fact remains, however, that the majority of surgeries performed on these children are strictly cosmetic.

One individual known to Laurent had twenty-two surgeries to make his body conform to male, one or more every year of his life. His genitals are so scarred that his penis feels, to him, like a piece of wood. What is terribly sad about this "standing to pee" issue is that there is usually nothing life-threatening about sitting to pee. It is, however, the "wrong" position for a boy. This behavior is considered so socially devastating that babies and toddlers are given painful, invasive surgery in an attempt to prevent it.

In the child assigned female, much of the genitals is removed, and when they mature, they experience little, if any, sexual sensation. Detecting arousal in one's own body can also be extremely difficult. Laurent showed me a 1992 photograph of such a child, just after surgery. The scarring looks like raw railroad tracks up the center of the tiny abdomen and chest, curling around the hips, dipping toward the groin. Laurent explained that the child in the photograph, who cannot be more than two years old, probably had an empty scrotum. "So there was more tissue than was considered acceptable for a female labia, but not enough for a male assignment. So they have removed a great deal of it, probably virtually all of the erectile tissue."

Laurent's explanation of the construction of the vagina was especially striking: "The vagina is surgically constructed using other tissue from the child's body, usually a piece of the bowel." In effect, incisions are made elsewhere in the child's body in order to harvest material to create a vagina, and the bowel is then pieced back together. One problem with this surgical intervention is that the bowel does not lubricate the way that a vagina lubricates. "It lubricates when it is stimulated by eating," explained Laurent, "and some people who have that kind of vaginoplasty have too much lubrication."

Laurent recommends that vaginoplasty not be undertaken on infants and small children. "The surgery is far more successful at the time of adolescence, because tissues are a lot larger and they've already gone through the morphological changes that come with adolescence." Laurent points out a psychologically critical factor that is often ignored: in order to keep the walls of the constructed vagina from closing, it must be dilated with an inflatable pump. This experience can traumatize and affect the psychosexual development of a child. By waiting until puberty, the surgery can be offered to the girl as a choice, and she can take responsibility for doing the dilation. She then would experience more control over her own body, particularly in such an intimate place.

Laurent thinks that intersexuals struggle much more with their sense of themselves because they "question themselves as worthwhile human beings, as somebody who might be lovable, because the surgery impresses them with how monstrous their body is. Something was so horrible about their bodies that it had to be removed, and it was never to be talked about again." Laurent, and activists like her, want the intersexed child to be told

"We love you exactly the way you are right now. There is nothing wrong with your body. When you grow up, if you want to change your body, we can do something about it."

Cheryl Chase recently attended a meeting of parents with inter-sexed children, where many parents conceded that they had wanted the baby to die rather than deal with the social stigma of having given birth to a hermaphrodite. This was a painful mo-ment for Cheryl, who only discovered in adulthood the truth about her own birth when she learned the source of the mysteri-ous railroad track scars on her abdomen, and that the operation she had at eight years old was not for "stomach aches," but to remove the testicular part of her ovatestes. She remembers about a half-dozen doctors continually drawing blood, taking X rays and poking their fingers up her vagina and rectum, but she never knew their true purpose.

In her late teenage years, she had a vivid, recurring nightmare of being chased by men who wanted to kill her. She had a gun to defend herself, but it was not loaded. She had a paper bag full of bullets, but she had to stop somewhere to load the gun. She ducked into a public bathroom, to hide in a stall and load the gun. She could not figure out if she should go into the men's room or the women's room, and so she decided arbitrarily. Inside the stall, the paper bag broke and the bullets fell and scattered onto the tile, making a big clatter. She looked down. The bullets were all different sizes and shapes, and she did not know which ones fit into the gun. Then she looked down between her legs, and saw that her genitals were all mangled. "My guts were coming out," she said. "Something was really wrong with them."

Cheryl was able to gain access to her medical records when she was twenty-two years old, and it was only then that she read, "Admitted to hospital as Charlie at 1-1/2 years." "Charlie" was crossed out by hand, and "Cheryl" was scribbled over it. Charlie had been admitted for determination of sex, and was determined to be a "true hermaphrodite." Charlie had both ovaries, testicular tissue and an enlarged clitoris.

Most intersexuals are described as "pseudo," which means the combination of traits is not as all-encompassing. "We call those ones pseudohermaphrodites," said Cheryl, "because that is how we fool ourselves that the world is not full of hermaphrodites."

When Cheryl was born, her parents would not let anyone see her genitals, and on the advice of doctors, they agreed to surgery. So much of her genitals was cut away that she was rendered physically incapable of clitoral orgasm. After the operations, her parents followed the standard instructions given by doctors to the parents of these children: move to a different town, and don't tell anybody where you went. It was horribly shameful for them, and painful, and it did not make them very warm toward Cheryl. "They got rid of all the blue baby clothes, toys and photos," she said. "Every trace of Charlie was gone."

When Cheryl first learned the truth, her fury and shame were consuming, but there was something in her that wanted to live, and to live with dignity. She realized she would have to do what every other person who is different must do. She must first accept herself. "I realized whatever it is that I am, or was, is okay. What is not okay is somebody else deciding to steal parts of my body, to make who I am so horrible that it could never be discussed or revealed. It took some time after I made that intellectual realization before I integrated it emotionally. I was deeply impressed with the horror of who I was by the total secrecy that surrounded who I am and what was done to me. My whole first year and a half was a lie. I was a boy. All my relatives knew it, and nobody ever breathed a word of it to me. They had my birth certificate changed, both name and sex." It became clear that the only way for Cheryl to make her way in the world was to find other people who shared her experience. They could help support and provide for each other, in ways they did not get as children. Most important, they would no longer feel alone.

"When I look in the mirror," said Cheryl, "I see a female

body, though scarred and missing some important genital parts. Sometimes, in my daily life, I experience a strange sort of bodily dissociation—my perception of myself is as a disembodied entity, without sex or gender. I view healing this split as an important element of personal growth that will allow me to reclaim my sexuality and to be more effective as an intersex advocate." Cheryl operates mostly from an intellectual place. Grief and rage dominate her emotional life, which she suppresses as much as possible. "There's a body here, beneath my eyes," she said, "but it doesn't exactly feel like that's who I am."

In 1993, Cheryl Chase founded the Intersex Society of North America (ISNA). Her first contact with another intersexed person came after writing a letter to the editor of *The Sciences* in response to Fausto-Sterling's article "The Five Sexes." The ISNA now has its own newsletter, "Hermaphrodites with Attitude," and they can be reached through E-mail at info@isna.org.

"I used to be so moved and cry when I read their stories," said Cheryl. "They were a lot worse than mine. But now that doesn't happen. I just think, 'Good. Another ally.' I had been told by surgeons for years that I had been unlucky with my surgery and treatment. 'Maybe there are one or two of you,' the doctors said. 'All these other people are happy. They're just fine. Nobody's ever contacted us and said, "You're crazy for doing this surgery." ' Now I know that's not true," she said. The ISNA has been contacted by people from most of the United States, and from several other countries. They are virtually unanimous: non-life-threatening surgery should wait until the child is at an age of consent.

I asked Cheryl if there was any one way to describe the intersexed people she reaches and who reach her. She laughed. "We're all over the map, every gender role. I imagined I would find people just like me. The only thing we share is that at first we want to kill doctors. A lot of people are disappointed. There are smart ones, retarded ones, feminines and masculines. Heterosexuals, homosexuals, bisexuals, asexuals. What's different about us is that all our lives, since medicine began, we've been treated as 'experiments of nature.' This is what I have to say to the surgeons and clinical psychologists: I am not here to help your research. One researcher wanted us to help him so he would know what sex to assign the babies! People, however, are angry about surgical mutilation, being treated like freaks and kept in the dark. We are working on a project to adopt kids of parents too uncomfortable to raise their intersexed children. Parents are not fond of us so far, but we're interested in talking to them. We'll be patient. They have to become strong first themselves."

That is just what is happening, particularly in England. In 1988, Mrs. Jackie Burrows, the mother of a six-year-old, formed the AIS Support Group for parents of children with Androgen Insensitivity Syndrome (male pseudohermaphrodites) and for the children themselves. Her support group was the first of its kind in the world.

When their child was born, Mrs. Burrows and her husband asked to be put in touch with other parents in similar situations. This was not possible, but they were led to a national group, Contact a Family, which was organized around families coping with disorders. Mrs. Burrows then found herself being contacted by adults who were treated for this condition as children, and who had spent a lifetime in secrecy and shame. Located in Nottinghamshire, the AIS Support Group now has its own newsletter, "ALIAS: The AIS Support Group," which even makes available, for a small fee, articles to help introduce "very young children" to the idea of genital diversity. For example, there is "The Baby Who Was Different—A Fairy Tale," an article produced by the Royal Children's Hospital in Melbourne, Australia. ALIAS also makes available the contact lists for self-help groups for intersexed individuals, like the ISNA, and another group recently formed in Germany.

One individual with a strong sense of himself who found his way to the ISNA was eager to share his story. Lynn Edward Harris, like Cheryl Chase, is a "true hermaphrodite," but he was never subjected to surgery. He explained that he "just fell between the cracks."

Lynn was announced as a girl by a doctor who "was half blind." "At approximately five, I distinctly remember my mother and I were on our way to the drugstore one day in the car, and we parked. I had been thinking about it for weeks. I pulled up my dress, lowered my panties, and exposed this budding penis. I said, 'Could you please explain this to me?' She said, 'Put your dress down, and don't look at it.' "

At puberty, Lynn could see that his body was simply not developing like a female's. He was not growing breasts, so he padded. He was, however, growing facial hair, and so he used depilatories. A resourceful individual, he didn't let too much of anything get in his way, and in 1968, at seventeen, he managed to be crowned the first Costa Mesa Junior Miss. But as he grew older, people began to mistake him for a man in drag, and so he entered on a course of female hormonal treatment. At the age of twenty-nine, he just could not keep it up anymore. He stopped the hormones and allowed his body to take its natural course.

He now lives as a gay man, which he finds ironic, since as far as he is concerned, he is still involved with the same sex he has always been involved with. As for his place within gay culture, he feels like an "accidental tourist," but physically, he is very comfortable. "Sure, my penis is just about the size of my thumb when erect, but it has a lot of good feeling, and I wouldn't trade it for a bigger one with no feeling, or for no penis at all." He believes that cosmetic surgery should be undertaken with the informed consent of the intersexed, postpubertal individual. He remains adamantly opposed to surgery on intersexed infants and children when their conditions are not life-threatening.

After winning the Junior Miss title at seventeen, Lynn was named in a national award competition for scholastic achievement, talent, poise and personality. He was "Miss Tinsel," and oversaw that year's Yuletide Decoration Contest for residential homes sponsored by the Junior Chamber of Commerce. "I won the tiara of genuine rhinestones and a college scholarship for two years." He notes that despite all the publicity on his case, no one has ever asked that the tiara be returned or the scholarship money repaid. There is no note of campiness in his voice as he tells of gaining his beauty contest titles. He went after these titles in earnest, and he respects the women who do the same.

Every four years, the world holds an Olympiad, wherein the greatest athletes compete, and every Olympiad has its rumors about a woman athlete being disqualified for being a man. The truth is, although individuals have been disqualified as not being female, nobody has ever been declared male. No man has ever masqueraded as a woman in the Olympics, and none of those disqualified were transsexuals. Instead, the disqualified athletes were determined to be genetically unusual females.

All Olympic athletes are given a test to determine their chromosomes, which are expected to be XX if you are female, and XY if you are male. However, as reported in the *Washington Post,* "In about one of every 500 cases, a woman contestant is found to have a Y chromosome, indicating that she is actually a male. The critics of this system note that a person's sex is not so simple a matter as X and Y chromosomes . . . The degrees and physical manifestations vary greatly, but there's little to indicate it gives the athlete any competitive advantage. Too often, in fact, the first a woman knows of it is when she takes the test. The result is frequently shock, followed by considerable anguish and humiliation, especially if word leaks out. 'There are a lot of women out there with a Y chromosome, and there are a lot of men without a Y,' said Dr. Albert de la Chapelle, a University of Helsinki geneticist." Ironically, one woman athlete, disqualified because she was not "female," went home, became pregnant and gave birth to a healthy baby.

When I asked Bo Laurent about the tests of Olympic athletes, and commented on how strange it must be to find out that your body is not what you thought, a mischievous smile slowly crossed her face. She asked me if I had ever had my chromosomes, or anything else, for that matter, tested, in terms of male and female. Did I have any evidence that I was what I believe myself to be? I have not had any tests, and my only proof is a "female" designation on my birth certificate and growing up on the pink side of the tracks.

There are, in fact, hundreds of thousands of us who do not fit into the strict physical categories of male and female. Many of these individuals have taken their places in society as homemakers, beauty queens, attorneys, therapists, soldiers and even movie stars. Many of them live in fear that the secret truth about their bodies will be discovered and their lives destroyed by fear and prejudice.

As our knowledge progresses, so much comes to light which has been hidden. Around every scientific bend there is another surprise, from alpha females among the pinyon jay birds to testosterone as the friendly hormone. Is it therefore medically sound to make any diagnosis, or recommend any treatment, based solely on masculine and feminine gender role expectations, when even male and female bodies are not two exclusive categories? It is time to look with new eyes at the biodiversity of nature. It is time to remember the most important idea in the Hippocratic oath, which is taken by most medical students: do no harm. Hippocrates separated medicine from superstition, and it is now time for us to separate the body from gender roles.

GENDER

INDEPENDENCE

Unlike Becky, the seven-year-old whose story opened this book, most girls do not grow up with a "bug-in-the-ear" device, over which a voice instructs from behind a one-way mirror, "You can press the wrist counter whenever you think about it after playing with the girls' toys." Unlike Kraig, the four-year-old in UCLA's feminine boy project, most boys do not grow up receiving blue chips for masculine behavior and red penalty chips for feminine behavior, with the red chips resulting in a spanking from Dad. Yet most of us received our gender training loud and clear. We knew from the time we could speak, perhaps before, what was expected of us as girls and boys. Using denial and suppression, we tried to cut out the parts of ourselves that weren't supposed to be there, beating back perfectly normal feelings and actions when they tried to surface. We learned our gender lessons, and were rewarded with social acceptance. Yet, like Becky and Jerry, the nine-year-old boy who was not athletic, the price is high.

We know that there are parts of us that are not gender appropriate: the boy knows he can rock a doll, the girl knows she can throw a football. When we first hide something natural about ourselves, even if we have loving friends and families, we believe that if they knew who we really were, they would not feel the same about us. We believe that inside, we are hiding something that is wrong, and so experience isolation, shame, and powerlessness.

The first step out is to take a deep breath and relax. Rather than trying to *do* something, we might simply notice what is happening with our bodies as we go about our business in the world. We can ask ourselves: Am I automatically locking my legs into one position? Am I self-conscious if I sit with my "legs crossed, foot on knee" because I am female? Am I afraid to sit with my "legs crossed, knee on knee" because I am male? If we want to have fun with this, it is not difficult: Using the Barlow Gender-Specific Motor Behavior Form, we might check out if our buttocks are four inches or more from the back of the chair! Using the Operational Definitions of Gestures developed by Rekers, we could assess ourselves for flexed elbow—"walking or standing with the arm(s) held such that the angle between the forearm and the upper arm is between 0 and 135 degrees." After all, we as taxpayers bankrolled these studies. We might as well get some use out of them.

At first, it is shocking to realize that we deny ourselves something so basic as certain body movements. Realization, however, is the first step toward gender independence. It is important to not expect ourselves to conform to yet another model, however, like androgyny. Androgyny was defined as having an exact balance of "masculine" and "feminine" traits. Gender independence does not have a litmus test. It simply means that an individual is not precluded from feeling or doing anything because of their body. Some of us might tend to have more traits traditionally associated with men or women, and there is absolutely nothing wrong with that. We can still be gender independent. If there is anything that should be taken from this book, it is that we are not all the same, but most of us have nevertheless barely tapped our potential because of gender role training.

The advantages of gender independence are extraordinary. People who are gender independent are more flexible, and have a wider range of strategies for dealing with diverse situations. They do not suppress a part of themselves for fear of not being masculine or feminine, and so they have access to more coping techniques and a wider range of problem-solving tools. For example, the gender independent man is more capable of retreating from a no-win situation without fear of appearing unmasculine, and the gender independent woman is more capable of holding her ground, when that is the most strategic action to take, without fear of appearing unfeminine. Although the gender independent person, like everyone else, will encounter situations in which he or she does not feel in control, their responses to these situations are more resilient than those of their sex-typed peers. Resilience and flexibility are key mental health components for the postmodern world, where the rules are no longer so simple.

Sex-typed gender roles, on the other hand, are the Trojan horse of social order. Just as the enemy soldiers hid within the huge wooden horse that was supposed to be a gift, adherence to the bipolar, sex-typed gender system has hidden within it the most debilitating of emotional illnesses, many of which literally affect the body.

Women who subscribe to the traditional feminine role stereotype are particularly vulnerable to depression in middle age. Depression has been linked to a lack of control over one's environment, resulting from what is known as learned helplessness. Learned helplessness means that an individual has come to believe themselves incapable of doing something that they could do. Depressed individuals believe that they cause their own failures, and that the failure is rooted within themselves, never within the situation. Many feminine sex-typed women spend their lives apologizing for just about everything that happens in the world around them, regardless of their control, or lack of control, over the actual events. Unmarried women are not as prone to depression, possibly because, for survival, they have to perform more tasks that would be considered masculine, and so view themselves as having more control of their environment.

Masculine sex-typed men have also been found to be suscep- tible to depression when they are in a situation that is out of their control, but they are not as vulnerable to this symptom because they tend to structure their world so that they avoid these situa- tions. Because of the complex nature of today's society, and the steady erosion of rigid sex roles among women, in particular, men are no longer as able to avoid situations in which they feel out of control. Their response is not usually depression, but anger, and a sense of being cheated, in that they no longer have the control that their fathers and grandfathers appeared to have.

Since the 1970s, masculine sex-typed individuals have been identified as coronary-prone, that is, at risk for coronary artery and heart disease. This so-called type A individual has been char- acterized as hostile, competitive and achievement-oriented, a per- sonality primarily associated with high masculinity. When social insecurity was tossed into the mix for the type A personality, these individuals were more likely to have coronary problems. One of the side effects of the treatment of type A men with antihypertensive drugs is sexual dysfunction, which causes anxi- ety and leads to depression.

The fact that men die before women has long puzzled scien- tists, with a man's life expectancy at 72.1 and a woman's life expectancy at 78.9, a difference of almost seven years. The seven- year difference has held up over time, despite the fact that the diseases of extreme old age, which affect primarily women, have received scant research and treatment attention. According to Dr. Ken Goldberg, a Dallas urologist and adviser to the Men's Health Network, a nonprofit group that sponsored a study on the life span gap, the problem can be traced to an aspect of the masculine sex role, or "men's mentality." While "smoking, drinking and reckless behavior" contribute significantly to earlier death, just as significant is the fact that men often experience the inability to ask for help, or to even acknowledge the onset of physical illness, because it does not seem manly. As a result, many conditions which could have been treated in their early stages become life-threatening or fatal. As the masculine sex role becomes less viable in a complex world, the stress of conforming to it can only have increasingly debilitating results.

There have been efforts to tie natural physical conditions in the male body, like testosterone, to the earlier demise of men, but this has not been shown to be the case. In late 1993, a German study was completed using biographical records through 1858 on fifty castrati, men castrated in boyhood to retain their soprano voices. Castration was performed to prevent the surge of hormones that lowers the voice. These data were then compared to data from bass, baritone and tenor male singers from the same time period. The researchers thought that testosterone itself might cause the male to die earlier than the female, but they found no connection. The castrati did not appear to live any longer than their noncastrated peers. As many studies have revealed, innate biological conditions take a backseat to masculine gender role behavior as a cause of lower life expectancy in men.

As masculine sex-typing has laid the foundation for coronary heart disease, feminine sex-typing has laid the foundation for many body image conditions among women concerning weight control. In *The Beauty Myth,* Naomi Wolf found that 95 percent of anorexics and bulimics are women. "While only one man in ten is 'strongly dissatisfied' with his body, one third of women are 'strongly dissatisfied' with theirs. Though the sexes are over-weight in equal proportions—about a third—ninety-five percent of enrollees in weight-loss programs are women. Women think they have a serious problem when they are fifteen pounds above the national average; men are not concerned until they are thirty-five pounds above." This obsession leads to low self-esteem, loss of control and sexual shame. Every year, 150,000 American women die of anorexia, and the disease has a death rate of up to 19 percent. Among those who survive, lack of nourishment commonly leads to sexual dysfunction and depression. Other industrialized countries are just as seriously affected, with at least 50 percent of British women, for example, suffering from eating disorders. "The United Kingdom now has 3.5 million anorexics or bulimics (95 percent of them female), with 6,000 new cases yearly." The numbers are increasing in Russia, Australia, Sweden, Italy, the Netherlands and Japan.

Eating disorders can be directly connected to wanting to appear feminine, as well as to a fear of masculinity. In 1990, researchers found that bulimic young women more often subscribed to the feminine sex-typed identity and ideology than their nonbulimic peers. If bulimia is partly induced by a desire to be attractive to men, bulimics experience a tragic Catch-22, because pleasure in sex is rare for them due to their strong body hatred. Yet this condition is not simply a courtship disorder, but a response to peer pressure, and the desire to be accepted as feminine among other sex-typed women.

Men are not immune to body image conditions, and for the sex-typed man, nothing wreaks more havoc than the size of his penis. In 1994, a Minnesota-based manufacturer of penile implants was named in the first class-action suit charging that the inflatable silicone devices, implanted into the penis and used by 300,000 men in the United States, are defective. Side effects can include infection, disfigurement, leakage, immune problems, pain and loss of sensation. In terms of the procedures to enlarge the penis, urologists are now advising that almost no one should undergo this surgery.

Obsession with penis size drives many men to attempt to enlarge penile circumference or length, but the surgery is easily botched. Researchers believe that, just as bulimic women do not understand that the female body tends to be rounded, men are not aware of the average size of a penis, and if they were, they would not be so vulnerable to this kind of body image distortion. In 1995, the American Urological Association reported that the "average penis was 3.5 inches long when flaccid, growing to an average of 5.1 inches when erect. The circumference was an average 3.9 inches, expanding to 4.9 inches when erect. 'Normal' length would be anything above 2.8 inches." This is certainly not the impression most men (and women) have about a normally sized penis.

In the 1990s, researchers created the term "gender role conflict," and attention is just now being paid to this condition among men. Male gender role conflict is defined as "occurring when rigid, sexist, or restrictive gender roles, learned during socialization, result in the personal restriction, devaluation, or violation of others or self." The overwhelming majority of researchers in this subject are men. For too long, questioning the health of the male gender role was thought to be a product of feminist ideology, which was viewed as emasculating and anti-male. Male researchers have now found that the masculine sex role is significantly related to psychological stress, and that the condition driving gender role conflict in men is a deep fear of being, or appearing, feminine.

In 1995, researchers reported that male gender role conflict has been associated with "lower self-esteem and higher anxiety, higher depression, lower social intimacy, more sexual aggression, and greater somatic [physical] complaints." Yet they also found that it took a lot for these men to seek out psychological counseling, because it goes against type. Since asking for help is a sign of vulnerability and weakness, psychologists concerned about mental health among men believe that there is a large population of men in deep need of counseling but unable to ask for it. In the men that they do see, they found that the level of psychological distress was notable, "midway between that of male psychiatric outpatient and inpatient norm groups." The severely disturbed profile of the men who do seek out help is probably due to the fact that they wait until the situation is in total crisis before reaching out.

From lower risks of suicidal behavior to greater psychological well-being, from life satisfaction to the ability to make and keep friends, from success in stepparenting to favorable outcomes in children after parental divorce, the demonstrated advantages of gender independence over sex-typed behavior are remarkable. Those individuals who have the ability to transcend traditional gender roles have been shown to have greater cognitive complexity than their sex-typed peers, which allows them to think abstractly, without tending to resort to either-or solutions. More flexible, they are willing to take risks, and their tolerance for ambiguity allows them to function with greater ease in an increasingly complicated society. Novel situations are not as threatening, because they have more resources for dealing with these situations. They are also not as judgmental, because their own identities are not wrapped up in others behaving in predictable sex-typed patterns. In the business world, even in male-dominated occupations, gender independent individuals are seen and experienced as stronger mentors, better salespeople and more desirable colleagues. Rated as better managers by those who work for them, the gender independent manager is particularly thought of as more effective at conflict management.

In the elderly population, those who are more gender independent experience greater emotional and psychological well-being. A 1984 study of sex role similarity in old age suggested that "if older adults were completely caught up in stereotyped male or female roles, it would be difficult for them to be the wise leaders who direct role development for younger members of society. Role complexity both frees them and gives them power." (Role complexity refers to taking on both traditionally male and traditionally female characteristics.) The researchers suggested that there is an evolutionary significance of complex roles in mature years, and then hypothesized that the traditional polarized masculine and feminine roles are "over-specializations" in response to the pressures of courtship and reproduction. "Like the flourish of the peacock's resplendent tail, they may be unusual, useful for guaranteeing new generations, but maladaptive before and after courtship when other needs are equally important." The question now becomes: Why are these sex roles considered "adaptive," even necessary, particularly during courtship?

The notion that "opposites attract," and that females and males are naturally at the opposite ends of one behavioral pole

240

during courtship and for reproductive reasons, is the root cause of the sometimes deadly conflicts in relationships. In a 1985 study of "courtship violence," researchers studied abuse between dating partners and found that the more traditionally masculine males were more likely to report having abused a dating partner than the males who were less sex-typed. Most sex crimes against women (and children) are perpetrated by men who have little tolerance for the ordinary problems of daily life, coupled with insecurities about their masculinity or masculine identity. Those most vulnerable to these attacks are feminine sex-typed women whose defensive styles lead to depression and anxiety, stemming from learned helplessness and feeling to blame for the abusive situation in which they find themselves.

It is important to remember that in the "measurements" of masculine identity in males and feminine identity in females, traits are self-selected and not necessarily real. Men might identify with the trait "independent," and select that as one of their attributes, because they know they are supposed to. Many men, particularly abusive men, are probably extremely dependent, not independent. Their dependency so terrifies them in terms of their identity that they must strike out at those they love who are perceived as causing, or triggering, their dependence. They often suspect the ones who love them of knowing the secret truth: that they are vulnerable, a truth so threatening to these men that sometimes only murder solves their dilemma.

So many self-help books on relationships between the sexes, primarily read by women, advise the woman to take responsibility for what she is assumed best at: communication. The man is presented and analyzed as mentally, even biologically, incapable of certain activities and thought processes. There is, indeed, a crisis among men and women, but it cannot possibly be solved by the gender gurus who repackage the bipolar myths that hack our psyches in two, then hold up the halves as ideal models.

John Gray, for example, explains that a man's sense of self "is defined through his ability to achieve results," and a woman's sense of self "is defined through her feelings and the quality of her relationships." Male and female "fulfillment" are given the same treatment: ". . . a man is fulfilled through working out the intricate details of solving a problem, a woman is fulfilled through talking about the details of her problems." Men are motivated and empowered "when they feel needed," and women "when they feel cherished." The most disturbing advice he gives to women is "When a man is in a negative state, treat him like a passing tornado and lie low," and "Never go into a man's cave or you will be burned by the dragon!" While he is in the cave, the woman is advised to distract herself by calling "a girlfriend for a good chat," listening "to self-improvement tapes" or taking "a bubble bath." Men are advised that they must support women when they are in their "wells," a sort of emotional vortex that women are incapable of escaping yet must enter, just as a man must enter his "cave." In his section on why women and men fight, Dr. Gray explains, "Men argue for the right to be free while women argue for the right to be upset." Most revealing are Gray's statements: "It is difficult for a man to listen to a woman when she is unhappy or disappointed because he feels like a failure," and "Most men strive for greater and greater success because they believe it will make them worthy of love."

The male role of "money tree" could not be clearer, nor the terrible price it exacts upon a relationship. The presentation as normal of the stereotypic male role of threatening and destructive behavior, comparable to fire-breathing dragons and tornadoes, and the female's stereotypic role of appeasement and self-blame, including listening to "self-improvement tapes," is a chilling elevation of emotional disturbance to cosmic truth. Gray cheerfully describes men and women as half-creatures who cannot function independently in the world, but must find someone who might as well be "from another planet" to complete themselves. He even provides a chapter on "Scoring Points with the Opposite Sex," which assigns a point system for sex-typed behaviors. By reducing relationships to a game, complete with penalty points and separate rules for men and women, Dr. Gray is part of the problem, not the solution.

Marianne Williamson drops us into the same trap, explaining that "most of us want a masculine man, but there's no way to have one unless we become feminine women." She advises that, despite whatever "masculine" energy she uses in her professional life, when she gets home, if she wants to experience herself as a "woman," she no longer "kid[s]" herself into thinking she can bring that "masculine" energy into her relationship. She must accept that "the dominant groove is that he's masculine and I'm feminine." Williamson writes that to accomplish this, women "are having to tie our hands behind our backs, bite our tongues, sit on our credit cards," in order to overcome "Amazon neurosis," which causes a woman to "go to him before he comes to us, to call first, to make the first move." Williamson finishes up her argument by explaining to women that they are basically the chosen people: "Men have got to realize—and so have we—that something of ancient significance is rising up from the bottom of things and spilling out through all of us. Men feel it; women feel it. Women, however, are going crazy around it because our nervous systems are tied to its expression. It's a pregnancy we can't abort; and when we try to, we get even crazier than we were. We might as well accept the fact that nature is turning the world on its ear, and she's chosen us to announce the news." Williamson asks women to choose between being "Glorious Queens or Slavegirls," a perfect example of constricted, either-or thinking.

Gray and Williamson have reduced intimate relationships to manipulative games in which people stifle parts of themselves that are not appropriately masculine or feminine, and mythologize biological and spiritual roots for dysfunctional sex roles. In a sense, they are helping to institutionalize the problems, rather than solve them. They offer coping strategies, which they advertise as the essential truths about the sexes. People who follow their guidelines probably experience a temporary relief, because we are comfortable with these familiar roles, whereas change and growth are,

at first, awkward and uncomfortable. That feeling of relief, however, is temporary, and cannot be sustained because it is pallia-
tive, not curative.

As we move out of courting rituals, and there is job stress, or
the arrival of a new baby, it becomes painfully obvious that masculine and feminine sex-typed roles are chosen, not natural, and
when that truth arrives, as it always does, there can be tremendous resentment on both sides. It is time to move beyond Mars
and Venus, Queens and Slavegirls, and Iron John. These models
no longer work, and in fact, they are destructive. Rationalizing the
problems between the sexes with the metaphor of being from two
different planets keeps people from solving their problems with
any meaningful growth, and instead sets relationships even more
firmly onto a crash course, isolating individuals in fantasy worlds.

One way out of the gender trap is to introduce the concept of
gender independence within relationships by bridging the gap
between the "ideal" sex-typed self and the actual self. Since most
human traits overlap, no one sex has a corner on any behavior. A
man can communicate, and still be decisive. A woman can lead,
and still be nurturing. The minute we look at our partner and
think, Just like a man, or Just like a woman, we know we have
fallen into the gender trap, and we are no longer seeing the individual we love, but a stereotype we have superimposed onto a
real, complex human being. That is the time to stop, take a deep
breath and find the parts of ourselves that could help us see past
the myths. Justifying unfair, selfish or thoughtless actions by saying "I'm a man!" or "I'm a woman!" is just as destructive. A
woman who clings to the "woman's prerogative" to change her
mind on a whim will never be given control over a complex corporate business. A man who clings to a "man's need to be free"
will never be given custody of his children.

Studies performed in 1982, 1989 and 1994 found that sex-
typed individuals had a more difficult time in long-term relationships than their more gender independent peers. In fact, the
"femininity level" of both spouses and the "masculinity level" of
the wife were major factors in the success of a relationship, and if

244

even one member of the couple had a mixture of masculine and feminine traits, the chances of greater sexual satisfaction increased. In 1992, the *Journal of Family Therapy* reported that, in the sex-typed relationship, "gender-based inequalities of power and culturally shared beliefs about gender and sexuality" result in greater sexual problems, because sex becomes a struggle over power.

In 1994, Cheryl Rampage looked at the connections among power, gender and marital intimacy. She found three major factors obscuring the power differences between husbands and wives: images of women, from romance novels to cartoons, depicting feminine submission as erotic and helplessness as attractive; convoluted concepts like "the power of powerlessness" which confuse the issue; and the irony that "men often *feel* powerless, even as they are exerting power over their wives."

I find myself cringing at the depictions of girls and women in cartoons as I sit beside my son and his male friends in the movie theater, watching them take it all in. Six and seven years old, they are not smiling or enjoying the swooning, screaming girl being saved by the brave, magically powerful boy: they are studying it. They are learning what is expected of them, and they are nervous. I can see it in their faces, in the way they clench their fists. They know they do not have special magical powers. They wonder what to do about it. They pretend, and fantasize, to cover up their tenderness and vulnerability. I want more for my son, and more for my friends' daughters, than these truncated roles.

Rampage also addresses the damage caused by the myth that women have "some inherent expertise at relating intimately." Men are treated as if they are emotionally handicapped because of some innate condition, and women, by claiming superior innate abilities to communicate, make it impossible for each partner to particpate "equally in the creation of meaning." In effect, this infantalizes the man, by declaring him constitutionally incapable of participating in the process.

Women must also ask themselves if, when their husband expresses vulnerability, they "feel revulsion." If they do, he is cer-

245

tain to know it, despite the myth that men are not intuitive. By looking at how we relate to our parents, women can see the roots of these feelings about men, and men can see the roots of their feelings about themselves. How do we feel if we see our mother cry? Our heart might open as we try to comfort her. But what happens if our father cries? Is there a moment of panic or fear, perhaps revulsion, even anger and shame?

If a woman pretends she is not strong, and if a man pretends he is not vulnerable, then they can never feel "known and utterly accepted" by each other in their relationship, which Rampage describes as "one of the essential and most delightful elements of being 'in love.'" Yet this feeling is often the result of idealized visions of each other, and after living together, and finding out the truth, these ideal visions crumble, leaving the real person standing there, the sex-typed roles exposed as the sham that they are. Perhaps if we began relationships as real people, without manufacturing identities for the purposes of courtship, we would be taking an important step toward the truth, which is not the fairy-tale story of a fire-breathing dragon in a cave, or a weeping maiden in a well. We could then give up the notion of finding our "other half." Relationships between two "halves" are a setup for stress, while relationships between whole individuals give us a real chance at communicating, building and growing. Rather than completing each other, when together, two whole people make something new; and when separate, they each remain whole, fully functioning and healthy.

In 1983, a case study was published by Peter Dowrick concerning a four-year-old named Jeremy, who was referred to a hospital-affiliated psychiatric unit for "extreme girl-stereotyped manner-isms and playing behaviors." There was the usual concern for his future social and sexual adjustment, but there was also this: "Observations at the Unit confirmed the reports and highlighted Jeremy's remarkable entertainment capacity in this role. The attention of other children was seen to be positively riveted by his performances with ironing boards and dolls' underwear, for example, and by his speech and mannerisms. His only sibling was two years younger, a boy whose first word was reportedly 'truck.' " Dr. Dowrick did not give Jeremy a hopeful prognosis for overcoming his gender disturbance. He lamented that Jeremy received far too much positive reinforcement for his "remarkable entertainment capacity." Let us hope that Jeremy's "cure" did not destroy his talent, and that he did not become frightened of tapping into that part of himself that brought to the world something positively riveting and "remarkable."

Studies of the most creative artists suggest that the production of art relies upon gender independent behavior. In 1988, researchers at Wake Forest University tested the 1972 hypothesis of June Wayne, in which she stated that the male artist is a stereotypical woman in terms of gender role behavior. In interviews with 544 male and female visual artists, all of whom had been nominated for national awards in visual arts, they found instead that all artists, male and female, tend to have gender independent self-images. At the Georgia State University School of Music in Atlanta, a 1994 study found that both music educators and music performers exhibited gender independence as a modal characteristic.

In Germany, the search for the source of creative musical talent has been undertaken at the University of Tübingen, particularly by Marianne Hassler. She found that composers and instrumentalists are not psychologically sex-typed. She also found that male and female composers had higher testosterone levels than their counterparts in the instrumentalist and nonmusician control groups, and that female composers attained the highest mean testosterone results of all female groups. The question arises, is she looking at the chicken or the egg? Is their creative behavior causing the rise in testosterone, or is the presence of higher testosterone triggering their particular form of creativity?

The testosterone level in the saliva of men was shown by Mazur and Lamb, in 1980, to rise and fall dependent upon their behavior, how in control of the situation they were and how much they perceived their own actions to be responsible for their success. In their first experiment, during a tennis match in which there was a decisive victory there was a rise in the winner's testosterone level. If it was a close match, there was no change in testosterone level. In their second experiment, a random lottery winner was drawn, and there was no change in testosterone levels for either the winner or the loser, because it was a situation over which they had no control. In their third experiment, recipients of M.D. degrees were shown to have a rise in testosterone level one and two days after receipt of the degree, something for which they had worked very hard. These researchers might consider repeating these experiments and measuring not just the testosterone but also the estrogen levels in these men, as well as the ratio of testosterone to estrogen both before and after each experiment. Finally, they might follow this up by testing for testosterone and estrogen rises in women during similar experiments, since it is probable that women, like men, experience hormonal shifts in response to creative or competitive behaviors.

Edited in 1988 by Loraine Obler and Deborah Fein, *The Exceptional Brain* explored the search for the neurological source of talent and special abilities. One of the chapters focused on the chess mind, and the fact that the top players in the world are overrepresented by youthful, left-handed men. (This does not, of course, mean that there are no top players who are right-handed.) There are, indeed, studies which show left-handedness to be a characteristic of many talented artists, engineers, musical composers and mathematicians. Left-handed homosexuals, in particular, are overrepresented in the category of prodigious mathematical geniuses. But is left-handedness, in and of itself, creating these special abilities? If one is left-handed, that trait might tend to expand a person's conceptualizing ability out of necessity, since society is set up for the right-handed. Whatever expands the ability to conceptualize, especially in unique ways, perhaps uses areas of the brain in somewhat different manners, thereby enhancing creativity in both spatial and linear terms.

248

The hypothesis was also advanced that testosterone fosters the brain organization of the mathematical abilities associated with the chess master. The theory of a testosterone-based *male* predisposition for chess, regardless of how strikingly male-dominated a game it is, has been put to rest by an extraordinary experiment in the early 1970s. A Hungarian educational psychologist, Laszlo Polgar, and his wife, Klara, believed that genius could be educated into any healthy child, and they decided to test this hypothesis on their own children, who were yet to be born. As chance would have it, they had three children, and they were all girls. The Polgars considered various subjects for the girls, including mathematics and foreign languages, but ultimately they selected chess because it is "very objective and easy to measure." They began to teach the girls the game at the age of four, and by eight, they could each outplay their father. Of their three daughters, two of them became chess grand masters, and the third daughter is closing in on that ranking. Their youngest is Judit, and in 1993, at sixteen years of age, she "trounced" Boris Spassky, the former world chess champion. Judit Polgar is the youngest grand master in history, achieving that status at the age of fifteen years and five months, a month younger than the American chess master, Bobby Fischer. We do not know, however, if the three Polgar sisters have created in their bodies higher levels of testosterone, or estrogen, or both, by engaging so intensely in the game.

In his book *Awakening Your Child's Natural Genius,* Dr. Thomas Armstrong has written that "the evolution of living things depends upon changes in the children of any given species." The most powerful survival and evolutionary traits in the human being are "a childlike nature, including sensitivity, curiosity, playfulness, creativity, imagination, a sense of wonder, and the need to learn." In writing of giftedness as a child's birthright, Armstrong highlights the work of Harvard's Dr. Howard Gardner on the seven different intelligences, from the interpersonal to the logical-mathematical. Dr. Gardner has said, "We are all so different largely because we all have different combinations of intelligences. If we recognize this, I think we will have at least a better chance of dealing appropriately with the many problems that we face in the world."

Nowhere in *Awakening Your Child's Natural Genius* are children divided into the two categories of boys and girls. Nowhere is it even suggested that a boy's brain is better at math, or that a girl's brain is better at linguistics. Dr. Armstrong, in fact, points out the destructive folly in such reasoning, in that it sets a child up for unnecessary failure based upon myth.

The creative power of the gender independent individual has always been recognized, but the pathologization of creativity because of its "cross-gendered" features continues. We see this especially in the analysis of children diagnosed with Gender Identity Disorder. Robert Stoller described the girls as possessing "unusual physical skills (as in athletics)," and in terms of the boys, he wrote specifically of the connection between boyhood femininity and artistic ability, which was reported as being obvious in the child by three years of age. Their talents included painting (with a "flamboyant use of colors"), dancing and mime, creative writing (in terms of storytelling), acting and inventive costuming abilities. Of these talents Stoller wrote, "We cannot tell if time or treatment will remove this lovely sign of nonetheless severe psychopathology, but at present, these children are remarkably creative." It was fashionable at the time to believe that males were driven to create because they could not give birth, which was described as "thwarted procreativity" or "feminine reproductive wishes." Stoller hypothesized, however, that these feminine, gender-disturbed boys were not necessarily compensating for their unconscious desire to have a baby. He instead speculated that their "artistic creativity is also inspired by a fear of death, fear of death being here considered a fear of absolute dissolution of identity . . ." Could they be creating for the sheer joy of it? Must everything they do be pathological?

Green and Money also observed special talents in these boys, particularly in terms of stage acting and role-taking. The boys they studied were sent to them in the mid-1960s "by family physicians, educators, or the pediatric clinics of the Johns Hopkins Hospital because of symptoms of effeminacy." One boy requested dancing lessons at the age of four. Another staged a production of *Carousel* at his home at the age of eleven. A thirteen-year-old produced "period" plays employing elaborate costumes. Many of the boys "constructed stages and recruited casts" (which does not seem to be an especially "effeminate" or "gender-deviant" activity). For whatever reason, these children tapped into those parts of themselves that inspired them to create and to be in the world in exceptional ways that are often closed to others. That gay men and lesbians might be overrepresented in the arts and in other endeavors where gender independent traits are desirable is no surprise. However, this has nothing to do with sexuality, and everything to do with gay people perceiving the option, and sometimes the necessity, of venturing beyond strict male and female gender roles, for both pleasure and survival.

Of all the traits that control cultural evolution, none is more powerful than creativity, and none is more intrinsically involved with exercising gender independence. As early as 1957, Frank Barron of Berkeley addressed this issue. Supported in part by the United States Air Force, he studied originality as it related to personality and intellect in one hundred officers, all of whom were ranked as captains. He found that originality was linked to an ability to integrate diverse stimuli, and that there were relationships in these men between "originality" and "femininity." Although he speculated that there could be a "biological bisexual disposition" in both men and women, he also knew that "the more original men would permit themselves to be more aware of tabooed interests and impulses, and would seek to integrate these superficially discordant phenomena into a more complex whole." Although Barron held on to the possibility of biologic drives, he also speculated that "some degree of cross-sex identification is important for creativity in men and perhaps women as well."

In 1962, Donald W. MacKinnon delivered a lecture at Yale University on the importance of the discovery and development of talented persons, and found that creative males scored relatively high on femininity. "In the language of the Swiss psychologist, Carl G. Jung (1956), creative persons are not so completely identified with their masculine persona roles as to blind themselves to or to deny expression to the more feminine traits of the anima. For some, to be sure, the balance between masculine and feminine traits, interests and identification is a precarious one, and for several of our subjects it would appear that their presently achieved reconciliation of these opposites of their nature has been barely effected and only after considerable psychic stress and turmoil." Because of rigid gender role stereotyping at work in society at the time of MacKinnon's study, the social stigmas and pressures stressed these creative individuals with such force that they had to fight to maintain their psychological balance. They were generally viewed as having within their natures an unnatural combination of "opposites" that were at once a gift and a curse. To his credit, Dr. MacKinnon did not argue for the innate instability of the creative individual, but instead pointed to the social problems encountered by the individual who is perceived as being both "masculine" and "feminine."

Dr. MacKinnon found that, rather than being psychopathological, the creative individual had "a good intellect, complexity and richness of personality, general lack of defensiveness, and candor in self-description," all of which describe the gender independent person. Intuitive perception, the antidote for either-or thinking, was another strong feature which especially included the ability to look "expectantly for a bridge or link between that which is given and present, and that which is not yet thought of, focusing habitually upon possibilities." He also noted that in the development of creative architects, for example, "in place of the more usual clear identification with one parent [usually the same-sex parent], there was a tendency for the architects to have identified either with both parents or with neither . . . What is perhaps more significant, though, is the high incidence of distinctly autonomous mothers among families of the creative architects, who led active lives with interests and sometimes careers of their own apart from their husbands'."

Donald MacKinnon delivered this lecture in 1962, one year prior to the publication of Betty Friedan's *The Feminine Mystique.* It must have come as quite a shock to those who heard it. He did not hypothesize about latent homosexuality present in creative men and women, or hormonal surges in the brain. He instead analyzed, for similarities, the families of the creative individual. He found that they all seemed to have an ethical code which emphasized integrity, quality, intellectual and cultural endeavor, success and ambition, being respectable and doing the right thing. He also found, perhaps most crucially, that the parents were not locked into sex-typed gender roles.

In 1966, Eleanor Maccoby of Stanford addressed the issues of intelligence and creativity. She reported that "a young child's interest in the games and activities characteristic of the opposite sex is positively correlated with I.Q.; that is, the brighter girls are more likely to enjoy baseball and other boys' games, while the brighter boys will more often engage in feminine activities." She noted that, with few exceptions, studies indicate that "analytic thinking, creativity, and high general intelligence are associated with cross-sex-typing, in that the men and boys who score high are more feminine, and the women and girls more masculine, than their low-scoring same-sex counterparts."

Yet creative individuals, subject to stress and turmoil in a rigidly sex-typed society, are often assumed to be temperamental and prone toward instability. These labels are imposed on the creative individual by a society distrustful of a gender independent identity, which has long been associated with latent or overt same-sex attraction. Maccoby anticipated this fear when she wrote, "It is important to note, however, that this cross-sex-typing does not imply that intellectual individuals are sexually uninterested in, or unattractive to, the opposite sex. It merely means that they share more of the interests and activities normally characteristic of the opposite sex."

In 1929, in *A Room of One's Own,* Virginia Woolf wrote of Coleridge's belief that the great mind is androgynous: "It is when this fusion takes place that the mind is fully fertilised and uses all

253

its faculties. Perhaps a mind that is purely masculine cannot create, any more than a mind that is purely feminine . . . [Coleridge] meant, perhaps, that the androgynous mind is resonant and porous; that it transmits emotion without impediment; that it is naturally creative, incandescent and undivided." Many prolific writers have long known that psychological, emotional and spiritual access to all parts of one's being is the secret well of creativity. F. Scott Fitzgerald said that the sign of genius is the ability to hold paradoxes within the mind, without having to make one thing or the other true or false. When asked of his source of inspiration for *Madame Bovary,* Flaubert replied: *"Madame Bovary, c'est moi!"* ("I *am* Madame Bovary!"). Anne Rice has said that her body is female but her mind is male. Joyce Carol Oates also took up the theme when she said that "imagination, in itself genderless, allows us all things."

Creativity, or genius, is not the province of the left-handed or the gender disturbed. Neither is it a temperamental demon of mental instability. As William James has said, genius "means little more than the faculty of perceiving in an unhabitual way." To this end, as we consider the concept of gender independence, we might ask ourselves: Am I pretending that I cannot do something because it is not a proper role for my sex? Is there something I have never tried—a way of dancing, sitting, competing or loving—because I have shut myself off from the experience? Am I pretending not to feel, to know, to see, to hear something inside of me because I think it inappropriate for my gender role? We can demonize those unfamiliar parts of ourselves and be frightened every time we feel them stirring, or we can recognize and embrace that which belonged to us in the first place. We can allow ourselves to see "in an unhabitual way," and by opening that door for ourselves, we open it also for those who come after us.

NOTES

PREFACE

Page

xiii "In Western Africa . . .": The Yoruban ceremonies were filmed by Dr. Raymond Prince, and recounted and interpreted by Rollo May in his essay "Psychotherapy and the Daimonic," anthologized by Joseph Campbell in *Myths, Dreams, and Religion,* New York: E. P. Dutton & Co., 1970, pp. 196–210.

xv "There were special . . .": Burke, Phyllis, *Family Values,* New York: Random House, 1993.

xvi "Bly writes . . .": Bly, Robert, *Iron John,* p. 94.

xxi "a mass pain . . .": Williamson, Marianne, *A Woman's Worth,* p. 4.
"masculine is active . . .": Ibid., p. 62.
"John Gray writes . . .": Gray, John, *Men Are from Mars, Women Are from Venus,* pp. 6–7.

BEHAVIOR

4 "In the words of . . .": Statement by Dr. Susan Coates at CLAGS public forum "Sissys and Tomboys: Gender Nonconformity and Homosexuality," New York City, on February 10, 1995.

BECKY

4 "In 1978, one month short . . .": Rekers, George A., and Mead, Shasta, "Early intervention for female sexual identity disturbance: Self-monitoring of play behavior."

7 "The evaluation that sealed . . .": Barlow, David H.; Hayes, Steven C.; Nelson, Rosemery O.; Steele, David L.; Meeler, Marie E., "Sex role motor behavior: A behavioral checklist."

9 "(In subsequent descriptions . . .": Rekers, George A., ed., *Handbook of Child and Adolescent Sexual Problems,* Chapter 12: "Differential diagnosis

and rationale for treatment of gender identity disorders and transvestism," p. 259.

11 "What Becky actually did . . .": Rekers now recommends, as an assessment method by doctors, that a play pattern be considered gender deviant if the child plays with a toy belonging to the opposite sex 70 percent of the time during baseline testing. Rekers, George A., ed., *Handbook of Child and Adolescent Sexual Problems,* Chapter 13: "Assessment and treatment methods for gender identity disorders and transvestism," p. 278.

12 "In fact, according to . . .": Interview with Dr. Laura Allen on January 26, 1995.

"The fact that most tomboys . . .": Phillips, G., and Over, R., "Differences between heterosexual, bisexual and lesbian women in recalled childhood experiences," and Plumb, Pat, and Cowan, Gloria, "A developmental study of destereotyping and androgynous activity preferences of tomboys, nontomboys, and males."

19 "Becky's mother proudly wrote . . .": It is ironic that the Barbie doll was modeled after Lilli, a German pornographic doll. Mothers were at first hesitant to buy Barbie because of the doll's maturity, feeling that it looked like a homewrecker, too sexy and racy, belonging in a man's drinking club, not in a girl's bedroom. Barbie was successfully marketed when the mothers' Achilles' heel was located. Marketers convinced mothers that Barbie would make a " 'poised little lady' out of her raffish, unkempt, possibly boyish child." Interview with Evelyn Burkhalter, Barbie Hall of Fame, Palo Alto, on March 25, 1995. *Forever Barbie* by M. G. Lord, p. 40.

"The same treatments . . .": Rekers, *Handbook of Child and Adolescent Sexual Problems,* Chapter 13: "Assessment and treatment methods for gender identity disorders and transvestism," pp. 281–283.

"and Becky's case history . . .": Rekers, *Handbook,* Chapter 12, pp. 258–259.

JERRY

20 "Jerry—Nine Years Old . . .": Myrick, Robert D., "The counselor-consultant and the effeminate boy."

23 "Frustrated by . . .": Rekers has described a method for identifying pathological sex role development in boys which includes comparing them with their same-aged male peers in ball skills, e.g., "distance in throwing the football" and "percentages of baskets made from the free throw line." This diagnostic technique was developed in the 1970s at UCLA, and he continues to recommend it in his *Handbook,* published in 1995.

"The problem was . . .": Interview with Dr. Robert Myrick on March 21, 1995.

25 "When I contacted . . .": Ibid.

28 "As early as 1959 . . .": Hartley, R. E., "Sex-role pressures and the socialization of the male child."

"In 1977, he devised . . .": Rekers, George A., "Assessment and treatment of childhood gender problems."

"Building on the 1977 study . . .": Rekers, G. A., and Rudy, J. P., "Differentiation of childhood body gestures."

29 "The year after . . .": Rekers, G. A., and Mead, S., "Human sex differ-

ences in carrying behaviors: A replication and extension." Rekers, George A., "Psychosexual assessment of gender identity disorders," p. 49.
31 "I asked Dr. Myrick . . .": Interview with Dr. Robert Myrick on October 17, 1995.

THE FEMININE BOY PROJECT AT UCLA
32 "Government records indicate . . .": I compiled the following list from a variety of federal sources:
National Institute of Mental Health Grants
NIMH Grant #24305
UCLA
Richard Green
1973 $ 41,138
1974 $ 43,500
             Total $ 84,638
For this research, an additional Foundations Fund for Research in Psychiatry Grant (G-69-471) was made to Richard Green.
NIMH Grant #26598
State University of New York at Stony Brook
Principal Investigator: Richard Green
Significant portions of these funds were also used at UCLA for the Feminine Boy Project.
When the grant was first made, the project was entitled: "Study of the Development of Atypical Sex Roles in Children."
1975 $ 32,714
1975 $ 11,256 (Supplement)
1976 $ 31,201
1976 $ 71,536
1976 $ 14,524 (Supplement)
1977 $109,508
1977 $ 5,546 (Supplement)
1978 $100,545
1979 $ 18,582 (Supplement)
             Subtotal $395,412
The title of this grant was changed when "re-competed" at the NIMH for the next five years. It was renamed: "Gender Identity Development: Atypical and Typical."
1980 $ 88,821
1981 $ 81,948
1982 $ 67,923
1982 $ 30,500 (Supplement)
1983 $ 95,837
1984 $120,224
             Subtotal $485,253
                 Total $880,665
NIMH Grant #20258
University of Mississippi at Jackson
Principal Investigators: David H. Barlow, W. Stewart Agras
"Modification of Deviant Behavior"

This study was conducted upon a seventeen-year-old. All other studies were on prepubescents.

1972 $ 38,899
1973 $ 38,444
1974 $ 37,477
                    Total $114,820

NIMH Grant #21803
University of California at Los Angeles
Principal Investigator: O. Ivar Lovaas
1973 $ 54,200
1974 $ 78,024
1975 $ 86,721
                    Total $218,945

NIMH Grant #28240
Fuller Theological Seminary
Principal Investigator: George Rekers
"Behavioral Treatment of Childhood Gender Problems"
1976 $ 96,153
                    Total $ 96,153

NIMH Grant #29945
Logos Research Institute
Principal Investigator: George Rekers
1978 $100,436
1979 $ 53,616
                    Total $154,052

National Institute of Health Biomedical Research
Support Grant #1-S07-RR05840
Roosevelt Institute, NYC
Principal Investigator: Seymour Lieberman
1985 $ 73,218

At least a portion of this grant was allocated to Dr. Susan Coates at the Childhood Gender Identity Project, St. Luke's-Roosevelt Hospital (in 1985, it was the Childhood Gender Identity Project; in 1990, the Childhood Gender Identity Unit, and in 1994, the Childhood Gender Identity Center). It supported her research on "Extreme boyhood femininity: Isolated behavior or pervasive disorder?" This journal article, which appeared in the *Annual Progress in Child Psychiatry and Development* in 1985, describes the grant as having been made to Dr. Susan Coates. However, in checking records, the PI is listed as Seymour Lieberman. Although the entire amount of this grant might have been allocated to the study of GIDC in children, I do not have access to those records, and therefore no amount has been added from this grant to the grand total awarded to institutions from the NIMH.
                    GRAND TOTAL $1,549,273

Presently, government funds could be awarded for the treatment of "gender deviance" and "Gender Identity Disorder" in children and youth under the guise of the study of "transsexualism," which makes the tracing of these funds almost impossible.

33 "Rekers himself . . .": Rekers, George A., *Growing up straight: What every family should know about homosexuality,* p. 10.

33 "Kraig—Four Years Old . . .": Rekers, George A., and Lovaas, O. Ivar, "Behavioral treatment of deviant sex-role behaviors in a male child."
"In 1973, Rekers and Lovaas devised . . .": Rekers recommends in 1995 a clinical interview protocol for children, in which the doctor asks the child fifteen specific questions, such as "What are the first names of your friends and playmates at home and school. (Note and compare the number of male and female friends.)," and "Most kids are called names at some time or another. What names do other kids call you?" Presumably, if the child has too many friends of the opposite sex, or is called "sissy" or "fag," those are diagnosable signs of the child's mental disorder. *Handbook,* p. 277.
34 "Dr. Green was the one . . .": Green, Richard, *The "Sissy Boy Syndrome" and the Development of Homosexuality,* pp. 12–13.
"Also on television . . .": Ibid., pp. 298–299.
"Kraig's mother was watching . . .": Ibid., p. 296.
"began with a genital examination . . .": Rekers, George A., "Psychosexual assessment of gender identity disorders," p. 56, and Wolfe, Barry E., "Behavioral treatment of childhood gender disorders," p. 554.
35 "Kraig was then sent . . .": Green, *The "Sissy Boy Syndrome,"* p. 300.
"Green's transcripts include . . .": Ibid., pp. 292–319.
"by Dr. Rekers to 'Craig' . . .": Rekers, *Handbook,* p. 257.
37 "and continues to recommend . . .": Rekers, *Handbook,* pp. 277–288.
38 "Kraig's memory . . .": Green, *The "Sissy Boy Syndrome,"* p. 300.
42 "Yet when Kraig was seventeen . . .": Ibid., p. 297.
43 "Richard Green's followup . . .": Ibid., pp. 292–319.
44 "Ironically, despite the publication . . .": Rekers, *Handbook,* Chapter 12: "Differential diagnosis and rationale for treatment of gender identity disorders and transvestism," pp. 257–258.
"There was a long . . .": Rekers, George A.; Lovaas, O. Ivar; and Low, Benson, "The behavioral treatment of a 'transsexual' preadolescent boy."
45 "One of the strangest . . .": Green, R., and Fuller, M., "Group therapy with feminine boys and their parents."
46 "Dr. Lovaas agreed to be interviewed . . .": Interview with Dr. O. Ivar Lovaas on April 19, 1995.
47 "He now describes . . .": Rekers describes his relationship with Lovaas quite differently. His official biography, on page 499 of the 1995 *Handbook of Child and Adolescent Sexual Problems,* reads as follows: "His clinical research career in child and adolescent sexual problems began in 1970 in UCLA, when the internationally acclaimed clinical child psychologist, Dr. O. Ivar Lovaas, his major professor, assigned him a dissertation research topic on the assessment and treatment of childhood gender identity disturbances."
48 "Another UCLA gender behaviorist . . .": Newman, Lawrence E., "Treatment for the parents of feminine boys."

49 "Despite this observation . . .": Green, *The "Sissy Boy Syndrome,"* p. 13.
The breakdown by age of boys in the study is:

4–5	years	7
5–6	years	12
6–7	years	9
7–8	years	8
8–9	years	16
9–12	years	<u>14</u>
	Total	66

"For example, in June of 1974 . . .": Rekers, George A.; Lovaas, O. Ivar,
and Low, Benson, "The behavioral treatment of a 'transsexual' preadolescent boy," p. 114.
"In the spring of 1977 . . .": Rekers, G. A.; Bentler, P. M., and Lovaas,
O. I., "Child gender disturbances: A clinical rationale for intervention,"
p. 4.

BLAMING THE PARENTS

51 "Kraig's mother had to sign . . .": Rekers, George A., and Lovaas,
O. Ivar. "Behavioral treatment of deviant sex-role behaviors in a male
child," pp. 180–181.
"Other parents were required . . .": Green, R., and Fuller, M., "Group
therapy with feminine boys and their parents."

52 "Feminine kids don't need . . .": Green, *The "Sissy Boy Syndrome,"*
p. 275.

53 "A recent interpretation . . .": Interview with Kenneth Zucker on
Feburary 24, 1995.
"There are many theories on parent culpability . . .": Zucker, Kenneth J.;
Green, Richard; Garofano, Chistina; Bradley, Susan J.; Williams, Katherine; Rebach, Howard M.; and Sullivan, Claire B. Lowry, "Prenatal gender
preference of mothers of feminine and masculine boys: Relation to sibling
sex composition and birth order," and
Zucker, Kenneth J.; Bradley, Susan J.; and Ipp, Moshe, "Delayed naming
of a newborn boy: Relationship to the mother's wish for a girl and subsequent cross-gender identity in the child by the age of two," and
Zucker, K. J., and Green, R., "Psychological and familial aspects of gender
identity disorder," p. 533, and
Stoller, Robert J., "The mother's contribution to infantile transvestic behaviour," and
Coates, Susan W., and Wolfe, Sabrina M., "Gender identity disorder in
boys: the interface of constitution and early experience," and
Greenacre, Phyllis, "Penis awe and its relation to penis envy."

54 "To treat these mothers . . .": Newman, Lawrence E., "Treatment for the
parents of feminine boys."
"In 1991, Janet Mitchell . . .": Mitchell, Janet N., "Maternal influences
on gender identity disorder in boys: Searching for specificity."
"despite Mitchell's research . . .": Zucker, K. J., and Green, R., "Psychological and familial aspects of gender identity disorder," p. 534.
"display separation anxiety disorder . . .": Coates, Susan, and Person,

Ethel S., "Extreme boyhood femininity: Isolated behavior or pervasive disorder?"

"Fathers . . .": Green, *The "Sissy Boy Syndrome,"* Chapter 3: "Parents and Sons," pp. 53–59, and Stoller, R. J., "Boyhood gender aberrations: Treatment issues," and

Zucker, K. J., and Green, R., "Psychological and familial aspects of gender identity disorder," pp. 535–536.

55 "The tragic results . . .": Silverstein, Olga, and Rashbaum, Beth, *The Courage to Raise Good Men.*

57 "In one experiment . . .": Smith, Caroline, and Lloyd, Barbara, "Maternal behavior and perceived sex of infant: Revisited."

"Another study identified . . .": Culp, Rex E.; Cook, Alicia S.; and Housley, Patricia C., "A comparison of observed and reported adult-infant interactions: Effects of perceived sex."

"In 1980, there was a study . . .": Sidorowicz, Laura S., and Lunney, G. Sparks, "Baby X revisited."

59 "In 1995, Dr. Green quipped . . .": *"Dateline"* interview with Richard Green at Charing Cross Hospital, London: 4/14/95.

THE CREATION OF A MENTAL ILLNESS

61 "a new mental illness appeared . . .": *Diagnostic and Statistical Manual of Mental Disorders 3rd edition* [DSM-III], Section "Psychosexual disorders," pp. 261–266.

"and again in the revised 1987 . . .": *Diagnostic and Statistical Manual of Mental Disorders 3rd Revised Edition* [DSM-III-R], Section "Disorders usually first evident in infancy, childhood, or adolescence," Gender Identity Disorder of Childhood, pp. 71–74.

"the stereotypical female behavior . . .": Coates, Susan, "Ontogenesis of boyhood gender identity disorder," p. 416.

62 "added a new criteria for girls . . .": Zucker, K., Bradley, S. J., and Lowry Sullivan, Claire B., "Gender identity disorder in children," p. 80.

"the publication of the DSM-IV in 1994 . . .": *Diagnostic and Statistical Manual of Mental Disorders 4th edition* [DSM-IV], "Sexual and gender identity disorders," Gender Identity Disorder, pp. 532–538.

63 "The rationale is that . . .": Zucker, K. J., and Green, R., "Psychological and familial aspects of gender identity disorder," p. 516, and

interview with Dr. Kenneth Zucker in Van Nuys, California, on February 24, 1995, and

Green, Richard, "Gender Identity Disorder in children," p. 2003, and Zucker, K.; Bradley, S. J.; and Lowry Sullivan, Claire B., "Gender identity disorder in children," p. 84.

64 "the Subcommittee on Gender Identity Disorders . . .": The 1994 definition of Gender Identity Disorder in children was devised by the DSM-IV Subcommittee on Gender Identity Disorders. The following individuals were the members of that subcommittee: acting as chair of the committee was Susan J. Bradley, M.D., Department of Psychiatry, The Hospital for Sick Children in Toronto, Ontario, Canada; Ray Blanchard, Ph.D., Gender Identity Clinic, Clarke Institute of Psychiatry, Toronto; Richard Green, M.D., J.D., Department of Psychiatry, UCLA (presently at Char-

ing Cross Hospital in London); Stephen B. Levine, M.D., Department of
Psychiatry, Case Western Reserve University, University Hospital, Cleve-
land, Ohio; Heino F. L. Meyer-Bahlburg, Dr. rer. nat., Program of Devel-
opmental Psychoendocrinology, Division of Child Psychiatry, New York
State Psychiatric Institute, New York City; Ira B. Pauly, M.D., Depart-
ment of Psychiatry, University of Nevada School of Medicine, Reno; Ken-
neth J. Zucker, Ph.D., Clarke Institute, Toronto; and Susan Coates, Ph.D.,
Childhood Gender Identity Unit, Department of Psychiatry, St. Luke's-
Roosevelt Hospital Center, New York City.
"This final DSM placement . . .": Zucker, K.; Bradley, S. J.; and Lowry
Sullivan, Claire B., "Gender identity disorder in children," p. 83.
"This could easily happen . . .": DSM-IV, pp. 532–538.

HOSPITALIZING THE CHILD
66 "In the DSM-III . . .": DSM-III, pp. 261–266.
"In the DSM-III-R . . .": DSM-III-R, pp. 71–74.
"In the DSM-IV . . .": DSM-IV, pp. 532–538.
"One could argue that GIDC . . .": Bradley, Susan J., and Zucker, Ken-
neth, "Gender identity disorder and psychosexual problems in children
and adolescents," p. 478.
"Therefore, in the United States . . .": Statistical Abstract of the United
States, "Projection of U.S. Resident Population for 1995," published
1994. Children under thirteen years: 5,444,300.
"If children and youth under the age . . .": Children NOW, Oakland,
California. Children under eighteen years: 64,000,000.

KIT
67 "In Albuquerque, New Mexico . . .": Interview with Attorney Ruth Cohen on October 24, 1995.
71 "A historic record of this pathologization . . .": MacDonald, Martha
Wilson, "Criminally aggressive behavior in passive, effeminate boys."
"Her work came to my attention . . .": Myrick, Robert D., "The counselor-consultant and the effeminate boy," p. 356.
73 "By 1941, boys and girls . . .": Bender, Lauretta, and Paster, Samuel,
"Homosexual trends in children."

JAMIE
75 "Jamie—Six Years Old . . .": Interview with "Jamie" in San Francisco
on April 9, 1995.
84 "Unless there is someone . . .": Interview with Shannon Minter in New
York City on February 10, 1995.
85 "If a doctor believes . . .": Rekers, *Handbook,* Chapter 14: "Homosexuality: development, risks, parental values, and controversies," p. 300

DAPHNE SCHOLINSKI
86 "Daphne Scholinski—Fourteen Years Old . . .": Interview with Daphne
Scholinski in San Francisco on April 13, 1995.
92 "Daphne's case came to my . . .": Interviews with Shannon Minter in
San Francisco, January through September 1995.

93 "Although not alone . . .": Interview with Lyn Duff in San Francisco on March 9, 1995.

94 "Most of the patients . . .": Interviews with Shannon Minter in San Francisco, January through September 1995.
"One fourteen-year-old . . .": Mirken, Bruce, "Setting them straight," p. 54.

95 "These schools advertise . . .": *Sunset Magazine,* February 1995, p. 143; August 1994, p. 129.

96 "The abuses of the diagnosis . . .": Dr. Susan Coates presented a paper and answered questions on GID in boys at a conference entitled "Sissies and Tomboys: Gender 'Nonconformity' and Homosexuality." The conference took place on February 10, 1995, at the Graduate School of the City University of New York, sponsored by the Center for Lesbian and Gay Studies (CLAGS), and organized by Matt Rottnek. Directed by its founder, Martin Duberman, the distinguished gay historian, CLAGS was organized in 1986 to encourage and disseminate groundbreaking research by lesbian and gay scholars, and to stimulate and help shape public debate on major issues of importance to the lesbian and gay community. The moderators for this conference were Suzanne Kessler and Justin Richardson. The panelists were Anne Fausto-Sterling, Leslie Feinberg, Naomi Scheman, Elias Farajaje-Jones, Chris Straayer, Susan Coates, Sabrina Wolfe, Ken Corbett, David Schwartz and Adrienne Harris.
"Referrals for one of her . . .": Coates, Susan, and Person, Ethel S., "Extreme boyhood femininity: Isolated behavior or pervasive disorder?" p. 201.

THE ANALYSTS

97 "In 1982, a five-year-old . . .": Loeb, Loretta, and Shane, Morton, "The resolution of a transsexual wish in a five-year-old boy."

STANLEY

98 "Stanley—Three Years Old . . .": Haber, Calvin, "The psychoanalytic treatment of a preschool boy with a gender identity disorder."

99 "Yet the mother prevailed . . .": Interview with Dr. O. Ivar Lovaas on April 19, 1995.
"As for the children . . .": DSM-III-R, p. 72.
"The gender identity doctors . . .": Green, Richard, "Gender Identity Disorder in children," p. 2005.

100 "In an interview with . . .": Interview with Dr. Kenneth Zucker in Van Nuys, California, on February 24, 1995.

105 "Psychoanalysis has not remained . . .": Green, *The "Sissy Boy Syndrome,"* pp. 48–49.

THE DOMESTIC SPHERE

108 "one of the symptoms for little girls . . .": DSM-III-R, p. 71.

ROBERT

109 "Robert—Five Years Old . . .": Lim, Meng Hooi, and Bottomley, Virginia, "A combined approach to the treatment of effeminate behaviour in a boy: A case study."

114 "To back themselves up . . .": Fenichel, Otto, *The Psychoanalytic Theory of Neurosis,* Chapter XVI, "Perversions and impulse neuroses," pp. 324–386.

120 "At a recent gender conference . . .": Statement by Richard Green, International Congress on Gender, Cross Dressing and Sex Issues, 2/25/95.

TABOO DOMESTIC BEHAVIOR

121 "ten-year-old Kevin . . .": Hay, William M.; Barlow, David H.; and Hay, Linda Rudin, "Treatment of stereotypic cross-gender motor behavior using covert modeling in a boy with gender identity confusion."

"In his *Sissy Boy* book . . .": Green, *The "Sissy Boy Syndrome,"* "Feminine boy, heterosexual man: Richard," pp. 218–233.

122 "In 1980, Arthur Horton . . .": Horton, A. M., "Behavioral treatment of childhood gender role confusion."

"In 1993, Kenneth Zucker . . .": Zucker, K. J., and Green, R., "Psychological and familial aspects of gender identity disorder," pp. 534–535.

123 "Yet even the Yale Child Study . . .": Herman, S. P., "Gender identity disorder in a five-year-old boy."

"A 1990 study conducted by . . .": Weisner, Thomas S., and Wilson-Mitchell, Jane E., "Nonconventional family life-styles and sex typing in six-year-olds."

125 "In 1986, Shelley Coverman . . .": Coverman, Shelley, and Sheley, Joseph F., "Change in men's housework and child-care time, 1965–1975."

126 "In 1976, *American Psychologist* . . .": Bryson, R. B.; Bryson, J. B.; Licht, M. H.; and Licht, B. G., "The professional pair: Husband and wife psychologists."

"In the 1990s, not much has changed . . .": Starrels, Marjorie E., "Husbands' involvement in female gender-typed household chores."

127 "Research shows that men become more rigid . . .": Cowan, P. A., "Becoming a father: A time of change, an opportunity for development."

128 "They often express . . .": Starrels, "Husbands' involvement in female gender-typed household chores."

129 "A family type not described . . .": Patterson, Charlotte J., "Families of the lesbian baby boom: Parents' division of labor and children's adjustment."

"For heterosexual wives . . .": Starrels, "Husbands' involvement in female gender-typed household chores."

130 "Patterson reviewed . . .": Patterson, "Families of the lesbian baby boom."

"Consider, then, the research . . .": McPherson, Dan, "Gay parenting couples: Parenting arrangements, arrangement satisfaction, and relationship satisfaction."

131 "A recent study by the Population Council . . .": Lewin, Tamar, "The decay of families is global, study says."

"A 1995 Whirlpool Foundation study . . .": Families and Work Institute, "Women: The new providers."

"Douglas Besharov, a resident . . .": Lewin, "The decay of families is global, study says."

132 "A man who is not thriving . . .": Gordon, Rachel, "1 in 4 U.S. kids now live in homes without fathers."

"Echoing Ms. Salisbury's sentiments . . .": Lewin, Tamar, "Creating fathers out of men with children."

134 "Twenty percent of preschool children . . .": McLeod, Ramon G., "More dads being Mr. Moms: Study finds 20% of preschool children cared for by fathers."

"now head 14 percent . . .": *New York Times,* Nation section, "Big increase in number of single fathers," August 31, 1993.

"In 1993, David Williams . . .": Verhover, Sam Howe, "At issue: Hold a baby or hold that line?"

APPEARANCE

OUTFITS, COSTUMES, UNIFORMS AND DISGUISES

141 "Originally, pink was a boy's color . . .": Garber, Marjorie, *Vested Interests: Cross-Dressing and Cultural Anxiety,* p. 1.

"In *Vested Interests* . . .": Ibid., Chapter 1: Dress codes, "None shall wear . . . ," pp. 25–32.

142 "Lest we think . . .": Kennedy, Elizabeth Lapovsky, and Davis, Madeline D., *Boots of Leather, Slippers of Gold,* p. 180, note 29, pp. 411–412.

"A 1992 *Washington Post* article . . .": Spake, Amanda, "Dressing for power."

143 "Only during World War II . . .": Wolf, Naomi, *The Beauty Myth,* pp. 62–64.

144 "By the mid-1970s . . .": Spake, "Dressing for power."

"*Newsweek* published a photograph . . .": Gelman, David, "Homoeroticism in the ranks."

145 "Angela Padilla was the second . . .": Interview with Angela Padilla in San Francisco on August 18, 1993.

146 "Marjorie Garber describes resources . . .": Garber, *Vested Interests,* p. 44.

DIANE TORR'S "DRAG KING WORKSHOP"

146 "Diane Torr is a performance artist . . .": interview with Diane Torr in New York City on February 8, 1995.

147 *"Washington Post* staff writer . . .": Span, Paula, "Guise and dolls."

148 Julie Wheelwright, writing . . .": Wheelwright, Julie, "Out of my way, I'm a man for a day."

"In New York, Paula Span . . .": Span, "Guise and dolls."

"Joy Press, a reporter . . .": Press, Joy, "Walk like a man."

"My favorite story . . .": Knapp, Caroline, "I was a drag king."

150 "A 1981 study out of Tulane . . .": Garwood, S. Gray; Baer, Susan; Levine, Douglas; Carroll, Sudie; and O'Neal, Ed, "Sex-role expectations of socially desirable first names."

"In 1995, two researchers . . .": Associated Press, "Sophie, Sophia top ultra-feminine names."

MISS VERA'S FINISHING SCHOOL

151 "Nothing took me more . . .": Glionna, John M., "Beneath the masquerade."

"Visiting Miss Vera . . .": Interview with Miss Veronica Vera in New York City on February 8, 1995.

156 "Studies have tended . . .": Brown, G. R., and Collier, L., "Transvestites' women revisited."

"In 1994, Dr. Brown conducted . . .": Brown, M.D., George R., "Women in relationships with cross-dressing men: A descriptive study from a nonclinical setting."

157 "a section on 'Significant Others . . .' ": Stevens, Jennifer Anne, *From Masculine to Feminine and All Points in Between,* Chapter 8: "Significant others," pp. 89–100.

"Studying these wives . . .": Hunt, Sallie, and Main, Terri L., "Sexual orientation confusion among spouses of transvestites and transsexuals following disclosure of spouse's gender dysphoria."

158 "To soften the experience . . .": Stevens, *"From Masculine to Feminine and All Points in Between,"* pp. 100–104.

STEFAN LYNCH

159 "When I met Stefan . . .": Interview with Stefan Lynch in San Francisco on May 4, 1995.

160 "Beginning in 1975 . . .": Zucker, K. J.; Bradley, S. J.; Steiner, B. W.; Doering, R. W.; Sullivan, J.; Finegan, J. K.; and Richardson, M., "Gender identity problems of children and adolescents: The establishment of a special clinic."

"The Clarke Institute . . .": Interview with Dr. Kenneth Zucker in Van Nuys, California, on February 24, 1995.

The Clarke Institute is presently listed in the 1994 catalog of Fuller Theological Seminary in Pasadena, California, as a clinical facility for field training in clinical psychology (p. 188). Fuller Theological Seminary received a grant of $96,153 from the NIMH in 1976 for the behavioral treatment of childhood gender problems, with George Rekers as principal investigator. They have received local, state and federal grants for issues pertaining to children. Fuller describes its "theological stance" as including a commitment to "an evangelical fervor which flows out of an emphasis on the character of God himself, the practice of evangelism in every culture of the world, and a constant engagement with Scripture, testing all things by it" (p. 6), which would include gender behavior and sexuality. Kenneth Zucker is listed in the Fuller Theological catalog as a clinical faculty member in clinical psychology, providing supervision to the seminary's graduate students placed at Clarke for field training (p. 184).

Susan Bradley, founder of the Clarke Institute, was the chair of the DSM-IV Subcommittee for Gender Identity Disorders in children, and the Institute's Ray Blanchard and Kenneth Zucker also sat on that subcommittee. They were instrumental in removing the requirement from the DSM that a child must explicitly state distress with his anatomy and the desire to have the body of the opposite sex before being diagnosed with GID.

THE BODY AS EVIDENCE

164 "In 1986, Michael Cunningham . . .": Cunningham, Michael R., "Measuring the physical in physical attractiveness: Quasi-experimentals on the sociobiology of female facial beauty."

165 "A particularly disturbing study . . .": Langlois, J. H., and Downs, A. C., "Peer relations as a function of physical attractiveness: The eye of the beholder or behavioral reality?"

166 "Physical unattractiveness in women . . .": Farina, A.; Fischer, E. H.; Sherman, S.; Smith, W. T.; Groh, T.; and Mermin, P., "Physical attractiveness and mental illness."

"Physically attractive children . . .": Barocas, Ralph, and Black, Harvey, "Referral rate and physical attractiveness in third-grade children."

"Even sentencing to jail terms . . .": Leventhal, Gloria, and Krate, Ronald, "Physical attractiveness and severity of sentencing."

167 "In 1974, Bem created . . .": Bem, Sandra L., "The measurement of psychological androgyny."

"The rigidity of sex-typed individuals . . .": Bem, Sandra L., "Sex role adaptability: One consequence of psychological androgyny."

"In 1981, in terms of appearance . . .": Andersen, Susan M., and Bem, Sandra Lipsitz, "Sex-typing and androgyny in dyadic interaction: Individual differences in responsiveness to physical attractiveness."

168 "researchers at Auburn University . . .": Gynther, M. D.; Davis, A. T.; and Shakes, L. G., "The perception of attractivness: What about the beholders?"

"The Macho Scale was developed . . .": Villemez, Wayne J., and Touhey, John C., "A measure of individual differences in sex stereotyping and sex discrimination: The 'Macho' Scale."

169 "The Survey of Heterosexual . . .": Twentyman, C.; Boland, T.; and McFall, R. M., "Heterosocial avoidance in college males: Four studies."

"A 1987 study at the University of Georgia . . .": Moore, J. S.; Graziano, W. G.; and Millar, M. G., "Physical attractiveness, sex role orientation, and the evaluation of adults and children."

THE BODY, GENDER IDENTITY AND SEXUALITY

170 "According to the Langlois study . . .": Langlois, J. H., and Downs, A. C., "Peer relations as a function of physical attractiveness: The eye of the beholder or behavioral reality?"

171 "As early as 1965 . . .": Zucker, K. J., and Green, R., "Psychological and familial aspects of gender identity disorder," pp. 525–526.

"In the 1970s, Richard Green . . .": Green, *The "Sissy Boy Syndrome,"* pp. 24–25.

"As recently as 1993 . . .": Zucker, Kenneth J.; Wild, Jennifer; Bradley, Susan J.; and Lowry, Claire B., "Physical attractiveness of boys with gender identity disorder."

172 "To that end . . .": Zucker, K. J., and Green, R., "Psychological and familial aspects of gender identity disorder," p. 526.

"In 1995, the Clarke Institute . . .": Fridell, Sari R.; Zucker, Kenneth J.; Bradley, Susan J.; and Maing, Dianne M., "Physical attractiveness of girls with gender identity disorder." (A version of this article was presented at the meeting of the International Academy of Sex Research, Edinburgh, Scotland, June 1994.)

175 "was dismissed as early as 1940 . . .": Wortis, Joseph, "Intersexuality and effeminacy in the male homosexual."

"and in 1945 by Margaret Mead . . .": Mead, Margaret, *Male and Female: A Study of the Sexes in a Changing World,* p. 109.

"In 1981, Dr. Muriel Wilson Perkins . . .": Perkins, Muriel Wilson, "Female homosexuality and body build." This study cites support by NIMH research fellowship grant #1-FO-MH53838-01.

"to refute the work of Meyer-Bahlburg . . .": Meyer-Bahlburg, Heino F. L., "Sex hormones and female homosexuality: A critical examination."

176 "In 1985, Mary Amanda Dew . . .": Dew, Mary Amanda, "The effect of attitudes on inferences of homosexuality and perceived physical attractiveness in women."

177 "A 1990 study at the State University of New York . . .": Dunkle, John H., and Francis, Patricia L., "The role of facial masculinity/femininity in the attribution of homosexuality."

"a strangest alliance was forged . . .": Vick, Karl, "An odd alliance tries to 'out' nominee Reno."

SEEING MALE, SEEING FEMALE

179 "In 1975, the Baby X study . . .": Seavey, Carol A.; Katz, Phyllis A.; and Zalk, Sue Rosenberg, "Baby X: The effect of gender labels on adult responses to infants."

"A 1977 study conducted at Michigan State . . .": Hildebrandt, K. A., and Fitzgerald, H. E., "Gender bias in observers' perceptions of infants' sex: It's a boy most of the time!"

"To answer that question . . .": Kessler, Suzanne J., and McKenna, Wendy, *Gender: An Ethnomethodological Approach.* Chapter 4: "Developmental aspects of gender," pp. 81–111.

"designed the Overlay Study . . .": Ibid., Kessler, Chapter 6: "Toward a theory of gender," pp. 142–169.

180 "As an alternative to . . .": Interview with Evelyn Kosack, Chairman of Jolen Bleach Company, from Connecticut, June 1995.

"I interviewed a woman . . .": Interview with "Kathy" in Palo Alto, California, on March 25, 1995.

181 "but the most revealing . . .": Goetinck, Sue, "Werewolf gene could shed light on hair growth."

182 "Margaret Mead asked a question . . .": Mead, *Male and Female,* Chapter 6: "Sex and temperament," pp. 102–112.

"Nowhere is the masculine stereotype . . .": Bly, Robert, *Iron John,* pp. 45–47.

SCIENCE

188 "on the scientific study of carrots . . .": Brody, Jane E., "Health factor in vegetables still elusive."

"In 1973, a study entitled . . .": Loehlin, J. C.; Vandenberg, S. G.; and Osborne, R. T., "Blood group genes and Negro-white ability differences."

ARE BOYS AND GIRLS DIFFERENT?

189 "we are dealing with a region . . .": Fausto-Sterling, Anne, *Myths of Gender,* p. 244.

190 "In terms of brain size . . .": *Ibid.,* p. 37.
"Fausto-Sterling also cites . . .": *Ibid.,* p. 227.
"Scientists studying fetal brains . . .": Begley, Sharon, "Gray matters," *Newsweek* cover story. Cover reads: "The New Science of the Brain: Why Men and Women Think Differently."
"when at rest, the brains . . .": Kolata, Gina, "Man's world, woman's world? Brain studies point to differences."

191 "There are many examples . . .": Interview with Dr. Laura Allen in Los Angeles, on August 20, 1993.
"A UCLA study by Dr. Lewis Baxter . . .": "Behavior therapy works like drugs on brain," *Los Angeles Times,* September 16, 1992.
"Dr. Lisa F. Berkman of Yale . . .": Raeburn, Paul (Associated Press), "Family is best heart medicine."
"The problems of categorizing humanity . . .": Begley, "Gray matters."
"Ironically, in *Myths of Gender* . . .": Fausto-Sterling, *Myths of Gender* p. 85.

192 "Begley tackled one of the biggest . . .": Begley, "Gray matters."
"These types of studies give the impression . . .": Interview with Dr. Angela Pattatucci, NIMH, August 1993.
"Dr. Ruben C. Gur . . .": Rosenthal, Harry F., "Researchers find brain differences based on gender."

193 "a 1994 study at Fresno State University . . .": Associated Press, "Women test better with right questions."

194 "According to Begley, Melissa Hines . . .": Begley, "Gray matters."
"Sex-typing in children has a profound . . .": Bauer, Patricia J., "Memory for gender-consistent and gender-inconsistent event sequences by twenty-five-month-old children."

195 "A 1982 study of third- . . .": Bussey, Kay, and Perry, David G., "Same-sex imitation: The avoidance of cross-sex models or the acceptance of same-sex models?"
"In 1994, a *New York Times*/CBS poll . . .": Lewin, Tamar, "Traditional family favored by boys, not girls."
"Ironically, journalist Michael D'Antonio . . .": D'Antonio, Michael, "The fragile sex."

196 "In a review of the literature . . .": Mead, B. J., and Ignico, A. A., "Children's gender-typed perceptions of physical activity: Consequences and implications."

197 "The world of sex-based biology . . .": Angier, Natalie, "Biologists hot on track of gene for femaleness."
"However, the big bang award . . .": Angier, Natalie, "Does testosterone equal aggression? Maybe not."

198 "That the male of a species . . .": Angier, Natalie, "Feminists and Darwin: Scientists try closing the gap."

199 "a 1995 ABC news special . . .": *Boys and Girls Are Different,* ABC News Special hosted by John Stossell and aired on February 1, 1995.

200 "As early as 1968, UCLA's Robert Stoller . . .": Coates, Susan W., and

Wolfe, Sabrina M., "Gender identity disorder in boys: The interface of constitution and early experience."

"Attempts to create objective tests . . .": Coates, Susan, and Person, Ethel S., "Extreme boyhood femininity: Isolated behavior or pervasive disorder?"

"to the play behavior ratio method . . .": Rekers, *Handbook,* p. 278.

201 "Dr. Coates has asked if . . .": Paper presented by Dr. Susan Coates at CLAGS public forum, New York City, on February 10, 1995.

"clearly challenges the belief . . .": Zucker, K. J., and Green, R., "Psychological and familial aspects of gender identity disorder," p. 518.

202 "Dr. Coates now contends . . .": Coates, Susan W., and Wolfe, Sabrina M., "Gender identity disorder in boys: The interface of constitution and early experience."

"Dr. David Schwartz has challenged . . .": Paper presented by Dr. David Schwartz at CLAGS public forum, New York City, on February 10, 1995.

203 "Coates herself has noted . . .": Coates, "Gender identity disorder in boys: The interface of constitution and early experience," p. 34.

"The hormone argument . . .": Berenbaum, Sheri A., and Snyder, Elizabeth, "Early hormonal influences on childhood sex-typed activity and playmate preferences: Implications for the development of sexual orientation."

"Yet they ignore . . .": Byne, William, and Parsons, Bruce, "Human sexual orientation: The biologic theories reappraised."

"The clitoris can be as enlarged . . .": Mazur, Tom, and Dobson, Kim, "Psychologic issues in individuals with genetic, hormonal, and anatomic anomalies of the sexual system," pp. 116–117.

"In a 1994 study of thirty CAH . . .": Byne and Parsons, "Human sexual orientation: The biologic theories reappraised."

"Coates also proposes . . .": Coates, Susan W., and Wolfe, Sabrina M., "Gender identity disorder in boys: The interface of constitution and early experience."

204 "who was reported to have . . .": Herman, S. P., "Gender identity disorder in a five-year-old boy."

"Stanley, our three-year-old . . .": Haber, Calvin, "The psychoanalytic treatment of a preschool boy with a gender identity disorder."

"Five-year-old Carlos . . .": Loeb, Loretta, and Shane, Morton, "The resolution of a transsexual wish in a five-year-old boy."

205 "parents were advised . . .": Interview with Shannon Minter, January 1996.

"Sports scientists have discovered . . .": Mead, B. J., and Ignico, A. A., "Children's gender-typed perceptions of physical activity: Consequences and implications."

"she is described in the psychiatric . . .": Stoller, R. J., "Etiological factors in female transsexualism: A first approximation."

"To this end, Rekers explains . . .": Rekers, *Handbook,* p. 280.

"Dr. David Schwartz asks . . .": Paper presented by Dr. David Schwartz at CLAGS public forum, New York City, on February 10, 1995.

"As girls have been encouraged . . .": Yannis, Alex, "Women's teams rise in colleges."

"gaps between male and female runners . . .": Fausto-Sterling, *Myths of Gender,* p. 219.

206 "In 1992, both *Nature* . . .": *Ibid.,* p. 269.

"That proper training . . .": Associated Press (Natick, Mass.), "Army study finds women can train for heavy jobs."

"Shifts in the performance . . .": Silverstein, Olga, and Rashbaum, Beth, *The Courage to Raise Good Men,* p. 265.

"Dr. Roger Sperry, a well-known . . .": Fausto-Sterling, *Myths of Gender,* p. 49.

"Rather than conceptualizing . . .": *Ibid.,* p. 256.

"As Fausto-Sterling eloquently writes . . .": *Ibid.,* p. 77.

SEXUALITY

207 "Heterosexuality and homosexuality . . .": Lehrman, Sally, " 'Gay gene' study under scrutiny."

"Just as in the studies of . . .": Byne, William, and Parsons, Bruce, "Human sexual orientation: The biologic theories reappraised."

"Recently, Dr. Sandra Witelson . . .": Ritter, Malcolm, "Brain structure may be gay clue."

"Dr. Paul Billings, an internist . . .": Billings, Paul, " 'Gay gene'—A new fish story?"

208 "One of the most high-profile . . .": Interviews with Dr. Laura Allen at UCLA on August 20, 1993, and by phone on various occasions, including January 26, 1995.

209 "For the past fifteen years . . .": Kolata, Gina. "Man's world, woman's world? Brain studies point to differences."

See also Fausto-Sterling, *Myths of Gender,* Chapter 5: "Hormones and aggression," pp. 123–154, for commentary on hormones and animal studies.

210 "Lesbians have *never* been shown . . .": Meyer-Bahlburg, Heino F. L., "Sex hormones and female homosexuality: A critical examination."

"In terms of the 'lesbian' rats . . .": Byne, William, and Parsons, Bruce, "Human sexual orientation: The biologic theories reappraised."

211 "This hunch is contrary . . .": Meyer-Bahlburg, "Sex hormones and female homosexuality."

212 "at the Clarke Institute . . .": Tkachuk, J., and Zucker, K. J., "The relation among sexual orientation, spatial ability, handedness, and recalled childhood gender identity in women and men."

213 "in 1993, Byne and Parsons . . .": Byne and Parsons, "Human sexual orientation."

214 "In 1995, researchers from Northwestern . . .": Bailey, J. M.; Bobrow, D.; Wolfe, M.; and Mikach, S., "Sexual orientation of adult sons of gay fathers."

"Studies on the children of lesbians . . .": Patterson, Charlotte J., "Children of lesbian and gay parents," and

Golombok, Susan, and Tasker, Fiona, "Do parents influence the sexual orientation of their children? Findings from a longitudinal study of lesbian families."

"The results of a . . .": Lehrman, Sally, " 'Gay gene' study under scrutiny."

215 "different genes can trigger . . .": Lehrman, Sally, "Same diseases, different genes in varied peoples."

"The exact location of a gene . . .": Brown, David, and Weiss, Rick, "Scientists reveal first rough map of genes."

"estimates suggest . . .": Fausto-Sterling, *Myths of Gender,* p. 71.

216 "are now referring to homosexuality . . .": Associated Press, "Christians trying to end talk of gays in school."

"comparable to alcoholism . . .": Mills, Kim, "Being gay similar to alcoholism."

"all recent studies have shown . . .": Berenbaum, Sheri A., and Snyder, Elizabeth, "Early hormonal influences on childhood sex-typed activity and playmate preferences: Implications for the development of sexual orientation."

"Studies claim that gay men . . .": Bailey, J. Michael, and Zucker, Kenneth J., "Childhood sex-typed behavior and sexual orientation: A conceptual analysis and quantitative review."

"To understand this phenomenon . . .": Dawes, Robyn M., *House of Cards: Psychology and Psychotherapy Built on Myth,* pp. 129–130.

218 "As the developmentalist . . .": Kakutani, Michiko, "Using memory to reorder, even transform, a life." Review of *White Gloves: How We Create Ourselves Through Memory,* by John Kotre.

"By adulthood . . .": Begley, Sharon, "Your child's brain."

"Oliver Sacks explained it best . . .": Sacks, Oliver, *An Anthropologist on Mars: Seven Paradoxical Tales,* p. xvii.

ALL GIRL, ALL BOY?

219 "In 1994, the male Dayak . . .": Diamond, Jared, "Father's milk," p. 83.

"In 1993, Dr. Anne Fausto-Sterling . . .": Fausto-Sterling, Anne, "The five sexes: Why male and female are not enough."

"on the Op-Ed page . . .": Fausto-Sterling, Anne, "How many sexes are there?"

"There were those who went so far . . .": Peer Review, *The Sciences,* July/August 1993, p. 3.

220 "Rather than exhibiting derangement . . .": Fausto-Sterling, "The five sexes."

"at a 1995 conference in New York . . .": Paper presented by Dr. Anne Fausto-Sterling at CLAGS public forum, New York City, on February 10, 1995.

"What seemed so preposterously . . .": Fausto-Sterling, "The five sexes."

221 "The hermaphrodite, today . . .": Interview with Bo Laurent in San Francisco on March 2, 1995.

"Laurent estimates that . . .": Using statistics available in medical textbooks, Bo Laurent assembled the frequency tables for all conditions that are classified as intersex: gonadal dysgenesis (Turner's and Klinefelter's syndromes); true hermaphroditism; female pseudohermaphroditism, including congenital adrenal hyperplasia; male pseudohermaphroditism, including androgen insensitivities and chromosomal mosaicisms, XX males, etc.; hypospadias (males); mullerian agenesis (females); micropenis; and adult cryptorchism. She listed without frequencies those conditions which are also intersex but which she did not include in her final estimate since there are no statistics available on their numbers. Under the category of female pseudohermaphroditism, these conditions include synthetic progestins and other teratogens; under the category of male pseudohermaphroditism, these include inborn errors of testosterone synthesis and metabolism of mullerian inhibiting factor. A final known condition without estimates is mullerian agenesis in females. This means that her estimates of intersexed individuals are conservative.

224 "Cheryl Chase recently attended . . .": Interview with Cheryl Chase on April 7, 1995.

226 "Her first contact with . . .": Peer Review, *The Sciences,* July/August 1993, p. 3.

"The ISNA now has . . .": The mailing address for the Intersex Society of North America is P.O. Box 31791, San Francisco, CA 94131.

227 "In 1988, Mrs. Jackie Burrows . . .": ALIAS, the support group for intersex children, can be reached in England at 2 Shirburn Avenue, Mansfield, Nottinghamshire, NG18 2BY, UK. Tel: +44(0)1623 661749. According to ALIAS, "The Baby Who Was Different—A Fairy Tale" was written by Dr. Garry Warne and published in *Maternal and Child Health,* May 1992, pp. 159–160. Dr. Warne is the Director of the Department of Endocrinology and Diabetes at the Royal Children's Hospital in Melbourne, Victoria, Australia.

"One individual with a strong sense . . .": Interview with Lynn Edward Harris on May 30, 1995.

229 "The truth is . . .": Interview with Bo Laurent in San Francisco on March 2, 1995.

"as reported in the *Washington Post* . . .": Editorial, "Sex tests for athletes."

GENDER INDEPENDENCE

Special Note: Many of the studies cited in this section used "androgyny" as the description for an alternative to sex-typed behavior. For our purposes, I will refer to "gender independence" as the alternative behavior, in that it is unlikely that those described as "androgynous" were ever neatly balanced, at all times, with a permanent blend of traditional male and female traits (the requirement for the technical label of psychological androgyny). In 1993, a journal article by Roos Vonk and Richard D. Ashmore, from Leiden University in the Netherlands (*Social Psychology Quarterly,* December, Vol. 56 (4): 278–287), pointed out that androgynous subjects used more situational qualifiers in describing their masculine, feminine and gender-neutral attributes. This suggested to the researchers that individuals, rather than being a permanent blend of traits, enact masculine and feminine qualities on different occasions. The hallmark of androgyny was found to be a more general situational flexibility, and there was no evidence that androgynous subjects enact their "masculine and feminine sides" simultaneously. The possible variations within the arena of "androgyny" are quite extraordinary, as a 1989 Canadian paper by Guy Bouchard, "Fifty-six conceptions of androgyny," demonstrated.

A great debt in the evolution of psychology is owed to Dr. Bem, the originator of the BSRI, and the concept of "androgyny," but as she herself has said, "If there is a moral to the concept of psychological androgyny, it is that behavior should have no gender. But there is an irony here, for the concept of androgyny contains an inner contradiction and hence the seeds of its own destruction. Thus, as the etymology of the word implies, the concept of androgyny necessarily presupposes that the concepts of femininity and masculinity themselves have distinct and substantive content. But to the extent that the androgynous message is absorbed by the culture, the concepts of femininity and masculinity will cease to have such content and the distinctions to which they refer will blur into invisibility. Thus, when androgyny becomes a reality, the concept of androgyny will have been transcended." (Bem, Sandra, "Theory and measurement of androgyny: A reply to Pedhazur-Tetenbaum and Locksley-Colten critiques.")

235 "People who are gender independent . . .": Rotter, Naomi G., and O'Connell, Agnes N., "The relationships among sex-role orientation, cognitive complexity, and tolerance for ambiguity."

"Women who subscribe to the traditional . . .": Studies consulted on Women and Depression:

Tinsley, Emiley G.; Sullivan-Guest, Sandra; and McGuire, John, "Feminine sex roles and depression in middle-aged women," and Sanfilipo, Michael P., "Masculinity, femininity, and subjective experiences of depression," and Elpern, Sarah, and Karp, Stephen A., "Sex-role orientation and depressive symptomatology," and

Feather, N. T. (South Australia), "Masculinity, femininity, self-esteem and subclinical depression," and

Krames, L.; England, R.; and Flett, G. L., "The role of masculinity and femininity in depression and social satisfaction in elderly females."

"Learned helplessness means . . .": Studies consulted on Learned Helplessness/Depression:

Baucom, Donald H., and Danker-Brown, Pamela, "Sex role identity and sex-stereotyped tasks in the development of learned helplessness in women," and

Baucom, Donald H., and Weiss, Bahr, "Peers' granting of control to women with different sex role identities: Implications for depression," and

Baucom, D. H., "Influence of sex roles on the development of learned helplessness," and

Baucom, D. H., "Sex role identity and the decision to regain control among women: A learned helplessness investigation," and

Abramson, Lyn Y., Seligman, Martin E. P.; and Teasdale, John D. (London), "Learned helplessness in humans: critique and formulation."

236 "Since the 1970s, masculine sex-typed . . .": Studies consulted on "Type A" Coronary-Prone Behavior:

Grimm, Laurence G., and Yarnold, Paul R., "Sex typing and the coronary-prone behavior pattern," and

Wright, L.; Abbanato, K. R.; Lancaster, C.; Bourke, M. L.; and Nielsen, B. A., "Gender-related subcomponent differences in high type A subjects," and

Yarnold, P. R.; Bryant, F. B.; and Litsas, F., "Type A behaviour and psychological androgyny among Greek college students," and

Rosen, Raymond C.; Kostis, John B.; Jekelis, Albert; and Taska, Lynn S.,

"Sexual sequelae of antihypertensive drugs: Treatment effects on self-report and physiological measures in middle-aged male hypertensives."

"The fact that men die . . .": Samuelson, Robert J., "Getting serious," p. 43.

"According to Dr. Ken Goldberg . . .": Reuters, "Doctors tie men's mentality to their shorter life span."

237 "In late 1993, a German study . . .": Nieschlag, Eberhard; Nieschlag, Susan; and Behre, Hermann M., "Lifespan and testosterone."

"95 percent of anorexics and bulimics . . .": Wolf, Naomi, *The Beauty Myth*, Chapter on "Hunger," pp. 179–217.

"While only one man in ten . . .": Wolf, *The Beauty Myth*, chapter on "Religion," p. 94.

238 "In 1990, researchers found that bulimic . . .": Brown, J. A.; Cross, H. J.; Nelson, J. M.; "Sex-role identity and sex-role ideology in college women with bulimic behavior."

"pleasure in sex is rare . . .": Wolf, *The Beauity Myth*, p. 193.

"Obsession with penis size . . .": Carlsen, William, "Suit filed against penile implant maker."

"In 1995, the American Urological Association . . .": Lehrman, Sally, "Procedure to enlarge penis gets low marks."

239 "In the 1990s, researchers created the term . . .": Studies consulted on Gender Role Conflict in men:

Good, G. E.; Robertson, J. M.; O'Neil, J. M.; Fitzgerald, L. F.; Stevens, M.; DeBord, K. A.; Bartels, K. M.; and Braverman, D. G., "Male gender role conflict: Psychometric issues and relations to psychological distress," and

Heppner, P. Paul, "On gender role conflict in men—Future directions and implications for counseling: Comment on Good et al. (1995) and Cournoyer and Mahalik (1995)," and

Cournoyer, Robert J., and Mahalik, James R., "Cross-sectional study of gender role conflict examining college-aged and middle-aged men."

"From lower risks of suicidal behavior . . .": Studies that revealed advantages of Gender Independence [Androgyny—See Special Note, p. 274] over sex-typed behavior:

Rotter, Naomi G., and O'Connell, Agnes N., "The relationships among sex-role orientation, cognitive complexity, and tolerance for ambiguity," and Blair, Kathryn-Anne, "Androgyny and tolerance of ambiguity: Predictors of stepparenting success," and

Scandura, T. A., and Ragins, B. R., "The effects of sex and gender role orientation on mentorship in male-dominated occupations," and

Lagace, R. R., and Twible, J. L., "The androgyny level of salespeople: Gooses and ganders, or all geese?" and

Arkkelin, D., and O'Connor, R., "The 'good' professional: Effects of trait-profile gender type, androgyny, and likableness on impressions of incumbents of sex-typed occupations," and

Jurma, W. E., and Powell, M. L., "Perceived gender roles of managers and effective conflict management," and

Ellis, Jon B., and Range, Lillian M., "Femininity and reasons for living," and

Grimmell, Derek, and Stern, Gary S., "The relationship between gender role ideals and psychological well-being," and

Hunt, Melissa G., "Expressiveness does predict well-being," and

Shichman, Shula, and Cooper, Ellen, "Life satisfaction and sex-role concept," and

Jones, D. C.; Bloys, N.; and Wood, M., "Sex roles and friendship patterns," and

Gately, D., and Schwebel, A. I., "Favorable outcomes in children after parental divorce. Special issue: Divorce and the next generation: Effects on young adults' patterns of intimacy and expectations for marriage," and

Lombardo, J. P., and Kemper, T. R., "Sex role and parental behaviors."

240 "In the elderly population . . .": Studies consulted on Sex Roles and Senior Citizens:

Dean-Church, L., and Gilroy, F. D., "Relation of sex-role orientation to life satisfaction in a healthy elderly sample," and

Wink, Paul, and Helson, Ravenna, "Personality change in women and their partners," and

Sinnott, Jan Dynda, "Older men, older women: Are their perceived sex roles similar?" and

Bernard, J. L.; Bernard, S. L.; and Bernard, M. L., "Courtship violence and sex-typing."

241 "Most sex crimes against women . . .": Rekers, *Handbook,* pp. 434–435.

"Those most vulnerable . . .": Anderson, T., and Leitner, L. M., "The relationship between the Defense Mechanisms Inventory and reported symptomatology in college females."

"a man's sense of self . . .": Gray, John, *Men Are from Mars, Women Are from Venus,* p. 16.

"A woman's sense of self . . .": Ibid., p. 18.

"a man is fulfilled through working . . .": Ibid., p. 39.

"when they feel cherished . . .": Ibid., p. 43.

"When a man is in a negative state . . .": Ibid., p. 203.

"Never go into a man's cave . . .": Ibid., p. 71.

"distract herself by calling . . .": Ibid., p. 77.

"Men are advised . . .": Ibid., p. 116.

"Men argue for the right . . .": Ibid., p. 124.

"It is difficult for a man to listen . . .": Ibid., p. 58.

"Most men strive for greater . . .": Ibid., p. 189.

"including listening to . . .": Ibid., p. 77.

"who might as well be . . .": Ibid., p. 5.

"He even provides a chapter . . .": Ibid., pp. 177–205.

243 "drops us into the same trap . . .": Williamson, Marianne, *A Woman's Worth,* p. 63.

"She advises that . . .": Ibid., p. 62.

"basically the chosen people . . .": Ibid., p. 126.

"Williamson asks women . . .": Ibid., pp. 3–21.

244 "Studies performed in 1982, 1989 and 1994 . . .": Safir, M. P.; Peres, Y.; Lichtenstein, M.; Hoch, Z.; and Shepher, J., "Psychological androgyny and sexual adequacy," and

Peterson, C.; Baucom, D. H.; Elliott, M. J.; and Farr, P. A., "The relationship between sex role identity and marital adjustment," and

Green, Beth L., and Kenrick, Douglas T., "The attractiveness of gender-typed traits at different relationship levels: Androgynous characteristics may be desirable after all."

245 "In 1992, the *Journal of Family Therapy* . . .": Foreman, Sally, and Dallos, Rudi, "Inequalities of power and sexual problems."

"In 1994, Cheryl Rampage . . .": Rampage, Cheryl, "Power, gender, and marital intimacy."

246 "In 1983, a case study . . .": Dowrick, Peter W., "Video training of alternatives to cross-gender identity behaviors in a 4-year-old boy."

247 "In 1988, researchers at Wake Forest . . .": Harris, Catherine T.; Perricone, Philip J.; and Smith, Margaret S., "The artist and androgyny: A study of gender identity in visual artists."

"a 1994 study found that both music . . .": Wubbenhorst, Thomas Martin, "Personality characteristics of music educators and performers."

"In Germany . . .": Hassler, Marianne, and Nieschlag, Eberhard, "Masculinity, femininity, and musical composition: Psychological and psychoendocrinological aspects of musical and spatial faculties," and

Hassler, Marianne, "Testosterone and artistic talents," and

Hassler, Marianne; Nieschlag, Eberhard; and de la Motte, Diether, "Creative musical talent, cognitive functioning, and gender: Psychobiological aspects."

"The testosterone level in the saliva . . .": Mazur, Allen, and Lamb, Theodore A., "Testosterone, status, and mood in human males."

248 "One of the chapters focused . . .": Obler, Loraine K., and Fein, Deborah, eds., *The Exceptional Brain: Neuropsychology of Talent and Special Abilities,* Chapter 7: "The Chess Mind," p. 156.

"Left-handed homosexuals . . .": Ibid., Introduction, p. 12.

249 "The hypothesis was also advanced . . .": Ibid., Chapter 7: "The Chess Mind," pp. 156–177.

"an extraordinary experiment in the early 1970s . . .": Myers, Linnet, "Teen-age girl topples chess legend Spassky."

"the evolution of living things . . .": Armstrong, Thomas, *Awakening Your Child's Natural Genius,* p. 5.

"In writing of giftedness . . .": Ibid., Chapter 12: "Giftedness: Every Child's Birthright," pp. 183–194.

250 "Nowhere is it even suggested . . .": Ibid., Chapter 5: "Math for the Real World," pp. 75–88.

"Robert Stoller described the girls . . .": Stoller, R. J., "Etiological factors in female transsexualism: A first approximation."

"and in terms of the boys . . .": Stoller, R. J., *Sex and Gender,* Volume I, Chapter 10:"Artistic Ability and Boyhood Femininity," pp. 126–130.

"It was fashionable . . .": Zucker, K. J., and Green, R., "Psychological and familial aspects of gender identity disorder," p. 525.

"Green and Money also observed . . .": Green, Richard, and Money, John, "Stage acting, role taking, and effeminate impersonation during boyhood."

251 "That gay men and lesbians . . .": Witt, Lynn; Thomas, Sherry; and Marcus, Eric, eds., *Out in All Directions.*

"As early as 1957 . . .": Barron, Frank, "Originality in relation to personality and intellect."

"In 1962, Donald W. MacKinnon . . .": MacKinnon, Donald W., "The nature and nurture of creative talent."

253 "prior to the publication . . .": Friedan, Betty, *The Feminine Mystique.*

"He did not hypothesize . . .": Zucker, K. J., and Green, R., "Psychological and familial aspects of gender identity disorder," p. 525.

"She reported that . . .": Maccoby, Eleanor E., "Sex differences in intellectual functioning," p. 34.

"She noted that . . .": Ibid., p. 35.

"Maccoby anticipated this fear . . .": Ibid., p. 35.

"the great mind is androgynous . . .": Woolf, Virginia, *A Room of One's Own,* p. 98.

254 "When asked of his source . . .": McDougall, Joyce, "The dead father: On early psychic trauma and its relation to disturbance in sexual identity and in creative activity."

"Anne Rice has said . . .": Ramsland, Katherine, *Prism of the Night: A Biography of Anne Rice.*

"Joyce Carol Oates also took . . .": Smith, Joan, "Dream weavings of Joyce Carol Oates."

"As William James has said . . .": Armstrong, Thomas, *Awakening Your Child's Natural Genius,* p. 193.

BIBLIOGRAPHY

JOURNAL AND NEWS ARTICLES:

ABELSON, GEOFFREY, and PALUSZNY, MARIA. "Gender identity in a group of retarded children." *Journal of Autism and Childhood Schizophrenia,* Vol. 8, No. 4, 1978.

ABRAMSON, LYN Y.; SELIGMAN, MARTIN E. P.; and TEASDALE, JOHN D. (London). "Learned helplessness in humans: critique and formulation." *Journal of Abnormal Psychology* 87: 49–74, 1978.

ADELMAN, MARCY R. "A comparison of professionally employed lesbians and heterosexual women on the MMPI." *Archives of Sexual Behavior,* Vol. 6, No. 3, 193–201, 1977.

AKERS, JEAN S., and CONAWAY, CLINTON H. "Female homosexual behavior in Macaca Mulatta." *Archives of Sexual Behavior,* Vol. 8, No. 1, 1979.

ALLEN, LAURA S., and GORSKI, ROGER A. "Sexual orientation and the size of the anterior commissure in the human brain." *Proceedings of the National Academy of Sciences, USA,* Vol. 89, pp. 7199–7202, August 1992.

ALLEN, LAURA S.; RICHEY, MARK F.; CHAI, YEE M.; and GORSKI, ROGER A. "Sex differences in the corpus callosum of the living human being." *Journal of Neuroscience* 11 (4): 933–942, April 1991.

ALLEY, THOMAS R. "Head shape and the perception of cuteness." *Developmental Psychology,* Vol. 17 (5): 650–654, 1981.

ALTSCHULER, JENNY. "Gender and illness: implications for family therapy." *Journal of Family Therapy* 15: 381–401, 1993.

AMERICAN PSYCHIATRIC ASSOCIATION, "She wants to be a boy." *DSM-III-R Casebook.* Washington, D.C.: American Psychiatric Press, pp. 349–351, 1989.

ANDERSEN, SUSAN M., and BEM, SANDRA LIPSITZ. "Sex typing and androgyny in dyadic interaction: Individual differences in responsiveness to physical attractiveness." *Journal of Personality and Social Psychology,* Vol. 41 (1): 74–86, 1981.

ANDERSON, T., and LEITNER, L. M. "The relationship between the Defense

Mechanisms Inventory and reported symptomatology in college females." *Personality and Individual Differences,* Vol. 12 (9): 967–969, 1991.

ANGIER, NATALIE. "Does testosterone equal aggression? Maybe not." *New York Times,* p. 1, June 20, 1995.

———. "How biology affects behavior and vice versa." *New York Times,* Section B, May 30, 1995.

———. "Biologists hot on track of gene for femaleness." *New York Times,* Section B, August 30, 1994.

———. "Feminists and Darwin: Scientists try closing the gap." *New York Times,* Section B, p. 7, June 21, 1994.

ARKKELIN, D., and O'CONNOR, R. "The 'good' professional: Effects of trait-profile gender type, androgyny, and likableness on impressions of incumbents of sex-typed occupations." *Sex Roles,* Vol. 27 (9/10): 517–532, 1992.

ASARNOW, JOAN ROSENBAUM. "Annotation: childhood-onset schizophrenia." *Journal of Child Psychology and Psychiatry and Allied Disciplines,* Vol. 35 (8): 1345–1371, 1994.

ASHTON, W. A., and FUEHRER, A. "Effects of gender and gender role identification of participant and type of social support resource on support seeking." *Sex Roles,* Vol. 28 (7/8): 461–476, 1993.

ASSOCIATED PRESS. "Christians trying to end talk of gays in school." *San Francisco Chronicle,* October 30, 1995.

———. "Sophie, Sophia top ultra-feminine names." *San Francisco Examiner,* p. B2, January 3, 1995.

———. "Women test better with right questions." *San Francisco Examiner,* p. A7, November 29, 1994.

BAILEY, J. M.; BOBROW, D.; WOLFE, M; and MIKACH, S. "Sexual orientation of adult sons of gay fathers." *Developmental Psychology,* Vol. 31 (1): 124–129, 1995.

BAILEY, J. MICHAEL, and ZUCKER, KENNETH J. "Childhood sex-typed behavior and sexual orientation: A conceptual analysis and quantitative review." *Developmental Psychology,* Vol. 31 (1): 43–55, 1995.

BAKWIN, HARRY. "Transvestism in children." *Journal of Pediatrics,* Vol. 56: 294–298, 1960.

BAKWIN, HARRY, and BAKWIN, RUTH. "Psychologic aspects of pediatrics: Homosexual behavior in children." *Journal of Pediatrics,* Vol. 43: 108–111, 1953.

BALLARD-REISCH, D., and ELTON, M. "Gender orientation and the Bem sex role inventory: A psychological construct revisited." *Sex Roles,* Vol. 27 (5/6): 291–306, 1992.

BARLOW, DAVID H.; HAYES, STEVEN C.; NELSON, ROSEMERY O.; STEELE, DAVID L.; MEELER, MARIE E. "Sex role motor behavior: A behavioral checklist." *Behavioral Assessment,* Vol. 1: 119–138, 1979.

BARLOW, DAVID H.; REYNOLDS, JOYCE; and AGRAS, STEWART. "Gender identity change in a transsexual." *Archives of General Psychiatry,* Vol. 28: 569–576, 1973.

BAROCAS, RALPH, and BLACK, HARVEY. "Referral rate and physical attractiveness in third-grade children." *Perceptual and Motor Skills,* Vol. 39: 731–734, 1974.

BARRON, FRANK. "Originality in relation to personality and intellect." *Journal of Personality* 25: 730–42, 1957.

BAR-TAL, DANIEL, and SAXE, LEONARD. "Physical attractiveness and its relationship to sex-role stereotyping." *Sex Roles,* Vol. 2 (2): 123–133, 1976.

BAUCOM, D. H. "Influence of sex roles on the development of learned helplessness." *Journal of Consulting and Clinical Psychology* 47: 928–936, 1979.

BAUCOM, D. H. "Sex role identity and the decision to regain control among women: A learned helplessness investigation." *Journal of Personality and Social Psychology,* Vol. 44: 334–343, 1983.

BAUCOM, DONALD H., and DANKER-BROWN, PAMELA. "Sex role identity and sex-stereotyped tasks in the development of learned helplessness in women." *Journal of Personality and Social Psychology* 46 (2): 422–430, 1984.

BAUCOM, DONALD H., and WEISS, BAHR. "Peers' granting of control to women with different sex role identities: Implications for depression." *Journal of Personality and Social Psychology* 51: 1075–1080, 1986.

BAUER, PATRICIA J. "Memory for gender-consistent and gender-inconsistent event sequences by twenty-five-month-old children." *Child Development* 64: 285–297, 1993.

BEBBINGTON, PAUL E. "Treatment of male sexual deviation by use of a vibrator: Case Report." *Archives of Sexual Behavior,* Vol. 6, No. 1: 21–24, 1977.

BEGLEY, SHARON. "Your child's brain." *Newsweek,* pp. 55–62, February 19, 1996.

———. "Gray matters." *Newsweek,* pp. 48–54, March 27, 1995.

"Behavior therapy works like drugs on brain." *Los Angeles Times,* September 16, 1992.

BELSKY, J. "Exploring individual differences in marital change across the transition to parenthood: The role of violated expectations." *Journal of Marriage and the Family,* Vol. 47: 1037–1044, 1985.

BEM, SANDRA. "Theory and measurement of androgyny: A reply to Pedhazur-Tetenbaum and Locksley-Colten critiques." *Journal of Personality and Social Psychology,* Vol. 37: 1047–1054, 1979.

BEM, SANDRA L. "Sex role adaptability: One consequence of psychological androgyny." *Journal of Personality and Social Psychology* 31 (4): 634–643, 1975.

———. "The measurement of psychological androgyny." *Journal of Consulting and Clinical Psychology,* Vol. 42 (2): 155–162, 1974.

BENDER, LAURETTA, and PASTER, SAMUEL. "Homosexual trends in children." *American Journal of Orthopsychiatry,* Vol. 11: 730–743, 1941.

BERENBAUM, SHERI A., and SNYDER, ELIZABETH. "Early hormonal influences on childhood sex-typed activity and playmate preferences: Implications for the development of sexual orientation." *Developmental Psychology,* Vol. 31 (1): 31–42, 1995.

BERNARD, J. L.; BERNARD, S. L.; BERNARD, M. L. "Courtship violence and sex-typing." *Family Relations,* Vol. 34 (4/October): 573–576, 1985.

BILLINGS, PAUL. "Gay gene—a new fish story?" Op-Ed page, *San Francisco Examiner,* p. A17, August 1, 1993.

BJORNSON, R., and WALDMAN, M. R., Eds. "Rethinking patterns of knowledge." *Papers in Comparative Studies,* Vol. 6, Ohio State University, Center for Comparative Studies in the Humanities, 1988–1989.

BLAIR, KATHRYN-ANNE. "Androgyny and tolerance of ambiguity: Predictors of stepparenting success." University of Missouri, Columbia. Dissertation Abstracts International: The Humanities and Social Sciences; 54, 5, Nov., 1965-A, 1993.

281

BLAKESLEE, SANDRA. "In brain's early growth, timetable may be crucial." *New York Times,* p. B5, August 29, 1995.

BLANCHARD, RAY. "A structural equation model for age at clinical presentation in nonhomosexual male gender dysphorics." *Archives of Sexual Behavior,* Vol. 23, No. 3, 1994.

————. "Varieties of autogynephilia and their relationship to gender dysphoria." *Archives of Sexual Behavior,* Vol. 22, No. 3, 1993.

————. "The classification and labeling of nonhomosexual gender dysphorias." *Archives of Sexual Behavior,* Vol. 18 (4), 315–334, 1989.

————. "Phallometric detection of fetishistic arousal in heterosexual male cross-dressers." *Journal of Sex Research* 22: No. 4, 452–462, 1986.

BLANCHARD, RAY, and FREUND, KURT. "Measuring masculine gender identity in females." *Journal of Consulting and Clinical Psychology,* Vol. 51 (2) 205–214, 1983.

BLANCHARD, RAY; CLEMMENSEN, LEONARD H.; and STEINER, BETTY W. "Heterosexual and homosexual gender dysphoria." *Archives of Sexual Behavior,* Vol. 16 (2), 139–152, 1987.

BOUCHARD, GUY. "Fifty-six conceptions of androgyny; Cinquante-six conceptions de l'androgynie." *Dialogue,* Vol. 28 (4): 609–636, 1989.

BRADLEY, SUSAN J.; BLANCHARD, RAY; COATES, SUSAN; GREEN, RICHARD; LEVINE, STEPHEN B.; MEYER-BAHLBURG, HEINO F. L.; PAULY, IRA B.; and ZUCKER, KENNETH J. "Interim report of the DSM-IV subcommittee on gender identity disorders." *Archives of Sexual Behavior,* Vol. 20, No. 4: 333–343, 1991.

BRADLEY, SUSAN J., and ZUCKER, KENNETH. "Gender identity disorder and psychosexual problems in children and adolescents." *Canadian Journal of Psychiatry,* Vol. 35: 477–486, 1990.

BRETHERTON, INGE. "The origins of attachment theory: John Bowlby and Mary Ainsworth." *Developmental Psychology,* Vol. 28 (5): 759–775, 1992.

BRODY, JANE E. "Health factor in vegetables still elusive." *New York Times,* p. B5, February 21, 1995.

BROWN, DAVID, and WEISS, RICK. "Scientists reveal first rough map of genes." *San Francisco Chronicle* (from the *Washington Post*), p. A16, September 28, 1995.

BROWN, G. R., and COLLIER, L. "Transvestites' women revisited." *Archives of Sexual Behavior,* Vol. 18: 73–83, 1989.

BROWN, M.D., GEORGE R. "Women in relationships with cross-dressing men: A descriptive study from a nonclinical setting." *Archives of Sexual Behavior,* Vol. 23, No. 5, 515–529, 1994.

BROWN, M.D., CAPT. USAF, GEORGE R. "Transsexuals in the military: flight into hypermasculinity." *Archives of Sexual Behavior,* Vol. 17, No. 6, 1988.

BROWN, J. A.; CROSS, H. J.; and NELSON, J. M. "Sex-role identity and sex-role ideology in college women with bulimic behavior." *International Journal of Eating Disorders,* Vol. 9 (5): 571–575, 1990.

BRYSON, R. B.; BRYSON, J. B.; LICHT, M. H.; and LICHT, B. G. "The professional pair: Husband and wife psychologists." *American Psychologist,* Vol. 31: 10–17, January 1976.

BUSSEY, KAY, and PERRY, DAVID G. "Same-sex imitation: The avoidance of cross-sex models or the acceptance of same-sex models?" *Sex Roles* 8: 773–784, 1982.

BYNE, WILLIAM, and PARSONS, BRUCE. "Human sexual orientation: The biologic theories reappraised." *Archives of General Psychiatry* 50: 228–239, March 1993.

CARLSEN, WILLIAM. "Suit filed against penile implant maker." *San Francisco Chronicle,* p. A1, May 21, 1994.

CARRIER, J. M. "Childhood cross-gender behavior and adult homosexuality" (Letter to the Editor). *Archives of Sexual Behavior* 15: 89–93, 1986.

CHIRA, SUSAN. "Push to revamp ideal for American fathers: Traditional male with some emotion." *New York Times,* Sunday National Edition, June 19, 1994.

COATES, SUSAN. "The etiology of boyhood gender identity disorder: An integrative model." *Interface of Psychoanalysis and Psychology,* Eds. James W. Barron, Morris N. Eagle, and David L. Wolitzky, American Psychology Association: Washington, D.C. Chapter 10, pp. 245–265, 1992.

COATES, SUSAN. "Ontogenesis of boyhood gender identity disorder." *Journal of the American Academy of Psychoanalysis* 18 (3): 414–438, 1990.

COATES, SUSAN, and MARANTZ, SONIA. "Mothers of boys with gender identity disorder: A comparison of matched controls." *Journal of the American Academy of Child and Adolescent Psychiatry,* Vol. 30 (2): 310–315, March 1991.

COATES, SUSAN, and PERSON, ETHEL S. "Extreme boyhood femininity: Isolated behavior or pervasive disorder?" *Annual Progress in Child Psychiatry and Child Development,* 197–213, 1986. (Reprint from *Journal of the American Academy of Child Psychiatry,* Vol. 24 (6): 702–709, Nov. 1985.)

COATES, SUSAN, and TUBER, STEVEN. "Indices of psychopathology in the Rorschachs of boys with severe gender identity disorder: A comparison with normal control subjects." *Journal of Personality Assessment,* Vol. 53 (1): 100–112, 1989.

COATES, SUSAN W., and WOLFE, SABRINA M. "Gender identity disorder in boys: The interface of constitution and early experience." *Psychoanalytic Inquiry* 15 (in press), January 1995.

COATES, SUSAN W.; HAHN-BURKE, S.; and WOLFE, SABRINA. "Do boys with gender identity disorder have a shy, inhibited temperament?" Paper presented at the Annual Meeting of the American Academy of Child and Adolescent Psychiatry, New York, 1994.

COATES, SUSAN; HAHN-BURKE, SARAH; WOLFE, SABRINA; SHINDLEDECKER, RICHARD; and NIERENBERG, ONA. "Sensory reactivity in boys with gender identity disorder: A comparison with matched controls." October 16, 1994. Unpublished.

COLEMAN, ELI; COLGAN, PHILIP; and GOOREN, LOUIS. "Male cross-gender behavior in Myanmar (Burma): A description of the Acault." *Archives of Sexual Behavior,* Vol. 21 (3): 313–321, 1992.

COLMAN, ANDREW M. " 'Scientific' racism and the evidence on race and intelligence." *Race,* Vol. 14 (2): 137–153, 1972.

CONSTANTINOPLE, ANNE. "Masculinity-Femininity: An exception to a famous dictum?" *Psychological Bulletin* 80 (5): 389–407, 1973.

————. "Sex-role acquisition: In search of the elephant." *Sex Roles* Vol. 5 (2): 121–133, 1979.

CONWAY, MICHAEL; GIANNOPOULOS, CONSTANTINA; and STIEFENHOFER, KARIN. "Response styles to sadness are related to sex and sex-role orientation." *Sex Roles* 22: 579–587, 1990.

COURNOYER, ROBERT J., and MAHALIK, JAMES R. "Cross-sectional study of gender role conflict examining college-aged and middle-aged men." *Journal of Counseling Psychology,* Vol. 42 (1): 11–19, 1995.

COVERMAN, SHELLEY, and SHELEY, JOSEPH F. "Change in men's housework and child-care time, 1965–1975." *Journal of Marriage and the Family,* Vol. 48: 413–422, May 1986.

COWAN, P. A. "Becoming a father: A time of change, an opportunity for development." In *Fatherhood Today: Men's Changing Role in the Family,* P. Bronstein and C. Cowan, Eds. New York: Wiley, 1988.

COWLEY, GEOFFREY. "It's time to rethink nature and nurture." *Newsweek,* pp. 52–53, March 27, 1995.

CRAWFORD, C. B. "Effects of sex and sex roles on same-sex touch." *Perceptual and Motor Skills,* Vol. 78 (2): 391–394, 1994.

CULP, REX E.; COOK, ALICIA S.; and HOUSLEY, PATRICIA C. "A comparison of observed and reported adult-infant interactions: Effects of perceived sex." *Sex Roles,* Vol. 9, No. 4: 475–479, 1983.

CUNNINGHAM, MICHAEL R. "Measuring the physical in physical attractiveness: Quasi-experimentals on the sociobiology of female facial beauty." *Journal of Personality and Social Psychology,* Vol. 50 (5): 925–935, 1986.

D'ANTONIO, MICHAEL. "The fragile sex." *Los Angeles Times Magazine,* p. 17, December 4, 1994.

DAVENPORT, CHARLES W. "A follow-up study of 10 feminine boys." *Archives of Sexual Behavior,* Vol. 15 (6): 511–517, Dec. 1986.

———. "Gender identity change in a female adolescent transsexual." *Archives of Sexual Behavior,* Vol. 6 (4): 327–340, 1977.

DAVIS, W. E., and JONES, M. H. "Negro vs. Caucasian psychological test performance revisited." *Journal of Consulting and Clinical Psychology,* Vol. 42 (5): 675–679, 1974.

DEAN-CHURCH, L., and GILROY, F. D. "Relation of sex-role orientation to life satisfaction in a healthy elderly sample." *Journal of Social Behavior and Personality,* Vol. 8 (1): 133–140, 1993.

DEHEER, N. D.; WAMPOLD, B. E.; and FREUND, R. D. "Do sex-typed and androgynous subjects prefer counselors on the basis of gender or effectiveness? They prefer the best." *Journal of Counseling Psychology,* Vol. 39 (2): 175–184, 1992.

DEMOSS, K.; MILICH, R.; and DEMERS, S. "Gender, creativity, depression, and attributional style in adolescents with high academic ability." *Journal of Abnormal Child Psychology,* Vol. 21 (4): 455–467, 1993.

DEVOR, HOLLY. "Sexual orientation identities, attractions, and practices of female-to-male transsexuals." *Journal of Sex Research,* Vol. 30 (4): 303–315, 1993.

DEW, MARY AMANDA. "The effect of attitudes on inferences of homosexuality and perceived physical attractiveness in women." *Sex Roles,* Vol. 12, Nos. 1/2: 143–155, 1985.

DIAMOND, JARED. "Father's milk." *Discover Magazine,* February 1995, pp. 82–87.

DIPIETRO, J. A. "Rough and tumble play: A function of gender." *Developmental Psychology* 17, No. 1, 50–58, 1981.

DIXON, DOROTHY. "See how they grow: The early childhood years." Twenty-Third Publications, 185 Willow Street, Box 180, Mystic, CT 06355, 1993.

DOWNEY, ANN M. "The relationship of sex-role orientation to self-perceived health status in middle-aged males." *Sex Roles,* Vol. 11, Nos. 3/4: 211–225, 1984.

DOWRICK, PETER W. "Video training of alternatives to cross-gender identity behaviors in a 4-year-old boy." *Child and Family Behavior Therapy,* Vol. 5 (2): 59–65, Summer 1983.

———. "Single dose medication to create a self-model film." *Child Behavior Therapy* 1 (2): 193–198, Summer 1979.

DULL, CECELIA YODER; GUIORA, ALEXANDER Z.; PALUSZNY, MARIA; BEIG-HALLAHMI, BENJAMIN; CATFORD, JOHN C.; and COOLEY, RALPH E. "The Michigan Gender Identity Test (MIGIT)." *Comprehensive Psychiatry,* Vol. 16, No. 6, 581–592, 1975.

DUNKLE, JOHN H., and FRANCIS, PATRICIA L. "The role of facial masculinity/ femininity in the attribution of homosexuality." *Sex Roles* 23: 157–167, 1990.

Editorial. "Sex tests for athletes." Op-Ed page, *Washington Post,* February 17, 1992.

EHRHARDT, ANKE A., and MCCAULEY, ELIZABETH A. "Follow-up of females with gender identity disorders." *Journal of Nervous and Mental Disease,* Vol. 172 (6): 353–358, June 1984.

———. "Sexual behavior in female transsexuals and lesbians." *Journal of Sex Research,* Vol. 16 (3), 202–211, August 1980.

EHRHARDT, ANKE A.; GRISANTI, GUDRUN; and MCCAULEY, ELIZABETH. "Female-to-male transsexuals compared to lesbians: Behavioral patterns of childhood and adolescent development." *Archives of Sexual Behavior,* Vol. 8, No. 6, 481–490, 1979.

EHRHARDT, ANKE A.; INCE, SUSAN E.; and MEYER-BAHLBURG, HEINO F. L. "Career aspiration and gender role development in young girls." *Archives of Sexual Behavior,* Vol. 10, No. 3, 281–299, 1981.

ELLIS, JON B., and RANGE, LILLIAN M. "Femininity and reasons for living." *Educational and Psychological Research,* Vol. 8 (1/Winter): 19–24, 1988.

ELPERN, SARAH, and KARP, STEPHEN A. "Sex-role orientation and depressive symptomatology." *Sex Roles* 10: 987–992, 1984.

EVANS, R. I.; TURNER, S. H.; GHEE, K. L.; and GETZ, J. G. "Is androgynous sex role related to cigarette smoking in adolescents?" *Journal of Applied Social Psychology,* Vol. 20 (6): 494–505, 1990.

FAGOT, B. "Consequences of moderate cross-gender behavior in preschool children." *Child Development* 48: 902–904, 1977.

FAMILIES AND WORK INSTITUTE. "Women: The new providers." Whirlpool Foundation Study, Part One, May 1995.

FARINA, A.; FISCHER, E. H.; SHERMAN, S.; SMITH, W. T.; GROH, T.; and MERMIN, P. "Physical attractiveness and mental illness." *Journal of Abnormal Psychology,* Vol. 86 (5): 510–517, 1977.

FAUSTO-STERLING, ANNE. "The five sexes: Why male and female are not enough." *The Sciences,* pp. 20–25, March/April 1993.

———. "How many sexes are there?" *New York Times,* March 12, 1993, Op. Ed. page, p. A29.

FEATHER, N. T. (South Australia). "Masculinity, femininity, self-esteem and subclinical depression." *Sex Roles* 12: 491–500, 1985.

FEINMAN, SAUL. "Why is cross-sex-role behavior more approved for girls than for boys? A status characteristic approach." *Sex Roles* 7: 289–299, 1981.

FINE, MICHELLE, and BOWERS, CHERYL. "Racial self-identification: The effects of social history and gender." *Journal of Applied Social Psychology,* Vol. 14 (2): 136–146, 1984.

FINLAY, BARBARA, and SCHELTEMA, KAREN E. "The relation of gender and sexual orientation to measures of masculinity, femininity, and androgyny: A further analysis." *Journal of Homosexuality,* Vol. 21 (3), 71–85, 1991.

FISHBAIN, DAVID A., and VILASUSO, ADOLFO. "Exclusive adult lesbianism associated with Turner's syndrome mosaicism." *Archives of Sexual Behavior,* Vol. 9 (4): 349–353, August 1980.

FLAKS, D. K.; FICHER, I.; MASTERPASQUA, F.; and JOSEPH, G. "Lesbians choosing motherhood: A comparative study of lesbian and heterosexual parents and their children." *Developmental Psychology,* Vol. 31 (1): 105–114, 1995.

FORD, DONNA Y., and HARRIS, J. JOHN III. "The elusive definition of creativity." *Journal of Creative Behavior,* Vol. 26 (3): 186–198, Third Quarter, 1992.

FOREMAN, SALLY, and DALLOS, RUDI. "Inequalities of power and sexual problems." *Journal of Family Therapy* 14: 349–369, 1992.

FRABLE, D. "If you are gender schematic, all members of the opposite sex look alike." *Journal of Personality and Social Psychology* 49: 459–468, 1985.

FRIDELL, SARI R.; ZUCKER, KENNETH J.; BRADLEY, SUSAN J.; and MAING, DIANNE M. "Physical attractiveness of girls with gender identity disorder." *Archives of Sexual Behavior,* in press. (A version of this article was presented at the meeting of the International Academy of Sex Research, Edinburgh, Scotland, June 1994.)

FRIEDRICHS, ROBERT W. "The impact of social factors upon scientific judgment: The 'Jensen thesis' as appraised by members of the American Psychological Association." *Journal of Negro Education,* Vol. 42 (4): 429–438, 1973.

GARWOOD, S. GRAY; BAER, SUSAN; LEVINE, DOUGLAS; CARROLL, SUDIE; and O'NEAL, ED. "Sex-role expectations of socially desirable first names." *Sex Roles,* Vol. 7, No. 3: 257–262, 1981.

GATELY, D., and SCHWEBEL, A. I. "Favorable outcomes in children after parental divorce." Special issue: Divorce and the next generation: Effects on young adults' patterns of intimacy and expectations for marriage. *Journal of Divorce and Remarriage,* Vol. 18 (3/4): 57–78, 1992.

GELMAN, DAVID. "Homoeroticism in the ranks." *Newsweek,* 28–29, July 26, 1993.

GIAMBRA, L. M.; CAMP, C. J.; and GRODSKY, A. "Curiosity and stimulation seeking across the adult life span: Cross-sectional and 6- to 8-year longitudinal findings." *Psychology and Aging,* Vol. 7 (1): 150–157, 1992.

GLIONNA, JOHN M. "Beneath the masquerade." *Los Angeles Times,* Life & Style, Cover Story, Section E, p. E1, February 22, 1995.

GOETINCK, SUE. "Werewolf gene could shed light on hair growth." *San Francisco Examiner* (from *Dallas Morning News*), p. A-15, June 1, 1995.

GOLOMBOK, SUSAN, and TASKER, FIONA. "Do parents influence the sexual orientation of their children? Findings from a longitudinal study of lesbian families." *Developmental Psychology,* Vol. 32, No. 1: 3–11, January 1996.

GOOD, G. E.; ROBERTSON, J. M.; O'NEIL, J. M.; FITZGERALD, L. F.; STEVENS, M.; DEBORD, K. A.; BARTELS, K. M.; and BRAVERMAN, D. G. "Male gender role conflict: Psychometric issues and relations to psychological distress." *Journal of Counseling Psychology,* Vol. 42 (1): 3–10, 1995.

GORDON, RACHEL. "1 in 4 U.S. kids now live in homes without fathers." *San Francisco Examiner,* p. A2, April 24, 1995.

GORNER, PETER. "Global brotherhood: It's in our genes." *San Francisco Examiner,* p. A-17, May 26, 1995.

GREEN, BETH L., and KENRICK, DOUGLAS T. "The attractiveness of gender-typed traits at different relationship levels: Androgynous characteristics may be desirable after all." *Personality and Social Psychology Bulletin,* Vol. 20 (3): 244–253, 1994.

GREEN, JAMISON, principal author. "Investigation into discrimination against transgendered people." A report by the Human Rights Commission, City and County of San Francisco, September 1994.

GREEN, R., and FULLER, M. "Group therapy with feminine boys and their parents." *International Journal of Group Psychotherapy,* Vol. 23 (1): 54–68, 1973.

GREEN, R.; NEUBERG, DONNA SHAPIRO; and FINCH, STEPHEN J. "Sex-typed motor behaviors of 'feminine' boys, conventionally masculine boys, and conventionally feminine girls." *Sex Roles,* Vol. 9, No. 5, 571–579, 1983.

GREEN, RICHARD. "Gender Identity Disorder in children," in *Treatments of Psychiatric Disorders* (2nd Ed.), Gabbard, Glen O., ed., American Psychiatric Press: pp. 2,000–2,014, 1995.

GREEN, RICHARD, and MONEY, JOHN. "Stage acting, role taking, and effeminate impersonation during boyhood." *Archives of General Psychiatry,* Vol. 15, 535–538, 1966.

GREEN, RICHARD; WILLIAMS, KATHERINE; and GOODMAN, MARILYN. "Parent-child factors in gender role socialization in girls." *Journal of the American Academy of Child Psychiatry* 26, 6: 720–731, 1985.

GREEN, RICHARD; MANDEL, JANE BARCLAY; HOTVEDT, MARY E.; GRAY, JAMES; and SMITH, LAUREL. "Lesbian mothers and their children: A comparison with solo parent heterosexual mothers and their children." *Archives of Sexual Behavior,* Vol. 15, No. 2, 167–184, 1986.

GREENACRE, PHYLLIS. "Penis awe and its relation to penis envy." In *Drives, Affects, Behavior,* Loewenstein, R.M., ed., International Universities Press, pp. 176–190, 1953.

GRIMM, LAURENCE G., and YARNOLD, PAUL R. "Sex typing and the coronary-prone behavior pattern." *Sex Roles,* Vol. 12, Nos. 1/2: 171–178, 1985.

GRIMMELL, DEREK, and STERN, GARY S. "The relationship between gender role ideals and psychological well-being." *Sex Roles,* Vol. 27, Nos. 9/10: 487–497, 1992.

GUNTER, N. C., and GUNTER, B. G. "Domestic division of labor among working couples: Does androgyny make a difference?" *Psychology of Women Quarterly,* Vol. 14 (3): 355–370, 1990.

GUPTA, SWAPNA. "Psychosocial development in a genetic male surgically reassigned as a female at birth." *American Journal of Psychotherapy,* Vol. XLIV, No. 2, April 1990.

GURMAN, ERNEST B., and LONG, KEITH. "Gender orientation and emergent leader behavior." *Sex Roles,* Vol. 27, Nos. 7/8: 391–400, 1992.

GYNTHER, M. D., DAVIS, A. T., and SHAKES, L. G. "The perception of attractiveness: What about the beholders?" *Journal of Clinical Psychology,* Vol. 46 (6): 745–748, 1991.

HABER, CALVIN. "The psychoanalytic treatment of a preschool boy with a gender identity disorder." *Journal of the American Psychoanalytic Association,* Vol. 39, (1): 107–129, 1991.

HACKEL, L. S., and RUBLE, D. N. "Changes in the marital relationship after the first baby is born: Predicting the impact of expectancy disconfirmation." *Journal of Personality and Social Psychology,* Vol. 62: 944–957, 1992.

HAEDERLE, MICHAEL. "The body builder." *Los Angeles Times,* Life Style, Section E, p. E1, January 23, 1995.

HARRINTON, DAVID M., and ANDERSEN, SUSAN M. "Creativity, masculinity, femininity, and three models of psychological androgyny." *Journal of Personality and Social Psychology,* Vol. 41 (4): 744–757, 1981.

HARRIS, CATHERINE T.; PERRICONE, PHILIP J.; and SMITH, MARGARET S. "The artist and androgyny: A study of gender identity in visual artists." *Empirical Studies of the Arts,* Vol. 6 (1): 67–78, 1988.

HARTLEY, R. E. "Sex-role pressures and the socialization of the male child." *Psychological Reports,* Vol. 5, 457–468, 1959.

HASSLER, M. "Testosterone and artistic talents." *International Journal of Neuroscience,* Vol. 56 (1–4): 25–38, 1991.

————. "Functional cerebral asymmetries and cognitive abilities in musicians, painters, and controls." *Brain and Cognition,* Vol. 13 (1): 1–17, 1990.

HASSLER, M., and NIESCHLAG, E. "Masculinity, femininity, and musical composition: Psychological and psychoendocrinological aspects of musical and spatial faculties." *Archiv für Psychologie,* Vol. 141 (1): 71–84, 1989.

HASSLER, M.; NIESCHLAG, E.; and DE LA MOTTE, D. "Creative musical talent, cognitive functioning, and gender: Psychobiological aspects." *Music Perception,* Vol. 8 (1): 35–48, 1990.

HAY, WILLIAM M.; BARLOW, DAVID H.; and HAY, LINDA RUDIN. "Treatment of stereotypic cross-gender motor behavior using covert modeling in a boy with gender identity confusion." *Journal of Consulting and Clinical Psychology,* Vol. 49, No. 3, 388–394, 1981.

HELLHAMMER, D. H., HUBERT, W., and SCHURMEYER, T. "Changes in saliva testosterone after psychological stimulation in men." *Psychoneuroendocrinology,* Vol. 10 (1): 77–81, 1985.

HEMMER, JOAN D., and KLEIBER, DOUGLAS A. "Tomboys and sissies: Androgynous children?" *Sex Roles* 7: 1205–1212, 1981.

HEPPNER, P. PAUL. "On gender role conflict in men—Future directions and implications for counseling: Comment on Good et al. (1995) and Cournoyer and Mahalik (1995)." *Journal of Consulting Psychology,* Vol. 42 (1): 20–23, 1995.

HERMAN, S. P. "Gender identity disorder in a five-year-old boy." *Yale Journal of Biology and Medicine* 56 (1): 15–22, Jan.-Feb. 1983.

HILDEBRANDT, K. A., and FITZGERALD, H. E. "Gender bias in observers' perceptions of infants' sex: It's a boy most of the time!" *Perceptual and Motor Skills,* Vol. 45: 472–474, 1977.

HINES, MELISSA; CHIU, LEE; McADAMS, LOU ANN; BENTLER, PETER M.; and LIPCAMON, JIM. "Cognition and the corpus callosum: Verbal fluency, visuospatial ability, and language lateralization related to midsagittal surface areas of callosal subregions." *Behavioral Neuroscience,* Vol. 106, No. 1, 3–14, 1992.

HOCKENBERRY, STEWART L., and BILLINGHAM, ROBERT E. "Sexual orientation and boyhood gender conformity: Development of the Boyhood Gender Conformity Scale (BGCS)." *Archives of Sexual Behavior,* Vol. 16, No. 6, 475–487, 1987.

HORTON, A. M. "Behavioral treatment of childhood gender role confusion." *Child Behavior Therapy* 2: 82–83, 1980.

HUNT, MELISSA G. "Expressiveness does predict well-being." *Sex Roles,* Vol. 29, Nos. 3/4, 147–169, 1993.

HUNT, SALLIE, and MAIN, TERRI L. "Sexual orientation confusion among spouses of transvestites and transsexuals following disclosure of spouse's gender dysphoria." In press, 1995.

JAFFE, LYNN J. "The unique predictive ability of sex-role identity in explaining women's response to advertising." *Psychology and Marketing,* Vol. 11 (5/Sept.-Oct.): 467–482, 1994.

JENSEN, ARTHUR R. "A theoretical note on sex linkage and race differences in spatial visualization ability." *Behavior Genetics,* Vol. 5 (2): 151–164, 1975.

JONES, D. C.; BLOYS, N.; and WOOD, M. "Sex roles and friendship patterns." *Sex Roles,* Vol. 23 (3/4): 133–145, 1990.

JURMA, W. E., and POWELL, M. L. "Perceived gender roles of managers and effective conflict management." *Psychological Reports,* Vol. 74 (1): 104–106, 1994.

KAKUTANI, MICHIKO. "Using memory to reorder, even transform, a life." Review of *White Gloves: How We Create Ourselves Through Memory,* by John Kotre. *New York Times,* Living Arts, Section C, p. C28, June 30, 1995.

KATZ, PHYLLIS A., and WALSH, P. VINCENT. "Modification of children's gender-stereotyped behavior." *Child Development* 62: 338–351, 1991.

KAYE, L. W., and APPLEGATE, J. S. "Men as elder caregivers: A response to changing families." *American Journal of Orthopsychiatry,* Vol. 60 (1): 86–95, 1990.

KERNS, JOHN G., and FINE, MARK A. "The relation between gender and negative attitudes toward gay men and lesbians: Do gender role attitudes mediate this relation?" *Sex Roles,* Vol. 31, Nos. 5/6: 297–307, 1994.

KNAPP, CAROLINE. "I was a drag king." *Boston Phoenix,* Section 2, April 30, 1993.

KOLATA, GINA. "Man's world, woman's world? Brain studies point to differences." *New York Times,* Section B, p. B5, February 28, 1995.

KRAMES, L.; ENGLAND, R.; and FLETT, G. L. "The role of masculinity and femininity in depression and social satisfaction in elderly females." *Sex Roles,* Vol. 19 (11/12, December): 713–721, 1988.

KWESKIN, S. L., and COOK, A. S. "Heterosexual and homosexual mothers' self-described sex role behavior and ideal sex role behavior in children." *Sex Roles* 8: 967–975, 1982.

LAGACE, R. R., and TWIBLE, J. L. "The androgyny level of salespeople: Gooses and ganders, or all geese?" *Journal of Social Behavior and Personality,* Vol. 5 (6): 641–650, 1990.

LAMKE, LEANNE K. "The impact of sex-role orientation on self-esteem in early adolescence." *Child Development,* Vol. 53 (6): 1530–1535, 1982.

LANGLOIS, J. H., and DOWNS, A. C. "Peer relations as a function of physical attractiveness: The eye of the beholder or behavioral reality?" *Child Development,* Vol. 50: 409–418, 1979.

LARSON, R. W.; RICHARDS, M. H.; and PERRY-JENKINS, M. "Divergent worlds: The daily emotional experience of mothers and fathers in the domestic and public spheres." *Journal of Personality and Social Psychology,* Vol. 67 (6): 1034–1046, 1994.

LAVOIE, J. C., and ANDREWS, R. "Facial attractiveness, physique, and sex role identity in young children." *Developmental Psychology,* Vol. 12 (6): 550–551, 1976.

LEHRMAN, SALLY. " 'Gay gene' study under scrutiny." *San Francisco Examiner,* p. 1, July 7, 1995.

———. "Procedure to enlarge penis gets low marks." *San Francisco Examiner,* p. A2, April 25, 1995.

———. "Same diseases, different genes in varied peoples." *San Francisco Examiner,* p. A4, January 19, 1995.

LESTER, DAVID. "Eye color and personality." *Perceptual and Motor Skills,* Vol. 73: 1074, 1991.

LEVAY, SIMON. "A difference in hypothalamic structure between heterosexual and homosexual men." *Science,* Vol. 253: 1034–1037, 1991.

LEVENTHAL, GLOIRA, and KRATE, RONALD. "Physical attractiveness and severity of sentencing." *Psychological Reports,* Vol. 40: 315–318, 1977.

LEV-RAN, ARYE. "Gender role differentiation in hermaphrodites." *Archives of Sexual Behavior,* Vol. 3 (5): 391–424, 1974.

———. "Sexuality and educational levels of women with the late-treated adrenogenital syndrome." *Archives of Sexual Behavior,* Vol. 3 (1): 27–32, 1974.

LEWIN, TAMAR. "The decay of families is global, study says." *New York Times,* p. A27, May 30, 1995.

———. "Creating fathers out of men with children." *New York Times,* Sunday National Edition, p. 1, June 18, 1995.

———. "Traditional family favored by boys, not girls." *New York Times,* National Edition, p. A1, July 11, 1994.

LIM, MENG HOOI, and BOTTOMLEY, VIRGINIA. "A combined approach to the treatment of effeminate behaviour in a boy: A case study." *Journal of Child Psychology and Psychiatry and Allied Disciplines,* Vol. 24, No. 3, 469–479, 1983.

LOEB, LORETTA, and SHANE, MORTON. "The resolution of a transsexual wish in a five-year-old boy." *Journal of the American Psychiatric Association* 30 (2): 419–434, 1982.

LOEHLIN, J. C.; VANDENBERG, S. G.; and OSBORNE, R. T. "Blood group genes and Negro-white ability differences." *Behavior Genetics,* Vol. 3 (3): 263–270, 1973.

LOMBARDO, J. P., and KEMPER, T. R. "Sex role and parental behaviors." *Journal of Genetic Psychology,* Vol. 153 (1): 103–111, 1992.

LOTTES, ILSA L. "Nontraditional gender roles and the sexual experiences of heterosexual college students." *Sex Roles,* Vol. 29, Nos. 9/10, 645–669, 1993.

LUBINSKI, DAVID; TELLEGEN, AUKE; and BUTCHER, JAMES N. "The relationship between androgyny and subjective indicators of emotional well-being." *Journal of Personality and Social Psychology,* Vol. 40, No. 4: 722–730, 1981.

MACDONALD, MARTHA WILSON. "Criminally aggressive behavior in passive, effeminate boys." *American Journal of Orthopsychiatry,* Vol. 8: 70–78, 1938.

MACKINNON, DONALD W. "The nature and nurture of creative talent." *American Psychologist* 17: 484–495, 1962.

MAHAN, JUNEAU. "Black and White children's racial identification and preference." *Journal of Black Psychology,* Vol. 3 (1): 47–58, 1976.

MANCIA, MAURO (Milan, translated by Maria Cristina Sollazzo). "The absent father: His role in sexual deviations and in transference." *International Journal of Psycho-Analysis* 74: 941–950, 1993.

MARTIN, CAROL LYNN. "Attitudes and expectations about children with nontraditional and traditional gender roles." *Sex Roles* 22: 151, 1990.

MAZUR, A., and LAMB, T. A. "Testosterone, status, and mood in human males." *Hormones and Behavior,* Vol. 14: 236–246, 1980.

MAZUR, TOM, and DOBSON, KIM. "Psychologic issues in individuals with genetic, hormonal, and anatomic anomalies of the sexual system," Chapter 6 in *Handbook of Child and Adolescent Sexual Problems,* Rekers, George, ed., Lexington Books, 1995.

MCDOUGALL, JOYCE. "The dead father: On early psychic trauma and its relation to disturbance in sexual identity and in creative activity." *International Journal of Psycho-Analysis* (Paris), Vol. 70, 205–219, 1989.

MCLEOD, RAMON G. "Single-parent families keep increasing: 'Never-married' group pushes tally." *San Francisco Chronicle,* p. A1, October 16, 1995.

———. "More dads being Mr. Moms: Study finds 20% of preschool children cared for by fathers." *San Francisco Chronicle,* p. A2, September 22, 1993.

MCPHERSON, DAN. "Gay parenting couples: Parenting arrangements, arrangement satisfaction, and relationship satisfaction." Unpublished dissertation, Pacific Graduate School of Psychology, Palo Alto, California, 1993.

MEAD, B. J., and IGNICO, A. A. "Children's gender-typed perceptions of physical activity: Consequences and implications." *Perceptual and Motor Skills,* Vol. 75: 1035–1042, 1992.

MEYER, ILAN H., and SCHWARTZ, SHARON. "Notes on gender identity disorder." Unpublished paper, Columbia University, School of Public Health, Division of Sociomedical Sciences, September 26, 1995.

MEYER, JON K. "The theory of gender identity disorders." *Journal of the American Psychoanalytic Asosciation* 30 (2): 381–418, 1982.

MEYER-BAHLBURG, HEINO F. L. "Intersexuality and the diagnosis of gender identity disorder." *Archives of Sexual Behavior,* Vol. 23, No. 1, 21–37, 1994.

———. "Sex hormones and female homosexuality: A critical examination." *Archives of Sexual Behavior,* Vol. 8, No. 2, 101–119, 1979.

MIHALIK, GARY J. "Sexuality and gender: An evolutionary perspective." *Psychiatric Annals,* Vol. 18 (1): 40–42, January 1988.

MILLS, KIM. "Being gay similar to alcoholism." *San Francisco Examiner,* p. A1, November 24, 1994.

MIRKEN, BRUCE. "Setting them straight." *10% Magazine,* 54, June 1994.

MILLER, M. J.; KNIPPERS, J. A.; BURLEY, K.; and TOBACYK, J. J. "Relationship between sex-role orientation and Holland's typology: Implications for career counselors." *College Student Journal,* Vol. 27 (3/Sept.): 356–361, 1993.

MITCHELL, JANET N. "Maternal influences on gender identity disorder in boys: Searching for specificity." Unpublished thesis, York University, Downsview, Canada, Nov. 18, 1991.

MONEY, JOHN. "Androgyne becomes bisexual in sexological theory: Plato to Freud and neuroscience." *Journal of the American Academy of Psychoanalysis,* Vol. 18 (3): 392–413, 1990.

———. "Pediatric sexology and hermaphroditism." *Advances in Developmental and Behavioral Pediatrics,* Vol. 7, 257–274, 1986.

———. "Gender-transposition theory and homosexual genesis." *Journal of Sex and Marital Therapy,* Vol. 10, No. 2, 75–82, 1984.

MONEY, JOHN (U.S.A.), and DALERY, JEAN (Paris). "Iatrogenic homosexuality:

Gender identity in seven 46,XX chromosomal females with hyperadrenocortical hermaphroditism born with a penis, three reared as boys, four reared as girls." *Journal of Homosexuality,* Vol. 1 (4), 357–371, Summer 1976.

MONEY, JOHN, and LAMACZ, MARGARET. "Gynemimesis and gynemimetophilia: Individual and cross-cultural manifestations of a gender-coping strategy hitherto unnamed." *Comprehensive Psychiatry,* Vol. 25, No. 4: 392–403, July/August 1984.

MONEY, JOHN, and NORMAN, BERNARD F. "Gender identity and gender transposition: Longitudinal outcome study of 24 male hermaphrodites assigned as boys." *Journal of Sex and Marital Therapy,* Vol. 13, No. 2, 75–92, Summer 1987.

MONEY, JOHN, and RUSSO, ANTHONY J. "Homosexual outcome of discordant gender identity/role in childhood: Longitudinal follow-up." *Journal of Pediatric Psychology,* Vol. 4, No. 1, 29–41, 1979.

MONEY, JOHN; DEVORE, HOWARD; and NORMAN, BERNARD F. "Gender identity and gender transposition: Longitudinal outcome study of 32 male hermaphrodites assigned as girls." *Journal of Sex and Marital Therapy,* Vol. 12, No. 3, 165–181, Fall 1986.

MOORE, J. S.; GRAZIANO, W. G.; and MILLAR, M. G. "Physical attractiveness, sex role orientation, and the evaluation of adults and children." *Personality and Social Psychology Bulletin,* Vol. 13 (1): 95–102, 1987.

MYERS, LINNET. "Teen-age girl topples chess legend Spassky." *San Francisco Examiner* (from *Chicago Tribune*), p. A1, February 18, 1993.

MYRICK, ROBERT D. "The counselor-consultant and the effeminate boy." *Personnel and Guidance Journal,* Vol. 48, No. 5, 355–361, January 1970.

NEWMAN, JUDITH, and HARRISON, LAIRD. "Horse sense." *People,* 51–52, December 6, 1993.

NEWMAN, K.; RANDOLPH, J.; and ANDERSON, K. "The surgical management of infants and children with ambiguous genitalia." *Annals of Surgery,* Vol. 215 (6): 644–653, 1992.

NEWMAN, LAWRENCE E. "Treatment for the parents of feminine boys." *American Journal of Psychiatry* 133 (6): 683–687, 1976.

NEW YORK TIMES. "Big increase in number of single fathers." *San Francisco Chronicle,* p. A2, August 31, 1993.

NIESCHLAG, EBERHARD; NIESCHLAG, SUSAN; and BEHRE, HERMANN M. "Lifespan and testosterone." Report of study from the Institute of Reproductive Medicine, Westfalian Wilhelm's University, Münster, Germany. *Nature* magazine (London), Letter to the Editor, Vol. 366, No. 6452, 215, November 18, 1993.

NORDYKE, NANCY S.; BAER, DONALD M.; ETZEL, BARBARA C.; and LEBLANC, JUDITH M. "Implications of the stereotyping and modification of sex role." *Journal of Applied Behavior Analysis* 10 (3): 553–557, Fall 1977.

NOVACEK, J.; RASKIN, R.; and HOGAN, R. "Why do adolescents use drugs? Age, sex, and user differences." *Journal of Youth and Adolescence,* Vol. 20 (5): 475–492, 1991.

PATTERSON, CHARLOTTE J. "Sexual orientation and human development: An overview." *Developmental Psychology,* Vol. 31 (1): 3–11, 1995.

———. "Families of the lesbian baby boom: Parents' division of labor and children's adjustment." *Developmental Psychology,* Vol. 31 (1): 115–123, 1995.

————. "Children of lesbian and gay parents." *Child Development* 63: 1025–1042, 1992.

PATTERSON, MARY JO. "Gender gap a mystery: Boys vastly outnumber girls in special ed." Newark, New Jersey Sunday *Star-Ledger,* Section One, February 5, 1995.

PAULY, I. B., and EDGERTON, M. T. "The gender identity movement: A growing surgical-psychiatric liaison." *Archives of Sexual Behavior* 15 (4): 315–329, August 1986.

PERKINS, MURIEL WILSON. "Female homosexuality and body build." *Archives of Sexual Behavior,* Vol. 10, No. 4, 337–345, 1981.

PETERSON, C.; BAUCOM, D. H.; ELLIOTT, M. J.; and FARR, P. A. "The relationship between sex role identity and marital adjustment." *Sex Roles,* Vol. 21 (11/12): 775–787, 1989.

PHILLIPS, G., and OVER, R. "Differences between heterosexual, bisexual and lesbian women in recalled childhood experiences." *Archives of Sexual Behavior,* Vol. 24 (1): 1–20, 1995.

PLUMB, PAT, and COWAN, GLORIA. "A developmental study of destereotyping and androgynous activity preferences of tomboys, nontomboys, and males." *Sex Roles,* Vol. 10, Nos. 9/10, 703–712, 1984.

PRESS, JOY. "Walk like a man." *The Guardian,* May 4, 1994.

QUAY, LORENE C. "Language dialect, age, and intelligence-test performance in disadvantaged Black children." *Child Development,* Vol. 45 (2): 463–468, 1974.

RAEBURN, PAUL (Associated Press). "Family is best heart medicine." *San Francisco Examiner,* p. A-9, January 19, 1995.

RAMPAGE, CHERYL. "Power, gender, and marital intimacy." *Journal of Family Therapy,* Vol. 16: 125–137, 1994.

REKERS, G. A., and MEAD, S. "Human sex differences in carrying behaviors: A replication and extension." *Perceptual and Motor Skills* 48: 625–626, 1978.

REKERS, G. A., and RUDY, J. P. "Differentiation of childhood body gestures." *Perceptual and Motor Skills* 46: 839–845, 1978.

REKERS, G. A.; BENTLER, P. M.; and LOVAAS, O. I. "Child gender disturbances: A clinical rationale for intervention." *Psychotherapy: Theory, Research and Practice* 14 (1): 2–11, Spring 1977.

REKERS, GEORGE A. "Psychosexual assessment of gender identity disorders." *Advances in Behavioral Assessment of Children and Families,* Vol. 4, 33–71, 1988.

————. "Assessment and treatment of childhood gender problems," in *Advances in Child Clinical Psychology,* Lahey, B. B., and Kazdin, A. E., eds., Vol. I, pp. 267–306, Plenum, 1977.

————. "Stimulus control over sex-typed play in cross-gender identified boys." *Journal of Experimental Child Psychology* 20: 136–148, 1975.

REKERS, GEORGE A., and LOVAAS, O. IVAR. "Behavioral treatment of deviant sex-role behaviors in a male child." *Journal of Applied Behavior Analysis* 7 (2): 173–190, Summer 1974.

REKERS, GEORGE A., and MEAD, SHASTA. "Early intervention for female sexual identity disturbance: Self-monitoring of play behavior." *Journal of Abnoraml Child Psychology,* Vol. 7, No. 4, 405–423, 1979.

REKERS, GEORGE A., and MOREY, SHASTA M. "The relationship of measures of sex-typed play with clinician ratings on degree of gender disturbance." *Journal of Clinical Psychology*, Vol. 46 (1): 28–34, January 1990.

———. "Relationship of maternal report of feminine behaviors and extraversion to clinician's rating of gender disturbance." *Perceptual and Motor Skills*, Vol. 69 (2): 387–394, Oct. 1989.

REKERS, GEORGE A.; LOVAAS, O. IVAR; and LOW, BENSON. "The behavioral treatment of a 'transsexual' preadolescent boy." *Journal of Abnormal Child Psychology*, Vol. 2, No. 2, June 1974.

REKERS, GEORGE A.; ROSEN, A. C.; and MOREY, S. M. "Projective test findings for boys with gender disturbance: Draw-A-Person Test, IT scale, and Make-A-Picture Story test." *Perceptual and Motor Skills* 71 (3 Pt. 1): 771–779, December 1990.

REKERS, GEORGE A.; SANDERS, JUDITH A.; and STRAUSS, CYD C. "Developmental differentiation of adolescent body gestures." *The Journal of Genetic Psychology* 138: 123–131, 1981.

REUTERS. "Doctors tie men's mentality to their shorter life span." *New York Times*, Section C, p. C14, June 14, 1995.

RITTER, MALCOLM. "Brain structure may be gay clue." *San Francisco Examiner*, p. B8, November 18, 1994.

ROSEN, RAYMOND C.; KOSTIS, JOHN B.; JEKELIS, ALBERT; and TASKA, LYNN S. "Sexual sequelae of antihypertensive drugs: Treatment effects on self-report and physiological measures in middle-aged male hypertensives." *Archives of Sexual Behavior*, Vol. 23 (2): 135–152, 1994.

ROSENBLITH, JUDY F. "A singular career: Nancy Bayley." *Developmental Psychology*, Vol. 28 (5): 747–758, 1992.

ROSENTHAL, HARRY F. "Researchers find brain differences based on gender." Associated Press, *San Francisco Examiner*, p. A21, January 27, 1995.

ROSS, MICHAEL W., and STALSTROM, OLLI W. "Exorcism as psychiatric treatment: A homosexual case study." *Archives of Sexual Behavior*, Vol. 8, No. 4: 379–383, 1979.

ROTTER, NAOMI G., and O'CONNELL, AGNES N. "The relationships among sex-role orientation, cognitive complexity, and tolerance for ambiguity." *Sex Roles*, Vol. 8, Part 2: 1209–1220, 1982.

RUBIN, T.; PROVENZANO, F.; and LURIA, Z. "The eye of the beholder: Parents' view on sex of newborns." *American Journal of Orthopsychiatry*, Vol. 44: 512–519, 1974.

RUBINI, V., and ANTONELLI, E. "Self-gender schemata and the processing of social information." *European Journal of Personality*, Vol. 6 (5): 359–370, 1992.

RUBLE, D. N.; FLEMING, A. S.; HACKEL, L. S.; and STANGOR, C. "Changes in the marital relationship during the transition to first time motherhood: Effects of violated expectations concerning division of household labor." *Journal of Personality and Social Psychology*, Vol. 55: 78–87.

SAFIR, M. P.; PERES, Y.; LICHTENSTEIN, M.; HOCH, Z.; and SHEPHER, J. "Psychological androgyny and sexual adequacy." *Journal of Sex and Marital Therapy*, Vol. 8 (3/Fall): 228–240, 1982.

SAMUELSON, ROBERT J. "Getting serious." *Newsweek*, pp. 40–44, September 18, 1995.

SANFILIPO, MICHAEL P. "Masculinity, femininity, and subjective experiences of depression." *Journal of Clinical Psychology*, Vol. 50 (2): 144–157, 1994.

294

SCANDURA, T. A., and RAGINS, B. R. "The effects of sex and gender role orientation on mentorship in male-dominated occupations." *Journal of Vocational Behavior,* Vol. 43 (3): 251–265, 1993.

SEAVEY, CAROL A.; KATZ, PHYLLIS A.; and ZALK, SUE ROSENBERG. "Baby X: The effect of gender labels on adult responses to infants." *Sex Roles,* Vol. 1, No. 2: 103–109, 1975.

SHICHMAN, SHULA, and COOPER, ELLEN. "Life satisfaction and sex-role concept." *Sex Roles,* Vol. 11, Nos. 3/4: 227–240, 1984.

SIDOROWICZ, LAURA S., and LUNNEY, G. SPARKS. "Baby X revisited." *Sex Roles,* Vol. 6, No. 1: 67–73, 1980.

SIMMONS, J. L. "Public stereotypes of deviants." *Social Problems,* Vol. 13: 223–232, 1965.

SINNOTT, JAN DYNDA. "Older men, older women: Are their perceived sex roles similar?" *Sex Roles,* Vol. 10, Nos. 11/12: 847–856, 1984.

SMITH, CAROLINE, and LLOYD, BARBARA. "Maternal behavior and perceived sex of infant: Revisited." *Child Development,* Vol. 49: 1263–1265, 1978.

SMITH, JOAN. "Dream weavings of Joyce Carol Oates." *San Francisco Examiner,* p. D3, August 22, 1993.

SPAKE, AMANDA. "Dressing for power." *Washington Post,* Section C, pp. C1, C4, January 5, 1992.

SPAN, PAULA. "Guise and dolls." *Washington Post,* Section C, p. C1, October 12, 1993.

SPENCE, JANET T. "Gender-related traits and gender ideology: Evidence for a multifactorial theory." *Journal of Personality and Social Psychology,* Vol. 64 (4): 624–635, 1993.

———. "Ratings of self and peers on sex role attributes and their relation to self-esteem and conceptions of masculinity and femininity." *Journal of Personality and Social Psychology,* Vol. 32 (1): 29–39, 1975.

SRIVASTAVA, ARUN; BORRIES, CAROLA; and SOMMER, VOLKER. "Homosexual mounting in free-ranging female Hanuman langurs (*Presbytis entellus*)." *Archives of Sexual Behavior,* Vol. 20, No. 5, 487–512, 1991.

STARRELS, MARJORIE E. "Husbands' involvement in female gender-typed household chores." *Sex Roles,* Vol. 31, Nos. 7/8, 473–491, 1994.

STOLLER, R. "The mother's contribution to infantile transvestic behavior." *International Journal of Psycho-Analysis* 47: 384–394, 1966.

STOLLER, R. J. "Etiological factors in female transsexualism: A first approximation." *Archives of Sexual Behavior,* Vol. 2 (1): 47–64, 1972.

———. *Sex and Gender,* Vol. I, Chapter 3: "The disruption of established gender identity," Science House, 1968.

———. *Sex and Gender,* Vol. I, Chapter 4: "The hermaphroditic identity of hermaphrodites," Science House, 1968.

———. *Sex and Gender,* Vol. I, Chapter 10: "Artistic ability and boyhood femininity," Science House, 1968.

———. "Boyhood gender aberrations: Treatment issues." *Journal of the American Psychoanalytic Association,* Vol. 26: 541–558, 1978.

STOPPARD, JANET M., and PAISLEY, KIM J. "Masculinity, femininity, life stress and depression." *Sex Roles* 16: 489–495, 1987.

TAYLOR, JOHN. "The third sex." *Esquire,* 102–114, April 1995.

TINSLEY, EMILEY G.; SULLIVAN-GUEST, SANDRA; and McGUIRE, JOHN. "Feminine sex roles and depression in middle-aged women." *Sex Roles* 11: 25–32, 1984.

TKACHUK, JAN, and ZUCKER, KENNETH J. "The relation among sexual orientation, spatial ability, handedness, and recalled childhood gender identity in women and men." Poster presented at the meeting of the International Academy of Sex Research, Barrie, Ontario, August 1991.

TWENTYMAN, C.; BOLAND, T.; and McFALL, R. M. "Heterosocial avoidance in college males: Four studies." *Behavior Modification,* Vol. 5 (4): 523–552, 1981.

VAN KEMENADE, JOHANNES F. L. M.; COHEN-KETTENIS, PEGGY T.; COHEN, LEO; and GOOREN, LOUIS J. G. (The Netherlands). "Effects of the pure antiandrogen RU 23.903 (anandron) on sexuality, aggression, and mood in male-to-female transsexuals." *Archives of Sexual Behavior,* Vol. 18, No. 3: 217–228, 1989.

VERHOVEK, SAM HOWE. "At issue: Hold a baby or hold that line?" *New York Times,* p. A1, October 20, 1993.

VICK, KARL. "An odd alliance tries to 'out' nominee Reno." *San Francisco Examiner* (from *St. Petersburg Times*), p. A1, February 21, 1992.

VILLEMEZ, WAYNE J., and TOUHEY, JOHN C. "A measure of individual differences in sex stereotyping and sex discrimination: The 'Macho' Scale." *Psychological Reports,* Vol. 41: 411–415, 1977.

VONK, ROOS, and ASHMORE, RICHARD D. "The multifaceted self: Androgyny reassessed by open-ended self-descriptions." *Social Psychology Quarterly,* Vol. 56 (4): 278–287, 1993.

WEINBERG, MARTIN S.; WILLIAMS, COLIN J.; and CALHAN, CASSANDRA. "Homosexual foot fetishism." *Archives of Sexual Behavior,* Vol. 23, No. 6: 611–626, 1994.

WEISNER, THOMAS S., and WILSON-MITCHELL, JANE E. "Nonconventional family life-styles and sex typing in six-year-olds." *Child Development* 61, Part II, 1915–1933, 1990.

WHEELER, P. T.; ADAMS, G. R.; and NIELSEN, E. C. "Effect of a child's physical attractiveness on verbal scoring of the Wechsler Intelligence Scale for Children (Revised) and personality attributions." *The Journal of General Psychology,* Vol. 114 (2): 109–116, 1987.

WHEELWRIGHT, JULIE. "Out of my way, I'm a man for a day." *The Independent,* November 11, 1994.

WILLEMSEN, TINEKE M. "On the bipolarity of androgyny: A critical comment on Kottke (1988)." *Psychological Reports,* Vol. 72 (1): 327–332, 1993.

WINK, PAUL, and HELSON, RAVENNA. "Personality change in women and their partners." *Journal of Personality and Social Psychology,* Vol. 65 (3): 597–605, 1993.

WINKLER, R. C. (New South Wales). "What types of sex-role behavior should behavior modifiers promote?" *Journal of Applied Behavior Analysis* 10 (3): 549–552, Fall 1977.

WOLFE, BARRY E. "Behavioral treatment of childhood gender disorders." *Behavior Modification,* Vol. 3, No. 4: 550–575, October 1979.

WORTIS, JOSEPH. "Intersexuality and effeminacy in the male homosexual." *American Journal of Orthopsychiatry* X, 3, 1940.

WRIGHT, L.; ABBANATO, K. R.; LANCASTER, C.; BOURKE, M. L., and NIELSEN, B. A. "Gender-related subcomponent differences in high type A subjects." *Journal of Clinical Psychology,* Vol. 50 (5): 677–680, 1994.

WUBBENHORST, THOMAS MARTIN. "Personality characteristics of music educators and performers." Special issue: Assessment in Music. *Psychology of Music,* Vol. 22 (1): 63–74, 1994.

YANNIS, ALEX. "Women's teams rise in colleges." *New York Times,* Sports section, p. B20, November 2, 1995.

YARNOLD, P. R.; BRYANT, F. B.; and LITSAS, F. "Type A behaviour and psychological androgyny among Greek college students." *European Journal of Personality,* Vol. 3 (4): 249–268, 1989.

ZUCKER, K.; BRADLEY, S. J.; and LOWRY SULLIVAN, CLAIRE B. "Gender identity disorder in children." *Annual Review of Sex Research* 3: 73–120, 1992.

ZUCKER, K. J. "It ain't the meat, it's the motion": Commentary on Rekers and Morey (1989) "Sex-typed body movements as a function of severity of gender disturbance in boys." *Journal of Psychology and Human Sexuality,* Vol. 5 (3): 69–73, 1992.

———. "Psychosocial and erotic development in cross-gender identified children." *Canadian Journal of Psychiatry* 35: 487–495, 1990.

ZUCKER, K. J., and GREEN, R. "Psychological and familial aspects of gender identity disorder," in Yates, A., ed., *Child and Adolescent Psychiatric Clinics of North America,* Sexual and gender identity disorders, W. B. Saunders, pp. 513–542, 1993.

ZUCKER, K. J., and MITCHELL, J. N. "The recalled childhood gender identity scale: Psychometric properties." Poster presented at the meeting of the International Academy of Sex Research, Barrie, Ontario, August 1991.

ZUCKER, K. J., and TORKOS, H. "Assessment of androgyny in children." *Annals of Sex Research* 2: 187–203, 1989.

ZUCKER, K. J.; COLE, H. J.; and BRADLEY, S. J. "Patterns of gender-role behaviour in children attending traditional and non-traditional day-care centres." *Canadian Journal of Psychiatry* 27: 410–414, 1982.

ZUCKER, K. J.; FINEGAN, J. K.; DOERING, R. W.; and BRADLEY, S. J. "Human figure drawings of gender-problem children: A comparison to sibling, psychiatric, and normal controls." *Journal of Abnormal Child Psychology* 11: 287–298, 1983.

ZUCKER, K. J.; GRIMSHAW, G.; BRADLEY, S. J.; LOWRY, C. B.; and MITCHELL, J. N. "Verbal and spatial ability in boys with gender identity disorder." Poster presented at the meeting of the International Academy of Sex Research, Barrie, Ontario, August 1991.

ZUCKER, K. J.; BRADLEY, S. J.; STEINER, B. W.; DOERING, R. W.; SULLIVAN, J.; FINEGAN, J. K.; and RICHARDSON, M. "Gender identity problems of children and adolescents: The establishment of a special clinic." *Canadian Psychiatric Association Journal* 23: 175–183, 1978.

ZUCKER, KENNETH J. "Gender identity disorders: A developmental perspective," in Diamant, L., and McAnulty, R. D., eds., *The Psychology of Sexual Orientation, Behavior, and Identity: A Handbook,* Greenwood Publishing Group, in press.

———. "Treatment of gender identity disorders in children," in Blanchard, Ray, and Steiner, Betty W., eds., *Clinical Management of Gender Identity Disorders in Children and Adults,* American Psychiatric Press, pp. 25–45, 1990.

———. Review of *Growing up straight: What every family should know about homosexuality* and *Shaping your child's sexual identity,* by George Rekers. *Archives of Sexual Behavior,* Vol. 13, No. 4: 387–390, 1984.

ZUCKER, KENNETH J.; BRADLEY, SUSAN J.; and HUGHES, HELEN E. "Gender dysphoria in a child with true hermaphroditism." *Canadian Journal of Psychiatry,* Vol. 32: 602–609, October 1987.

ZUCKER, KENNETH J.; BRADLEY, SUSAN J.; and IPP, MOSHE. "Delayed naming of a newborn boy: Relationship to the mother's wish for a girl and subsequent cross-gender identity in the child by the age of two." *Journal of Psychology and Human Sexuality,* Vol. 6 (1): 57–68, 1993.

ZUCKER, KENNETH J.; DOERING, ROBERT W.; BRADLEY, SUSAN J.; and MACINTYRE, ROBERT B. "Effects of neutral toys on sex-typed play in children with gender identity disorder." *Journal of Abnormal Child Psychology,* Vol. 17, No. 5: 563–574, 1989.

ZUCKER, KENNETH J.; FINEGAN, JO-ANNE K.; DOERING, ROBERT W.; and BRADLEY, SUSAN J. "Two subgroups of gender-problem children." *Archives of Sexual Behavior,* Vol. 13, No. 1: 27–39, 1984.

ZUCKER, KENNETH J.; LOZINSKI, JODI A.; BRADLEY, SUSAN J.; and DOERING, ROBERT W. "Sex-typed responses in the Rorschach protocols of children with gender identity disorder." *Journal of Personality Assessment* 58 (2): 295–310, 1992.

ZUCKER, KENNETH J.; WILD, JENNIFER; BRADLEY, SUSAN J.; and LOWRY, CLAIRE B. "Physical attractiveness of boys with gender identity disorder." *Archives of Sexual Behavior,* Vol. 22, No. 1: 23–36, 1993.

ZUCKER, KENNETH J.; BRADLEY, SUSAN J.; SULLIVAN, CLAIRE B. LOWRY; KUKSIS, MYRA; BIRKENFELD-ADAMS, ANDREA; and MITCHELL, JANET N. "A gender identity interview for children." *Journal of Personality Assessment* 61 (3): 443–456, 1993.

ZUCKER, KENNETH J.; GREEN, RICHARD; GAROFANO, CHRISTINA; BRADLEY, SUSAN J.; WILLIAMS, KATHERINE; REBACH, HOWARD M.; and SULLIVAN, CLAIRE B. LOWRY. "Prenatal gender preference of mothers of feminine and masculine boys: Relation to sibling sex composition and birth order." *Journal of Abnormal Child Psychology,* Vol. 22, No. 1: 1–13, 1994.

BOOKS:

ARMSTRONG, THOMAS. *Awakening Your Child's Natural Genius.* New York: Jeremy P. Tarcher/Perigee Books (Putnam), 1991.

BLY, ROBERT. *Iron John.* New York: Vintage Books, 1992. (Originally published by Addison-Wesley in 1990.)

BORNSTEIN, KATE. *Gender Outlaw.* New York: Routledge, 1994.

BURKE, PHYLLIS. *Family Values.* New York: Random House, 1993.

CAMPBELL, JOSEPH, ed. *Myths, Dreams and Religion.* New York: E.P. Dutton & Co., 1970.

DAWES, ROBYN M. *House of Cards: Psychology and Psychotherapy Built on Myth.* New York: The Free Press, A Division of Macmillan, Inc., 1994.

DEVOR, HOLLY. *Gender Blending.* Bloomington and Indianapolis: Indiana University Press, A Midland Book, 1989.

Diagnostic and Statistical Manual of Mental Disorders 3rd Edition [DSM-III]. Washington, D.C.: American Psychiatric Association, 1980.

Diagnostic and Statistical Manual of Mental Disorders 3rd Revised Edition [DSM-III-R], Washington, D.C.: American Psychiatric Association, 1987.

Diagnostic and Statistical Manual of Mental Disorders 4th Edition [DSM-IV], Washington, D.C.: American Psychiatric Association, 1994.

FAUSTO-STERLING, ANNE. *Myths of Gender.* New York: Basic Books (Harper Collins), Second Edition, 1992.

FENICHEL, OTTO. *The Psychoanalytic Theory of Neurosis.* New York: W. W. Norton & Company, 1945.

FENNEMA, ELIZABETH, and LEDER, GILAH C., eds. *Mathematics and Gender.* New York: Teachers College Press, Columbia University, 1990.

FRIEDAN, BETTY. *The Feminine Mystique.* New York: W. W. Norton & Company, 1963.

GARBER, MARJORIE. *Vested Interests: Cross-Dressing and Cultural Anxiety.* New York: Routledge, 1992.

GOLDBERG, H. *The Hazards of Being Male.* New York: Signet, 1976.

———. *The New Male.* New York: Morrow, 1979.

GRAY, JOHN. *Men Are from Mars, Women Are from Venus.* New York: Harper Collins, 1992.

GREEN, RICHARD. *The "Sissy Boy Syndrome" and the Development of Homosexuality.* New Haven: Yale University Press, 1987.

IRVINE, JANICE M. *Disorders of Desire.* Philadelphia: Temple University Press, 1990.

KENNEDY, ELIZABETH LAPOVSKY, and DAVIS, MADELINE D. *Boots of Leather, Slippers of Gold.* New York: Routledge, 1993.

KESSLER, SUZANNE J., and MCKENNA, WENDY. *Gender: An Ethnomethodological Approach.* Chicago: University of Chicago Press, 1978.

LAPON, LENNY. *Mass Murderers in White Coats.* Springfield, Massachusetts: Psychiatric Genocide Research Institute, 1986.

LEVAY, SIMON. *The Sexual Brain.* Cambridge, Massachusetts: MIT Press, 1993.

LORD, M. G. *Forever Barbie.* New York: William Morrow and Company, 1994.

MACCOBY, ELEANOR E. *The Development of Sex Differences.* Stanford, California: Stanford University Press, 1966.

MEAD, MARGARET. *Male and Female: A Study of the Sexes in a Changing World.* New York: New American Library, Mentor Book, Sixth Printing, 1962. (Original copyright through William Morrow, 1949.)

OBLER, LORAINE K., and FEIN, DEBORAH, eds. *The Exceptional Brain: Neuropsychology of Talent and Special Abilities.* New York: Guilford Press, 1988.

RAMSLAND, KATHERINE. *Prism of the Night: A Biography of Anne Rice.* New York: Plume (Penguin), 1992.

REKERS, GEORGE A. *Growing Up Straight: What Every Family Should Know About Homosexuality.* Chicago: Moody Press, 1982.

REKERS, GEORGE A., ed. *Handbook of Child and Adolescent Sexual Problems.* New York: Lexington Books, Free Press, 1995.

SACKS, OLIVER. *An Anthropologist on Mars: Seven Paradoxical Tales.* New York: Knopf, 1995.

SEDGWICK, EVE KOSOFSKY. *Tendencies.* Durham: Duke University Press, 1993.

SILVERSTEIN, OLGA, and RASHBAUM, BETH. *The Courage to Raise Good Men.* New York: Viking, 1994.

STEVENS, JENNIFER ANNE. *From Masculine to Feminine and All Points in Between: A Practical Guide for Transvestites, Cross-Dressers, Transgenderists, Transsexuals, and Others Who Choose to Develop a More Feminine Image . . . and for the Curious and Concerned.* Cambridge, Massachusetts: Different Path Press, 1990.

STOLLER, R. J. *Sex and Gender: On the Development of Masculinity and Femininity.* Volume II. New York: Science House, 1968.

THORNE, BARRIE. *Gender Play: Girls and Boys in School.* New Brunswick, New Jersey: Rutgers University Press, 1993.

WILLIAMSON, MARIANNE. *A Woman's Worth.* New York: Ballantine Books, 1993.

WITT, LYNN; THOMAS, SHERRY; and MARCUS, ERIC, eds. *Out in All Directions.* New York: Warner Books, 1995.

WITTIG, MONIQUE. *The Straight Mind and Other Essays.* Boston: Beacon Press, 1992.

WOLF, NAOMI. *The Beauty Myth.* New York: Anchor Doubleday, 1992. (Originally published by William Morrow, 1991.)

WOOLF, VIRGINIA. *A Room of One's Own.* New York: Harcourt, Brace & World (A Harvest Book), 1989. (Original publication in 1929.)

WORLD HEALTH ORGANIZATION. *International Classification of Diseases (ICD-10).* Volumes I, II, III: 1992, 1993, 1994.

INDEX

ABOUT THE AUTHOR

Phyllis Burke is the author of the highly acclaimed novel *Atomic Candy,* as well as the memoir *Family Values: Two Moms and Their Son.* She lives in San Francisco.